Bartender Magazine's
Ultimate
Bartender's guide

More than 1,300 Recipes from the World's Best Bartenders, Plus Everything You Need to Set Up and Serve

Ray Foley

SOURCEBOOKS, INC.
NAPERVILLE, ILLINOIS

Published by Sourcebooks, Inc.
P.O. Box 4410, Naperville, Illinois 60567-4410
(630) 961-3900
Fax: (630) 961-2168
www.sourcebooks.com

Library of Congress Cataloging-in-Publication Data

Foley, Ray.
  Bartender magazine's ultimate bartender's guide : more than 1,300 recipes from the world's best bartenders, plus everything you need to set up and serve / Ray Foley.
      p. cm.
  Includes index.
  ISBN 978-1-4022-0915-4 (hardcover)
  1. Bartending. 2. Cocktails. I. Bartender magazine. II. Title.

TX951.F588 2007
641.8'74--dc22

                                  2007014595

Printed and bound in the United States of America.
        IN 10 9 8 7 6 5 4 3 2 1

To all the great bartenders, bar people, and readers of *Bartender* Magazine, now and in the future, and to all those who logged on to www.bartender.com.

Acknowledgments

To all the brand managers, public relation firms, agencies, and suppliers who made *Bartender* Magazine successful and for all their input to this, *Bartender* Magazine's Ultimate Bartender's Guide.

I would also like to thank Peter Lynch and the people at Sourcebooks; Loretta NatFo; the Famous Foleys: Ray, William, Amy, and Ryan; and also those on the other side of the bar tolerating me, and of course, the bartenders all over the world who take the chance and serve me! And to Jaclyn Marie Foley, the love of my life, who makes my cup overflow, and of course my main man Ryan. Erin Mackey for her tremendous assistance on putting this book together.

Contents

Introduction

We have been publishing *Bartender* Magazine for over twenty-eight years and are now presenting this up-to-date *Bartender Magazine Ultimate Bartender's Guide.*

The ONLY Book You'll Ever Need!

I have tended bar for over seventeen years and I am a bartender, not a mixologist, or master mixologist, or bar chef—just a bartender who loves the business and the people. This book is a collection of recipes from readers of *Bartender* Magazine and our website (www.bartender.com).

There are recipes from my collection of cocktail books (over 950). I have been collecting them for over thirty years. I have selected only great brands and products. When you start with great products, you make great cocktails.

Use premium brands; they represent you, your establishment, and your cocktail. I have not (hopefully) included cocktails with items you'll have difficulty finding, i.e., no Chinese sesame syrup, puree of cucumber, kumquat leaves (if kumquats have leaves), or pearl caviar from Kazakhztan.

We have enjoyed the success of *Bartender* Magazine and thank all the readers, advertisers, and those who made it possible. I hope you have fun reading and making all the cocktails in this book. If we can be of any service, please email us at barmag@aol.com.

But, please remember not to drink in excess. Moderation is the key word. Good judgment for yourself and your guests is most important to any successful party. Drinking and driving do not mix! The cocktail recipes herein are for your pleasure. Enjoy in moderation.

Have fun!

Names and Origins

Alabama Slammer

A cocktail popularized at the University of Alabama made with sloe gin, amaretto, Southern Comfort, and orange juice.

Alizé

Evocative of the gentle tropical trade winds of the French Caribbean islands for which it is named, Alizé de France is a totally unique product in a new category of its own creation.

Ambrosia

A cocktail reputedly first concocted at Arnaud's restaurant in New Orleans immediately following the end of Prohibition.

Bacardi Cocktail

A cocktail made with lime juice, sugar, grenadine, and Bacardi Light Rum. The name dates back to 1934 and was associated with the firm Bacardi Imports, Inc., of Miami, Florida. In 1936, a New York State Supreme Court ruled that to be authentic, a "Bacardi Cocktail" had to be made with Bacardi Rum, since the name Bacardi was a registered trademark.

Bamboo Cocktail

A cocktail said to have been invented about 1910 by bartender Charlie Mahoney of the Hoffman House in New York. Drink is made with a dash of orange bitters, 1 oz. sherry and 1 oz. dry vermouth, stirred with ice, strained, and served in a wine glass with a lemon peel.

Bellini
Invented at Harry's Bar in Venice, Italy, around 1943.

Black Russian
By bartender Gus Tops at the Hotel Metropoli in Brussels. Gus also dispensed scarves with his silhouette and recipe of his cocktail.

Black Velvet—Also known as Bismarck or Champagne Velvet
Created in 1861 at Brooks's Club, London.

Bloody Mary
Invented by Pete Petiot at Harry's Bar, 5 Rue Daunou, Paris, France, in 1921; he later became Captain of Bars at the St. Regis Hotel, New York, NY.

Blue Lagoon
Created around 1960 at Harry's Bar, Paris, by Harry's son, Andy MacElhone.

Bobby Burns
Named after Robert Burns (1759-96), the Scottish poet and songwriter best known for "Auld Lang Syne."

The Bronx
By Johnny Solon of the Waldorf Bar in New York's Waldorf Astoria. Johnny created it the day after a trip to the Bronx Zoo.

Cuba Libre

This drink is a political statement as well as a cocktail. It translates to "Free Cuba," a status the country enjoyed in 1898 at the end of the Spanish-American war. Cuban/American relations were friendly around the turn of the century, when a US Army lieutenant in Havana mixed some light native rum with a new-fangled American soft drink called Coca Cola and braced the libation with a lime.

Daiquiri

Connived by workers from Bethlehem Steel during a malaria epidemic in the Village of Daiquiri, near Santiago, Cuba.

French 75

If one requests this drink, he might receive a mix of gin and champagne. In the French trenches of World War I, however, gin was scarce but cognac and champagne were not. American doughboys soon discovered that a combination of the two produced an effect similar to getting zapped by an artillery piece known as a French 75.

The Gibson

Named after New York artist Charles Dana Gibson by his bartender, Charles Connoly, of the Players Club in New York. Another version credits Billie Gibson, a fight promoter.

Gin Rickey

By a bartender at Shoemaker's in Washington, DC, for his customer "Colonel Jim" Rickey, a lobbyist.

Harvey Wallbanger

Created by Bill Doner at Newport Beach, CA. The Harvey Wallbanger started as a fad by Bill and was first served at a bar called The Office. Bill was last seen as Vice President of Marketing at Caesars Palace in Las Vegas. Before that, he ran a fleet of fishing boats in Cabo San Lucas, Mexico. Thank you, Bill, for a great drink and legend...wherever you are.

Irish Coffee

Was originated at the Buena Vista Cafe in San Francisco, which the late Chronicle columnist and travel writer Stanton Delaplane often frequented. On a trip to Ireland during the early fifties, Delaplane noted the custom of bolstering airport coffee with whiskey. Intending to elaborate on these crude airport toddies, he and his cronies at the Buena Vista settled on the perfect recipe: three sugar cubes, an ounce and a half of Irish whiskey, coffee, and a float of quickly agitated whipped cream.

Kioki Coffee

Created by George Bullington, founder of Southern California's Bully's restaurant chain. During the sixties, Kahlua-based coffee drinks were popular at his La Jolla location. Perhaps to defray costs, Bullington made a drink with one half-jigger of Kahlua, one half-jigger of the less expensive but similar-tasting dark crème de cacao, a float of brandy and whipped cream. Bullington's Hawaiian customers started referring to the drink as a Coffee Kioki—"Kioki" meaning "George" in Hawaiian.

Kir

After the Mayor of DiJon (Major Kir) to increase sales of cassis.

Long Island Iced Tea

Hails from Long Island, specifically the Oak Beach Inn in Hampton Bays. Spirits writer John Mariani credits bartender Robert "Rosebud" Butt as the inventor, whose original recipe calling for an ounce each of clear liquors (vodka, gin, tequila, light rum), a half ounce of triple sec, lemon juice and a splash of cola is still popular with young drinkers (though not with those who have to get up early the next day!)

Mai Tai

Invented by Vic Bergeron in 1944 at his Polynesian-style Oakland bar. He did not want fruit juices detracting from the two ounces of J. Wray Nephew Jamaican Rum he poured as the base for his creation. He merely added a half ounce of French orgeat (an almond-flavored syrup), a half ounce of orange curacao, a quarter ounce of rock candy syrup, and the juice of one lime. Customer Carrie Wright of Tahiti was the first to taste the concoction, to which she responded, "Mai tai...roe ae," (Tahitian for "Out of this world...the best"). The Mai Tai became famous, and conflicting stories about its origins aggravated Bergeron so much that he elicited a sworn statement from Mrs. Wright in 1970, testifying to his authorship of the cocktail.

Margarita

One story tells of a bartender in Pueblo, Mexico, named Daniel Negrete who had a girlfriend named Margarita. She took a dab of salt with everything she drank. To please her, Negrete created a drink of ice, cointreau, tequila and lime juice and put salt around the rim of the glass.

Another legend says that Margarita Sames of San Antonio, Texas, was a frequent visitor to Acapulco and a patron of the bar at the Flamingo Hotel. She had a special passion for tequila and encouraged the bartenders to create variations using the Mexican liquor. Her special favorite was a combination of tequila, cointreau and lime juice.

And then there's the tale of the ship that lost most of its provisions during a violent storm. All was lost save a supply of cointreau, tequila, and limes. An imaginative ship's mate combined the ingredients, was delighted with the result, and named the mixture after his beloved—you guessed it— Margarita!

Mimosa
Created around 1925 at the Ritz Hotel Bar, Paris. It took its name from the mimosa flowering plant, whose color it resembled.

The Manhattan
By John Welby Henderson, a bartender for a John A. Hopkins of Fairfax, Virginia. Hopkins had been wounded in a duel with Baron Henri de Vrie at Challono at Bladesburg, Maryland, in April 1846. Hopkins was rushed to Hotel Palo Alto, where Henderson was working. Henderson filled a glass with Maryland Rye, some syrup, and some bitters. The Manhattan survived; whether Hopkins did is unknown.

The Martini
1. By bartender Professor Jerry Thomas of San Francisco from a stranger on his way to Martinez. Made with gin, vermouth, bitters, dash of maraschino.
2. By a bartender in Martinez, California, for a gold miner who struck it rich. The miner ordered champagne for the house. But there was none. The bartender offered something better, a "Martinez Special," some sauterne and gin. The rich miner spread the word ordering throughout California a "Martinez Special."
3. After the British army rifle: the Martini and Henry. The rifle was known for its kick, like the first sip of Gin and It ("It" being vermouth).
4. After Martini and Rossi Vermouth, because it was first used

in the drink Gin and It, with one-half gin and one-half Martini and Rossi Vermouth.

5. At the Knickerbocker Hotel in the early 1900s, a bartender named Martini di Arma Tiggia mixed a Martini using only a dry gin and only dry vermouth.

Moscow Mule
Unveiled at Hollywood's Cock N' Bull by owner Jack Morgan and one Jack Martin in 1946 to rid himself of an overstock of ginger beer.

Negroni
It seems that a certain Count Negroni of Florence once requested a drink that would stand apart from all the Americanos ordered at his favorite neighborhood cafe. The bartender answered his request with a cocktail composed of equal parts gin, sweet vermouth, and Campari, and he garnished the result with a tell-tale orange slice. Unfortunately for the Count, the drink became as popular as the Americano.

Old Fashioned
Originated by a bartender at the Louisville Pendennis Club in Kentucky for Colonel James E. Pepper, a distiller of bourbon whiskey.

Pina Colada
Two stories, take your pick. On a plaque at 104 Forales Street, once the Barrchina Bar and now a perfumery, reads: "The house where in 1963 the Pina Colada was created by Don Ramon Portas Mingat." Across town at the Caribe Hilton, bartender Ramon (Monchito) Marrero says he created the Pina Colada in 1954...

Planters Punch

To a bartender at Planters Hotel in St. Louis; also credited to a Jamaican planter's wife offering a drink one part sour, two parts sweet, three parts strong and four parts weak to cool off from the Jamaican sun.

Ramos Fizz

By the proprietor of the Old Stagg Saloon in New Orleans' French Quarter, called Ramos, of course. Stories say it took eight to ten waitresses to shake this drink.

Rob Roy

From Robert MacGregor, Scotland's Robin Hood, Roy being the Scottish nickname for a man with red hair.

Screwdriver

By Texas oil rig workers who stirred vodka and orange juice with their screwdrivers.

Side Car

Harry's New York Bar in Paris, according to the owner at that time, Harry MacElhone, after a motorcycle sidecar in which a customer was driving into the bar.

Silk Panties

Created by Sandra Gutierrez of Chicago, Illinois, and winner of *Bartender* Magazine's 1986 Schnapps contest.

Singapore Sling

By a bartender at the Long Bar in Singapore's Raffles Hotel around 1915.

Tom Collins

By John Collins, a waiter at Lipmmer's Old House, Coduit Street, Hanover Square, in England. "Tom" was used instead of John from the use of Old Tom Gin. Today a "John Collins" would use whiskey.

Tom and Jerry

Created by Jerry Thomas around 1852 at the Planters' House Bar, St. Louis, Missouri.

The Ward Eight

From Boston's Ward Eight, a dominant political subdivision of the community, known for its bloody political elections. A Whiskey Sour with a splash of grenadine. Locke-O'Ber's in Boston is a great place to try one.

Zombie

Inventor Don Beaches was an innovator of the Polynesian-style, umbrella-bedded fufu drink. Real Polynesians never drank such things. But the tropical atmosphere at Beaches' Los Angeles restaurant inspired him. Don the Beachcomber made Scorpions, Beachcombers, and Zombies seem as island-indigenous as poi. He invented the Zombie back in the thirties as a mix of three different rums, papaya juice, orange juice, pineapple juice, lemon juice, grenadine, orgeat, Pernod, and curacao. What has survived is the 151 Float. That and the effect its name suggests.

Bar Tools

You need the proper tools to make outstanding drinks. Below are a few of the tools that will help to make you a real pro.

Bar Spoon: A long spoon for stirring cocktails or pitchers.

Blender: Blending drinks or crushing ice. Remember to save your blade by always pouring in the liquid before the ice.

Cocktail Shaker and Mixing/Measuring Glass: There are countless designs to choose from, but the standard is the Boston. It's a mixing glass that fits snuggly into a stainless steel cone.

Ice Bag: To crush ice use a rubber mallet and a lint free or canvas ice bag, often referred to as a Lewis Ice Bag.

Ice Bucket: Should have a vacuum seal and the ability to hold three trays of ice.

Ice Scoop/Tongs/Ice Pick: Never use your hands to pick up ice, use a scoop or tongs. The ice pick can help you unstick ice or break it up.

Jigger/Measuring Glass: Glass or metal, all drinks should be made using these bar tools. Remember that drinks on the rocks and mixed drinks should contain no more than 2 oz. of alcohol.

Knife and Cutting Board: A sturdy board and a small, sharp paring knife are essential to cutting fruit garnishes.

Muddler: Use this small wooden bat or pestle to crush fruit, herbs, or cracked ice. Muddlers come in all different sizes and are used for making Stixx drinks.

Napkins/Coasters: To place a drink on, hold a drink with and for basic convenience.

Pitcher of water: Keep it clean. Someone always wants water and you certainly will use it.

Pourer: A helpful way to pour directly into the glass. A lidded spout helps keep everything but the drink out.

Stirrers/Straws: Use them to sip, stir, and mix drinks. Glass is preferred for the mixer/stirrer.

Strainer: The strainer, quite simply, prevents ice from pouring out of the shaker. The two most common types in use are the Hawthorne, with its distinctive coil rim, most often used when pouring from the metal part of the Boston Shaker, and the Julep, a perforated metal spoon-like strainer used when pouring from the glass part of the Boston.

Wine/Bottle Opener: They come in all shapes and sizes. The best is the industry standard Waiter's opener. It can open cans as well as snap off those bottle tops and has a sharp blade.

Cuts and Garnishes

You drink with your eyes, and the prettier you can make a drink, the more appealing it is. You can have a great tasting drink, but if it does not look good then no one will want to taste it. In this case, you do judge a book by its cover and a drink by its garnish. Below are some ideas for garnishes and a simple lesson on cutting shapes of some basic fruits and vegetables. But remember: use your imagination and personality; you can get wild with garnishes.

Always make sure your garnishes are fresh and clean.

TYPES OF CUT

Slice: A thinly cut portion, with a bit of peel on top, or half a wheel.

Twist: Made by using a paring knife to cut away a thin portion of peel, which will naturally twist.

Wedge: A triangular cut portion of the fruit or veggie.

Wheel: A whole slice, the fruit or veggie from peel to peel.

TYPES OF GARNISH

Apples, Apricots, Peaches, and Plums: They look best sliced. Peaches in particular make a great champagne garnish.

Bananas: Slices or wheels. Make sure the bananas are not too ripe.

Celery: Whole stalk with flower.

Chocolate Sticks: They make a great stirrer and garnish in one. (And I know these are available at Bloomingdales!)

Cinnamon Sticks: Great for hot drinks.

Cloves: Add them whole to hot drinks.

Cocktail Onions: Whole onions are usually used in a Gibson Cocktail.

Coffee Beans: Three beans are usually dropped into sambuca, sometimes flamed. I do not recommend flaming.

Cucumber: A slice or a twist makes a very nice decoration.

Flowers: Rose petals, small baby orchids or any other flowers look great in most tall cocktails and add a great visual effect.

Fresh Herbs: Mint is the most popular, but you can use cilantro, basil, rosemary, and thyme. Many herbs work well in Bloody Marys and of course mint is commonly known for being in the Mint Julep or Mojito. But remember, mint can be used in a garnish as you see fit. It looks nice and it smells great. Use your imagination!

Lemons: Twist, slices, wheels, and wedges.

Limes: Twist, slices, wheels, and wedges.

Maraschino Cherries: The fun fruit. It looks good, tastes good, and adds value to any drink or desert. The maraschino originates from an Italian liqueur that used the local "Marasca" cherry as its base. Originally brought to the United States in the 1890s from regions of Yugoslavia and Italy, by 1920 the American maraschino had replaced the foreign versions. American producers used a domestic sweet cherry called the Royal Anne cherry and eliminated the use of liquor in the processing, substituting it with almond oil.

The modern day maraschino is primarily grown in Oregon, Washington, and Michigan and is characterized by its bright, uniform color and fruit cherry flavor with just a mere hint of almond.

Olives: Whole black and green, both can be stuffed with almonds, anchovies, blue cheese, or pimentos.

Oranges: Twist, slices, wheels, and wedges.

Pineapples: Wedges; also use the whole pineapple as a serving container.

Pink grapefruit: Though bitter, large grapefruit slices or wheels can add a burst of flavor.

Raspberries: Whole or muddled.

Salt: Table salt, sea salt, and kosher salt are used to coat the rim of the glass and are mostly for Margaritas or a Salty Dog. You can also add half sugar to the salt, which makes for an interesting taste. Colored salts are also available and fun.

Sugar: Can be used to coat drinks. Cubes can be used in champagne drinks, and there are colored sugars available as well.

Strawberries: Sliced and hung on the side of the glass.

"Toys": Non-edible plastic mermaids, Barrel of Monkeys, baby ducks, umbrellas, fancy straws and stirrers, and little boats add a fun element to a drink. Make sure they are small enough to fit in the drink and large enough so you can't swallow them. Remember these "toys" are not for children under twenty-one.

Cutting Fruit

Different kinds of fruit are used to garnish different kinds of drinks. Remember to wash all fruit and vegetables before cutting.

Lemon twist: 1) Cut off both ends. 2) Using a sharp knife or spoon, insert between rind and meat, carefully separating. 3) Cut skin into 1/4 inch strips.

Celery: 1) Cut off bottom of celery; you may also cut off top. 2) If leaf is fresh, you may use this as garnish. 3) Cut celery stalk in half.

Oranges: 1) Cut oranges in half. 2) Slice orange into half moon cuts.

Limes: 1) Cut ends of lime. 2) Slice lime into half. 3) Cut in half moons.

Wedges (lemon/lime): 1) Slice lime in half. 2) Place cut halves flat down and halve again. 3) Cut into 1/4 inch to 1/2 inch wedges.

Pineapple: 1) Cut off top and bottom. 2) Cut pineapple in half. 3) Cut in half again. 4) Cut 1/2 inch slices. 5) Cut wedges.

Mixers and Enhancers

Here's a great way to add creativity and sparkle to a drink, by adding a great mix or enhancer. Changing the color, texture, and taste of the alcohol with a juice or other product can make it memorable. Mixers and enhancers should also be on hand for people who do not drink alcohol. (Be sure to check the section on nonalcoholic drinks.)

When using juices, make sure you check the expiration date and use the liquid quickly after opening; there is nothing worse than a juice that has gone bad. Don't let your enhancer be a distracter.

FRUIT JUICE

Apple Juice: Bottled apple juice is the best. Check dates.

Clamato Juice: A mixture of clam and tomato juice.

Cranberry Juice Cocktail: Excellent bottled.

Grapefruit Juice: Fresh is best, but like orange juice, some carton and frozen varieties can do the job.

Lime Juice: If you cannot get fresh squeezed, I highly recommend Rose's Lime Juice.

Orange Juice: Fresh squeezed is the best but there are great frozen and carton varieties available.

Pineapple Juice: Bottled is best.

Tomato Juice: Bottled juice is best. For Bloody Marys try using V-8.

OTHER MIXERS

Try your local grocery store for a variety of new and mixed juice drinks like cran-apple. Ocean Spray has a ton of new juice mixes; go out and try some, have fun, and experiment. You may surprise yourself.

SODA:

Cola or diet cola, Dr. Pepper, ginger ale, lemon-lime soda, root beer, seltzer water or club soda, tonic water. Check your local store; there are many regional specific sodas that can add zest to a drink.

OTHER MIXERS:

Beef bullion, cappuccino, clam juice, Coco Lopez cream of coconut, coffee, espresso, half-and-half, heavy cream, honey, ice cream, lemon juice or lemon mix, and tea.

ENHANCERS:

Angostura Bitters

Chocolate Syrup: A good quality, fine chocolate syrup can make a great chocolate martini and add flavor to any ice cream drink.

Egg Whites: Not recommended for use due to food safety reasons.

Falernum Syrup: A rum based syrup from Barbados with a refined infusion of lime laced with fine cane syrup and "botanicals" including almonds and cloves.

Fruit Syrups: There are many available such as strawberry, raspberry, and other berries. For more information on the syrups available contact Monin. (www.monin.com)

Horseradish

Orgeat Syrup: Flavored with almonds and orange flavored water.

Peychauds Bitters: Available from the Sazerac Company. (www.sazerac.com/bitters.html)

Rose's Grenadine

Rose's Lime Juice

Worcestershire Sauce

Types of Drinks

There are seven basic ways of preparing a drink: you can blend, build, shake, stir, mix, layer, or muddle. Within these ways of preparing, though, come many types of drinks, and here are a few interesting ones. First off, I will quickly go over some of the older types of drinks.

Aperitif: A light alcohol drink served before lunch or dinner, sometimes bitter.

Cobbler: A tall drink usually filled with crushed ice and garnished with fruit or mint.

Crusta: Served in a wine glass with a sugarcoated rim and the inside of the glass lined with a citrus rind.

Cups: A traditionally British category of wine-based drinks.

Daisy: An oversized cocktail sweetened with fruit syrup served over crushed ice.

Eggnog: A blend of milk or cream, beaten eggs, sugar, and liquor, usually rum, brandy, or whiskey, and sometimes sherry, topped with nutmeg.

Flip: Cold, creamy drinks made with eggs, sugar, alcohol, and citrus juice.

Highball: A tall drink usually served with whiskey and ginger ale. (The favorite drink of many drinkers' grandparents!)

Grog: A rum-based drink made with fruit and sugar.

Julep: A tall, sweet drink usually made with bourbon, water, sugar, crushed ice, and occasionally mint. The most popular julep being, of course, the Kentucky Derby's famous Mint Julep.

Puff: Made with equal parts alcohol and milk topped with club soda.

Pousse-Café: A drink made of layers created by floating liqueur according to their density.

Rickey: A cocktail made of alcohol (usually whiskey, lime juice, and soda water).

Sling: A tall drink made with lemon juice and sugar, and topped with club soda.

Smash: A short julep.

Toddy: Served hot, it's a mixture of alcohol, spices, and hot water.

The following are more recent and popular drinks:

Blended Drinks: Blender drinks consisting of ice, ice cream, and a variety of other ingredients blended to a smooth though thick consistency.

Cream: Any drink made with ice cream, heavy cream, half-and-half, or any of the famous bottled cream drinks.

Mist: Any type of alcoholic beverage served over crushed ice.

Mojito: A Cuban-born drink prepared with sugar, muddled mint leaves, fresh lime juice, rum, ice, and soda water, and garnished with mint leaves.

Shooter: A straight shot of alcohol, also sometimes called serving a drink "neat."

Sours: Drinks made with lemon juice, sugar, and alcohol.

The next two types of drinks are new on the scene and sure to be filling the glasses of trendsetters at a bar near you:

Stixx: Tall muddled cocktails using different sized muddlers from six inches to twelve inches. Now they are muddling herbs, fruits, spices, and a variety of ethnic and regional ingredients including beans, roots, and spices.

Toppers: Blended drinks with ice cream or crushed ice, the thicker the better, which is why these drinks are served with a spoon and a straw. They are made using cordials, flavored rums, flavored vodkas, blended fresh fruits, and tropical juices. They are topped with crushed candy, fruits, nuts, and just about anything you can eat with a spoon.

COCKTAILS

Bourbon

ALPHABET SOUP

2 oz. Elijan Craig Bourbon
2 dashes Angostura Bitters
½ oz. curacao

Strain the mixture into a cocktail glass.

AMERICANA

¼ oz. George Dickel No. 12
  Tennessee Whiskey
½ tsp. sugar
1-2 dashes bitters
2 oz. champagne
1 peach slice

Combine the bourbon, bitters and sugar. Stir until the sugar is dissolved. Add champagne and a slice of peach.

ANGELIC

1 oz. bourbon
½ oz. white creme de cacao
dash grenadine
2 oz. half & half

Shake with ice and serve on rocks or strain into cocktail glass.

APPETIZER #4

2 oz. Old Fitzgerald Bourbon
½ tsp. cointreau
3 dashes bitters
1 lemon twist.

Pour the bourbon, cointreau and bitters into a mixing glass half-filled with ice cubes.

ATLANTA BELLE

1 oz. bourbon
¾ oz. green creme de menthe
¾ oz. white creme de cacao
3 oz. half & half

Shake with ice and serve on the rocks.

BEEHIVE

1½ oz. Rebel Yell
2 oz. grapefruit juice
¾ oz. honey

Shake well and serve on the rocks.

BISHOP

1 oz. Rebel Yell
½ oz. sweet vermouth
1 oz. orange juice
dash yellow chartreuse

Shake with ice and serve on the rocks.

BOURBON A LA CREME

2 oz. Old Charter
1 oz. dark creme de cacao
1-2 vanilla beans

Combine with ice and allow to stand in the refrigerator for at least 1 hour. When ready, shake well and serve straight up.

BOURBON COLLINS

2 oz. bourbon
4-5 oz. sweetened lemon mix
club soda

Shake with ice and pour into tall glass with ice.

BOURBON DELIGHT

1½ oz. Old Fitzgerald
½ oz. sweet vermouth
¼ oz. creme de cassis
¼ oz. lemon juice

Shake with ice and serve on the rocks.

BOURBON MILK PUNCH

2 oz. Elijah Craig Bourbon
4 oz. milk
1 tsp. superfine sugar
¼ tsp. vanilla extract
¼ tsp. grated nutmeg
¼ tsp. ground cinnamon

Shake.

BOURBON SLOE GIN FIX

1½ oz. bourbon
½ oz. sloe gin
2 oz. sweetened lemon mix

Shake. Add slice of fresh or brandied peach.

BOURBON SLUSHIE

1½ oz. bourbon
1 tsp. sugar
ice
lemon wedge
cherry

Blend. Serve with lemon wedge.

BRASS KNUCKLE

1½ oz. Elijah Craig
½ oz. triple sec
2 oz. sweetened lemon mix

Shake with ice and serve on the rocks.

BULL AND BEAR

1½ oz. Old Charter
¾ oz. curacao
1 Tbsp. grenadine
juice ½ lime

Shake. Garnish with cherry and orange slice.

CHOCOLATE CLOVER LIQUEUR

1¾ cups George Dickel No. 12
  Tennessee Whiskey
1 cup whipping cream
4 fresh eggs
2 Tbsp. chocolate syrup
2 tsp. instant coffee
1 tsp. vanilla extract
½ tsp. almond extract

Combine all ingredients in blender. Blend until smooth. Store in refrigerator. Shake or stir before serving. Makes about 5 cups.

THE CITRUS TURKEY

1½ oz. Wild Turkey
1 oz. club soda
1 oz. orange juice
ice to fill
orange wheel garnish

Squeeze lemon. Mix. Garnish with orange wheel. Drop lemon wedge into drink.

———⚬⚬⚬———

COLONEL HAYDEN

1½ oz. Old Grand Dad
¾ oz. apricot brandy
3 oz. pineapple juice

Shake with ice and serve on the rocks.

———⚬⚬⚬———

COMMODORE

1 part Evan Williams Bourbon
1 part creme de cacao
1 part sweetened lemon juice
dash grenadine

Shake with ice and serve on the rocks.

———⚬⚬⚬———

CRANBERRY COOLER

1½ oz. W. L. Weller
1 cup crushed ice
1½ oz. cranberry juice
½ oz. lime juice
1 tsp. sugar

Place crushed ice in blender; add ingredients in order listed. Blend on slow speed, 15-30 seconds, or until frozen stiff. Makes one 12-oz. serving.

DAISY DUELER

1½ oz. George Dickel No. 12
Tennessee Whiskey
1½ tsp. lemon juice
1½ tsp. sugar syrup
several drops cointreau
club soda

Combine all ingredients except soda with ice; shake well. Strain; add ice and fill the glass with soda. Decorate with fruit slices.

———⚬⚬⚬———

DIXIE

2 oz. Elijah Craig
¼ oz. white creme de menthe
¼ oz. triple sec
dash Angostura Bitters

Shake with ice and serve on rocks with lemon twist.

———⚬⚬⚬———

DIZZY IZZY

¾ oz. Elijah Craig
¾ oz. sherry
½ oz. pineapple juice
½ oz. sweetened lemon mix

Shake with ice and serve on the rocks.

———⚬⚬⚬———

DOWNHOME PUNCH

1 part Jack Daniel's
1 part peach schnapps
2 parts whiskey sour mix
2 parts orange juice
1 part 7-Up or Sprite
splash grenadine

Garnish with orange and cherry.

BOURBON

DUBONNET MANHATTAN
1 part bourbon
1 part Dubonnet
dash Angostura Bitters

Stir on the rocks or strain into cocktail glass.

—∞∞—

EGGNOG
1 egg
1 tsp. fine-grain sugar
2 oz. Old Charter
8 oz. fresh milk

Shake well with cracked ice. Strain into a tall glass and serve with grated nutmeg and cinnamon stick.

—∞∞—

EVAN AND COLA
1½ oz. Evan Williams
2 oz. cola

In a tall glass, fill with cola.

—∞∞—

EZRA BLIZZARD
1½ oz. Ezra Brooks
1½ oz. cranberry juice
½ oz. lime juice
½ oz. grenadine
1 tsp. sugar

Blend.

—∞∞—

EZRA SUNRISE
1½ oz. Ezra Brooks
3 oz. orange juice
1 tsp. grenadine

Mix. Add grenadine.

FAY RYE COCKTAIL
2 oz. rye whiskey
1 oz. sweet vermouth
1 tsp. absinthe substitute
  (Pernod, Ricard, or Herbsaint)
3 dashes Angostura Bitters
1 maraschino cherry

Stir. Strain the mixture into the chilled cocktail glass; garnish with cherry.

—∞∞—

FLORIDA PUNCH
2 oz. Evan Williams
2 oz. pineapple juice
½ tsp. sugar

In a tall glass with ice, fill with club soda.

—∞∞—

GEORGE AND GINGER
2 oz. George Dickel

In a tall glass with ice, fill with ginger ale.

—∞∞—

GRAND FELLOW
3 parts Old Grand Dad bourbon
1 part sweet vermouth
dash Angostura Bitters

Stir on the rocks or strain into cocktail glass.

—∞∞—

GRANDFATHER
2 parts Old Grand Dad
1 part amaretto

Stir on the rocks.

JIM BEAM BOURBON AND COLA

1½ oz. Jim Beam Kentucky
 Straight Bourbon Whiskey
cola to fill

Pour over ice in a highball glass. Fill with cola.

JOHN COLLINS

3 oz. Evan Williams Bourbon
1 oz. fresh lemon juice
1 tsp. superfine sugar
3 oz. club soda
1 cherry
1 orange slice

In a shaker half-filled with ice cubes, combine the bourbon, lemon juice and sugar. Shake well and pour into a collins glass. Top with club soda. Garnish with cherry and orange slice.

JOHNNY RISE

1½ oz. bourbon
orange juice
dash grenadine

In tall glass with ice, fill with orange juice.

KENTUCKY BLIZZARD

1½ oz. Old Charter
1 cup crushed ice
1½ oz. cranberry juice
½ oz. lime juice
½ oz. grenadine
1 tsp. sugar

Shake all ingredients briskly with cracked ice. Strain into cocktail glass or over fresh ice in an old-fashioned glass. Garnish with half slice of orange.

KENTUCKY COCKTAIL

1 part Evan Williams
1 part pineapple juice

Shake with ice and serve on rocks or strain into cocktail glass.

KENTUCKY FLOAT

2 oz. Jim Beam Kentucky
 Straight Bourbon Whiskey
scoop of vanilla or chocolate ice
 cream
cola, chilled

Pour Jim Beam over ice cream in a tall glass and fill with cola.

KENTUCKY KOLA

1½ oz. Elijah Craig Bourbon
cola to fill

Stir.

LOUISVILLE COOLER
1½ oz. W. L. Weller
1 oz. orange juice
1 Tbsp. lime juice
1 tsp. superfine sugar

Shake all ingredients briskly with cracked ice. Strain into cocktail glass or over fresh ice in old-fashioned glass. Garnish with half slice of orange.

LOUISVILLE LADY
1 oz. Old Charter
¾ oz. creme de cacao
¾ oz. cream

Shake. Strain into cocktail glass.

LYNCHBURG LEMONADE
1 part Jack Daniel's
1 part triple sec
1 part whiskey sour mix
2 parts 7-Up or Sprite

Garnish with lemon and cherry.

MAGNOLIA MAIDEN
1¼ oz. W. L. Weller
splash club soda
1¼ oz. Grand Marnier
splash simple syrup

Shake bourbon, Grand Marnier and simple syrup with crushed ice in shaker. Strain into old-fashioned glass with ice. Top with club soda.

MANHATTAN
2 oz. Maker's Mark
1½ oz. sweet vermouth
1 dash Angostura Bitters

Stir with cracked ice. Strain into 3 oz. cocktail glass; add cherry.

MINT JULEP
3 oz. Maker's Mark
2-3 sprigs of mint
1 tsp. sugar

In a tall glass, muddle mint, sugar, and 2 tsp. water. Fill with crushed ice and add bourbon. Stir till well frosted.

MINTY JULEP
1½ oz. bourbon
½ oz. greene creme de menthe

Add splash of water and stir on the rocks.

OLD FASHIONED
2½ oz. Maker's Mark
several drops sugar syrup
few dashes of Angostura Bitters

Combine and stir. Top with an orange slice, a cherry, or a lemon twist.

PERFECT BOURBON MANHATTAN
4 parts Maker's Mark
1 part sweet vermouth
1 part dry vermouth

Stir on the rocks or strain into cocktail glass. Add lemon twist.

REMEMBER THE MAINE

1½ oz. Evan Williams Bourbon
¾ oz. sweet vermouth
2 tsp. cherry brandy
½ tsp. absinthe substitute
(Pernod, Ricard, or Herbsaint)
2 dashes Angostura Bitters.

Stir. Strain the mixture into a chilled cocktail glass.

SHRAPNEL

1½ oz. bourbon
½ oz. sweet vermouth
½ oz. dry vermouth
½ oz. apricot brandy

Stir on the rocks. Add orange slice.

SOUTHERN BELL

1¼ oz. George Dickel No. 12
Tennessee Whiskey
2 oz. pineapple juice
¾ oz. triple sec
splash grenadine
2 oz. orange juice

Combine bourbon, triple sec, orange juice, and pineapple juice in a tall glass with ice. Top with grenadine. Stir once.

SOUTHERN SOUR

¾ oz. Jack Daniel's
¾ oz. Southern Comfort
3 oz. sweetened lemon mix

Shake with ice and serve on rocks or strain into cocktail glass. Add cherry and orange slice.

STEVE'S SOUR

2½ oz. Old Grand Dad Bourbon
1½ oz. orange juice
1½ oz. sweetened lemon juice

Shake with ice and serve on the rocks.

STUMP LIFTER #1

2 oz. Elijah Craig Bourbon
3 oz. hard cider

Stir well in old-fashioned glass.

STUMP LIFTER #2

2 oz. Elijah Craig Bourbon
5 oz. apple juice.

Stir well in collins glass.

SUGARBUTTIE COCKTAIL

1½ oz. bourbon
1 oz. tawny or ruby port

Serve in snifter or over ice.

TENNESSEE MUD

1 part Jack Daniel's
1 part amaretto
coffee
whipped cream

TENNESSEE TEA

1 part Jack Daniel's
1 part triple sec
1 part whiskey sour mix
2 parts cola

Garnish with lemon wedge.

TURKEY TWIST

¾ oz. Wild Turkey 101
¾ oz. Arrow Triple Sec
1½ oz. sweet & sour mix
lemon-lime soda to fill

Shake. Pour into tall glass. Fill with lemon-lime soda and stir. Garnish with twist of lime.

WARD EIGHT

2 oz. rye whiskey or bourbon
1 oz. fresh lemon juice
½ oz. fresh orange juice
1 tsp. grenadine

Shake and pour into an old-fashioned glass. Garnish with a lemon twist.

WARD FOURTEEN

2 parts bourbon
1 part orange juice
1 part sweetened lemon mix
dash grenadine

Shake and serve on the rocks.

WELLERITA

1 oz. W. L. Weller
1½ oz. sweet & sour mix
½ oz. triple sec
½ oz. pineapple juice

Mix all ingredients in shaker with crushed ice. Strain into sour glass or pour over ice cubes into old-fashioned glass.

WHISKEY COBBLER

2½ oz. Old Charter
1 Tbsp. lemon juice
2 tsp. grapefruit juice
1½ tsp. almond extract
1 peach slice

Combine ingredients except peach slice. Stir well, add ice, and decorate with peach slice.

WHISKEY SOUR

1½ oz. Jack Daniel's
juice ½ lemon
½ tsp. sugar

Shake well with cracked ice, strain into sour glass. Lemon and cherry garnish.

WHISKEY TCHING

1½ oz. bourbon
rye or Tennessee whiskey
1 oz. Canton Ginger Liqueur
1 lemon twist

Stir well; garnish with a lemon twist.

WILD ICED TEA

1½ oz. Wild Turkey 101
2½ oz. sweet & sour mix
cola to fill
splash triple sec

Pour Wild Turkey and sweet and sour mix over ice in a tall glass. Fill with cola and garnish with lemon slice.

WILD TURKEY AND 7-UP

1½ oz. Wild Turkey 101
7-Up to fill

Garnish with a lime wedge.

WILD TURKEY AND O. J.

1½ oz. Wild Turkey 101
orange juice to fill

Stir.

WILD TURKEY CRIMSON SOUR

1½ oz. Wild Turkey 101
1½ oz. grenadine
3 oz. sweet & sour mix

Shake. Pour into tall glass. Garnish with orange wheel and maraschino cherry.

WILD TURKEY GOBBLER

1½ oz. Wild Turkey 101
5½ oz. hot apple cider

Pour hot apple cider and Wild Turkey into a mug and garnish with a cinnamon stick.

WILD TURKEY LEMON FIZZ

1½ oz. Wild Turkey 101
seltzer
splash lemon
squeeze lemon

Mix; top with seltzer or club soda.

WILD TURKEY LIME FIZZ

1½ oz. Wild Turkey 101
seltzer
splash Rose's Lime Juice
squeeze lime

Mix; top with seltzer or club soda.

WILD TURKEY ORANGE FIZZ

1½ oz. Wild Turkey 101
seltzer
splash orange juice
squeeze orange

In a tumbler filled with ice, top with seltzer or club soda.

WILD TURKEY PRESBYTERIAN

1½ oz. Wild Turkey 101
equal parts: ginger ale and club
 soda

Stir gently. Garnish with
lemon peel.

———∞∞———

WILD TURKEY SOUR

1½ oz. Wild Turkey 101
dash club soda
3 oz. sour mix

Shake well with cracked ice
and strain into sour glass. Add
good dash of soda. Garnish
with slice of orange and
maraschino cherry.

———∞∞———

WILD TURKEY SPLASH

2 oz. Wild Turkey 101
splash soda water

———∞∞———

WILD TURKEY TODDY

2 oz. Wild Turkey 101
1 oz. orange juice
1 tsp. granulated sugar
¼ pat butter
1 whole clove

Place in a mug. Fill with boiling water and stir. Float a pat
of butter on top.

———∞∞———

WYOOTER HOOTER

1 part Jack Daniel's
4 parts 7-Up or Sprite
splash of grenadine

Cordials

ALABAMA SLAMMER
1½ oz. amaretto
1 oz. Southern Comfort
½ oz. sloe gin
½ oz. lemon juice

ALBINO MONKEY
¼ oz. Bols White Creme de Cacao
¼ oz. Bols Creme de Banana
½ oz. half & half
¾ oz. white rum

Shake, strain and serve.

B & B STINGER
2½ oz. B & B
½ oz. Bols White Creme de Menthe

In a mixing glass half-filled with ice cubes, combine the B & B and creme de menthe. Stir well.

B-52
1 oz. Grand Marnier
¾ oz. Kahlua
½ oz. Baileys Irish Cream

Shake well. Strain into a cocktail glass.

BAILEYS CREAM DREAM
2 oz. Baileys Irish Cream
2 oz. half & half
4 oz. ice cubes

Blend for 30 seconds.

BAILEYS ITALIAN DREAM
1½ oz. Baileys Irish Cream
½ oz. Disaronno Amaretto
2 oz. half & half
3 ice cubes or crushed ice

Blend for 30 seconds.

BAILEYS RUSSIAN DREAM
1½ oz. Baileys Irish Cream
½ oz. vodka
2 oz. half & half
4 oz. ice cubes

Blend for 30 seconds.

BANANA SPLIT
1½ parts Hiram Walker Swiss Chocolate Almond
½ part Hiram Walker Creme de Banana
3 parts cream

Blend.

BEER NUTS

¾ oz. DeKuyper Old Tavern Root
  Beer Schnapps
1 oz. DeKuyper Hazelnut
  Liqueur

Shake, serve over rocks or in a shot glass.

———— ∞ ————

BEETLEJUICE

1 oz. white creme de cacao
1 oz. dark creme de cacao
½ oz. coffee liqueur
2 tsp. peppermint schnapps
1 oz. light cream

Combine all the ingredients in a shaker with ice cubes. Shake and strain into a cocktail glass.

———— ∞ ————

BERMUDA TRIANGLE

¾ oz. cointreau
1½ oz. Mount Gay Eclipse Rum
splash Rose's Lime Juice

Shake with ice into a chilled martini glass.

———— ∞ ————

BLACK MAGIC

Top 1 oz. Opal Nera Sambuca with club soda and ice. Garnish with lemon peel.

BLACK SUN

¾ oz. cointreau
1½ oz. Mount Gay White Rum
cola

In a highball glass, pour ingredients over ice; fill with cola and stir.

———— ∞ ————

BLACK WIDOW

2 oz. Hiram Walker Strawberry
  Schnapps
½ oz. Opal Nera
½ oz. cream

———— ∞ ————

BLUE LAGOON

1 oz. Hiram Walker Blue Curacao
1 oz. Fris Vodka
½ oz. pineapple juice

———— ∞ ————

BUTTER BEAM

1½ oz. DeKuyper ButterShots
  Schnapps
1½ oz. Jim Beam Bourbon

Serve in a rocks glass.

———— ∞ ————

BUTTERSWIRL

2 oz. Hiram Walker Butternips
  Schnapps
1 scoop vanilla ice cream

Blend. Top with sprinkles.

CAFE FRANGELICO

1½ oz. Frangelico
3 oz. hot coffee

Top with whipped cream and crushed hazelnuts.

CANDI APPLE

¾ oz. Mozart Liqueur
¾ oz. Schonauer Apfel Schnapps

Mix in a shot glass or over rocks.

CHAMBORD & COGNAC

½ oz. Chambord
½ oz. cognac

Place in a snifter glass and heat in a microwave for 25 seconds.

CHAMBORD ADRENALIN

equal parts: Chambord and Absolut Vodka

Serve chilled.

CHAMBORD SPIRIT

½ oz. Chambord
½ oz. Wild Spirit

Pour over lots of ice.

CHERRY BOMB

¾ oz. Mozart Liqueur
¾ oz. cherry-flavored brandy

Shake, serve over rocks or straight up.

CHOCOLATE SOLDIER

½ oz. Mozart Liqueur
½ oz. bourbon
dash grenadine

Shake, serve on the rocks.

CORKSCREW

1 part Hiram Walker Peach
 Flavored Brandy
1½ parts light rum
1 Tbsp. dry vermouth
3 or 4 ice cubes

Shake.

CRANBERRY LARGO

1½ oz. DeKuyper Key Largo
 Tropical Schnapps
2 oz. cranberry juice

Garnish with lemon or lime.

DISARONNO GODFATHER

1½ oz. J&B Scotch
½ oz. Disaronno Amaretto

Stir.

DISARONNO SEA BREEZE

1 oz. Disaronno Amaretto
1 oz. Malibu Rum
½ oz. pineapple juice
½ oz. cranberry juice

Combine and serve over crushed ice.

DIRTY HARRY

1 oz. Grand Marnier
1 oz. Tia Maria

Shake with ice and strain.

DREAM SHAKE

1 part Baileys Irish Cream
1 part Tia Maria

Shake, strain into a shot glass.

DYNASTY

1½ oz. amaretto
1½ oz. Southern Comfort

Shake or blend.

ERIE TOUR

1 part Irish Mist
1 part Carolans Irish Cream
1 part Tullamore Dew

Combine over ice.

ERIN GO BURR

3 oz. Carolans Irish Cream

Serve chilled, straight up in a chilled cocktail glass.

FERRIS WHEEL

1½ oz. Romana Sambuca
1 oz. brandy
1 lemon twist

Stir well. Strain into a cocktail glass. Garnish with a lemon twist.

FIFTH AVENUE

½ oz. Baileys Irish Cream
½ oz. apricot brandy
½ oz. white creme de cacao

Shake with ice. Strain into a cocktail glass.

FIRE AND ICE

½ parts Hiram Walker Sambuca
½ parts Hiram Walker Triple Sec
½ parts brandy

Mix.

FRENCH ICED TEA

In a high ball glass, add 1½ oz. Marie Brizard Anisette to your favorite flavored iced tea.

FRUITY IRISHMAN
2 parts Baileys Irish Cream
1 part Midori Melon Liqueur

Stir well over ice.

FUZZY NAVEL
1½ oz. DeKuyper Peachtree
  Schnapps
2 oz. orange juice

Stir.

GINGERSNAP
1 part Hiram Walker Ginger
  Flavored Brandy
1 part vodka
2 parts pineapple juice
4 parts lemonade

Combine in glass, stir. Garnish
with lemon twist.

GIRL SCOUT COOKIE
1½ oz. DeKuyper Peppermint
  Schnapps
1½ oz. coffee liqueur
3 oz. half & half

Shake with ice and serve on
the rocks.

GOLDEN CADILLAC
1½ oz. Hiram Walker White
  Creme de Cacao
¾ oz. Galliano
1 oz. light cream

Shake well. Strain into a cocktail
glass.

GOLDEN FLEECE
1½ oz. yellow Chartreuse
1 oz. Goldwasser

Stir well. Strain into a cocktail
glass.

GOOD N'PLENTY SHOOTER
½ oz. Marie Brizard Anisette
1 oz. Marie Brizard Amour

GRASSHOPPER
1 oz. Bols Green Creme de
  Menthe
1 oz. Bols White Creme de Cacao
1 oz. light cream

Shake well. Strain into a cocktail
glass.

HARVEY WALLBANGER
1½ oz. Smirnoff Vodka
4 oz. orange juice
½ oz. Galliano

Top off glass with the Galliano
so that it floats on top.

HIGH VOLTAGE
¾ oz. cointreau
1 oz. scotch whiskey
juice of ½ lemon or lime

Shake.

ITALIAN SPEAR

1 part DeKuyper Peppermint
  Schnapps
1 part amaretto

Stir on the rocks.

JAGUAR

2 oz. Galliano
1 oz. white creme de cacao
1 oz. heavy cream
1 scoop crushed ice

Combine all the ingredients
in a blender. Blend.

JELLY BEAN

1 part Hiram Walker Blackberry
  Flavored Brandy
1 part Hiram Walker Anisette

Combine.

JUNGLE FEVER

3 oz. DeKuyper Harvest Pear
  Schnapps
splash of pineapple juice

Pour Schnapps over ice. Add a
splash of pineapple juice.
Garnish with a cherry.

KAHLUA & SODA

1 oz. Kahlua
3 oz. soda

Pour over ice, garnish with a
twist of lime.

KAHLUA BLACK RUSSIAN

1 oz. Kahlua
1½ oz. Fris Vodka Skandia

Pour over ice and stir.

KAMIKAZE

¾ oz. cointreau
1½ oz. vodka
juice of 1/2 lime

Shake.

KAMIKAZE

1 oz. Smirnoff Vodka
½ oz. cointreau
¼ oz. Rose's Lime Juice

Shake with ice and strain into
a shot glass.

KEY LARGO

½ oz. cointreau
1½ oz. grapefruit juice
¾ oz. Campari

In a highball glass, pour
ingredients over ice; fill with
club soda and stir.

THE LEAF

1 oz. Midori Melon Liqueur
½ oz. Puerto Rican Rum
2 oz. cream

Stir.

LICOR 43 MINI-BEER
1 oz. Licor 43

Top with cream.

THE LIFT
1 part DeKuyper Peppermint Schnapps
2 parts Old Grand Dad Bourbon
1 dash Angostura Bitters

Stir on the rocks.

M&M
1 part Kahlua
1 part Disaronno Amaretto

Layer the amaretto over the Kahlua.

MELON MATAZZ
1 oz. DeKuyper Melon Liqueur
1 oz. DeKuyper Razzmatazz
sour mix to fill
splash lemon-lime soda

Garnish with lemon wedge.

MELONADE
2 parts Marie Brizard Watermelon
1 part vodka
3 parts fresh lemonade

MELONBALL
2 oz. Midori Melon Liqueur
1 oz. Banzai Vodka
3 oz. orange juice

Mix together in a tall glass and fill with orange juice.

MIDNIGHT MOZART
¾ oz. Mozart Liqueur
¾ oz. coffee flavored brandy
3 oz. coffee

Pour into coffee, top with milk or heavy cream.

MIST & JUICE
one part Irish Mist
three parts juice of your choice (orange or cranberry is great)

Blend, serve in a tall glass.

MISTICO MARTINI
1 oz. Jose Cuervo Mistico
1 oz. Chambord
1 oz. sweet & sour mix

Stir with ice and strain into a martini glass.

MISTY DEW
equal parts:
Irish Mist
Tullamore Dew Irish Whiskey

Pour over ice in a rocks glass.

MUCHO MELON

2 parts Marie Brizard
  Watermelon
2 parts rum
2 parts pineapple juice

NEON CACTUS

1 oz. DeKuyper Cactus Juice
2 oz. lime juice

Chill, pour into shot glass.

PACIFIER

1 scoop crushed ice
1½ oz. white creme de menthe
several dashes Fernet Branca

Pack a sherry glass with the
crushed ice. Pour in the creme
de menthe and top off with a
float of Fernet Branca.

PEARL DIVER

½ oz. coconut rum
½ oz. Midori
½ oz. pineapple juice

PINK FLAMINGO

1 oz. DeKuyper WilderBerry
  Schnapps
2 oz. cranberry juice
shot of sweet & sour mix

Pour together over ice and
stir.

PURPLE HAZE

1 part Chambord
1 part vodka
1 part cranberry juice or sour
  mix

Combine in a shot glass.

QUIET NUN

1 oz. Benedictine
½ oz. cointreau
1 oz. light cream
1 scoop crushed ice

Shake well and strain into a
chilled cocktail glass.

RATTLESNAKE

2 oz. Hiram Walker Red Hot
  Schnapps

Serve in a shot glass with a
dash of Tabasco sauce.

RED HOT & ICE COLD

1½ parts Hiram Walker Red Hot
  Schnapps in shot glass

Serve with your favorite glass
of beer.

ROMAN SCREW DRIVER

1½ parts Hiram Walker Sambuca
3 oz. orange juice

Pack a tall glass with ice. Add 1
1/2 parts Hiram Walker sambuca. Top with orange juice and
orange slice.

ROOT BEER FLOAT

2 parts Hiram Walker Old
  Fashioned Root Beer Schnapps
2 parts milk or cream
4 parts lemon-lime soda

Blend.

RUM RUNNER

½ part Hiram Walker Blackberry
  Flavored Brandy
½ part Hiram Walker Creme de
  Banana
1½ parts light rum
splash grenadine
splash lemon/lime juices

Blend. Garnish with pineapple
and cherry.

THE RUSTY NAIL

half Drambuie
half premium scotch

SEX ON THE BEACH

½ oz. Stoli Vodka
½ oz. Midori
½ oz. raspberry liqueur
½ oz. pineapple and cranberry
  juice

SICILIAN KISS

1 part Disaronno Amaretto
1 part Southern Comfort

Stir on the rocks.

SICILIAN MARTINI

1½ oz. Opal Nera Sambuca
2 oz. Fris Vodka

Stir with ice and strain.

SIDE CAR

¾ oz. cointreau
1½ oz. Remy Martin cognac
juice of ½ lemon

Shake with ice and strain into
a chilled martini glass.

SILENT MONK

1 oz. Benedictine
½ oz. cointreau or triple sec
1 oz. light cream

Shake well.

SIMPLY BONKERS

1 part Chambord
1 part Bacardi Rum
1 part cream

Combine in a shot glass.

SLAMPIRE (A.K.A. FIREBALL)

1½ oz. Hot Damn! Hot
  Cinnamon Schnapps
twist of Tabasco

Chill and add a twist of
Tabasco. Serve as a shot.

SLOE GIN COCKTAIL

1 ½ oz. sloe gin
½ oz. dry vermouth

Shake well.

—⊗⊗⊗—

SOL Y SOMBRE (SUN & SHADE)

1½ oz. Marie Brizard Anisette
1½ oz. Gautier Cognac

Run with the bulls!

—⊗⊗⊗—

STAR WARS

1 oz. Disaronno Amaretto
1 oz. cointreau
1 oz. Southern Comfort
1 oz. grenadine

Blend.

—⊗⊗⊗—

STOPLIGHT

2 oz. sloe gin
1 oz. gin
1 oz. lemon juice
1 scoop crushed ice
1 maraschino cherry

Mix.

—⊗⊗⊗—

SUNBLOCK 42O

1 oz. DeKuyper Peachtree
  Schnapps
½ oz. DeKuyper Amaretto
3 oz. cranberry juice

Pour over ice in a 16-oz. glass. Stir and garnish with an orange wedge.

SWEET TART

1 oz. Absolut Vodka
¼ oz. Chambord
¼ oz. Rose's Lime Juice
¼ oz. pineapple juice

Shake and strain into a shot glass.

—⊗⊗⊗—

TIA MOCHATINI

⅓ Tia Maria
⅓ Fris Vodka
⅓ chocolate liqueur

Shake well over ice. Serve in a martini glass with a chocolate shaving.

—⊗⊗⊗—

TIA RUMBA

2 oz. Tia Maria
2 oz. rum

Shake well over ice, serve in a martini glass with a coffee bean.

—⊗⊗⊗—

TRINITY

½ oz. Bols Peach Schnapps
½ oz. Bols Apricot Flavored
  Brandy
½ oz. Grand Marnier

Combine all ingredients over ice in a 4-oz. rocks glass.

TUACA COOL GIRL

1½ oz. Fris Vodka
¾ oz. Tuaca Liqueur
3 oz. cranberry juice

Mix Fris Vodka with Tuaca
Liqueur. Add cranberry juice.
Serve in a chilled martini glass
with a lemon twist.

———∞∞∞———

TUACA HOT APPLE PIE

1 oz. Tuaca Liqueur
3½ oz. hot apple cider

Add Tuaca liqueur to a steaming mug of hot apple cider.
Top with a whisper of
whipped cream and kiss of
cinnamon.

———∞∞∞———

VELVET HUMMER

1 part Hiram Walker Creme de
  Cacao Brown
1 part Hiram Walker Triple Sec
4 parts vanilla ice cream

Blend.

———∞∞∞———

VERY CONTINENTAL STINGER

Combine 1½ parts Hiram Walker
  Amaretto and cognac
with ¾ parts Hiram Walker
  Peppermint Schnapps

Gin

1951 MARTINI RINSE

3 oz. Gordon's Gin
½ oz. cointreau rinse
anchovy stuffed olive

Stir and serve in a chilled Martini glass.

————

ABBEY COCKTAIL

1 ½ oz. gin
1 oz. orange juice
1 dash orange bitters
maraschino cherry

Shake.

————

ALABAMA FIZZ

1½ oz. gin
juice of ½ lemon
1 tsp. sugar
2 oz. chilled club soda
sprig of fresh mint

Shake and strain.

————

ALASKA COCKTAIL

2 oz. gin
½ oz. yellow Chartreuse
2 dashes orange bitters

Stir.

ALEXANDER COCKTAIL

1 oz. gin
1 oz. white creme de cacao
1 oz. cream
¼ tsp. nutmeg

Shake.

————

ALEXANDER'S SISTER

1 oz. dry gin
1 oz. cream
1 oz. creme de menthe

Shake and strain.

————

ALFONSO SPECIAL

1½ oz. Grand Marnier
¾ oz. gin
¾ oz. dry vermouth
4 dashes sweet vermouth
1 dash Angostura Bitters

Stir or shake.

————

ALLIES COCKTAIL

1 oz. gin
1 oz. dry vermouth
2 dashes Kummel

Stir.

ANGEL FACE

1 oz. gin
1 oz. apricot brandy
1 oz. apple brandy or Calvados

Shake.

ARCADIA

1½ oz. gin
½ oz. Galliano
½ oz. creme de bananes
½ oz. grapefruit juice

Shake and strain.

AUTHENTIC GIN MARTINI

1 oz. Gilbey's Gin
½ oz. dry vermouth
olive

Shake well with ice. Strain into martini glass. Add olive.

BALD HEAD MARTINI

4 parts Gordon's Gin
1 part French vermouth
1 part Italian vermouth
1 or 2 dashes Pernod
green olive

Sprinkle the oil from a twist of lemon peel on top.

BARBARY COAST COCKTAIL

¾ oz. gin
¾ oz. scotch
¾ oz. creme de cacao
¾ oz. cream

Shake.

BEAUTY SPOT

1½ oz. gin
2 tsp. white creme de cacao
½ tsp. grenadine

Shake and strain.

BEEKMAN PLACE

1 oz. gin
2 oz. sloe gin
1 tsp. lemon juice
1 oz. grenadine

Shake.

BEL AIR COCKTAIL

2 oz. gin
1 oz. apricot brandy
1 tsp. grenadine

Shake.

BELMONT COCKTAIL

2 oz. gin
1 tsp. grenadine
¾ oz. cream

Shake.

BENNETT COCKTAIL

1½ oz. gin
½ oz. lime juice
½ tsp. sugar
2 dashes Angostura Bitters

Shake.

BERMUDA HIGHBALL

¾ oz. gin
¾ oz. dry vermouth
¾ oz. brandy
3 oz. chilled ginger ale or club soda
twist of lemon peel

Pour over ice.

BITCH ON WHEELS

2 oz. Gordon's Gin
½ oz. extra dry vermouth
¼ oz. Pernod and white creme de menthe

Shake ingredients with ice and strain into a chilled martini glass.

BLACK CURRANT MARTINI

1 oz. Gordon's Gin
1 oz. Godiva Liqueur
¼ oz. creme de cassis
⅛ oz. each lemon juice and lime juice

Combine with ice; shake well. Served chilled. Garnish with cherry.

BLACK MARTINI

2½ oz. Gordon's Gin

splash of Chambord

BLONDE BOMBSHELL

1½ oz. gin
½ oz. white curacao
1 tsp. white creme de menthe
2 tsp. heavy cream

Shake and strain.

BLUE COWBOY

crushed ice
1½ oz. gin
½ oz. blue curacao

Stir and strain.

BLUE LADY

1 oz. Bombay Sapphire Gin
¼ oz. blue curacao
1 oz. sweet & sour mix

Shake, serve over ice.

BLUE MOON COCKTAIL

1½ oz. gin
¾ oz. blue curacao
twist of lemon

Shake and strain.

GIN

BLUES MARTINI

½ oz. Gordon's Gin
½ oz. Gordon's Vodka

Add a few drops of blue curacao.

BOMBAY MARTINI

1½ oz. Bombay Saphire Gin
dash extra dry vermouth

Stir in cocktail glass with ice.
Strain and serve straight up or
on the rocks. Add lemon twist
or olive.

BOMBAY SPIDER

1¼ oz. Bombay Saphire Gin
dash bitters
3 oz. ginger ale

In a tall glass filled with ice,
add Bombay and bitters and
fill with ginger ale.

BOOMERANG

2 oz. gin
½ oz. dry vermouth
2 dashes bitters
½ tsp. maraschino liqueur
1 maraschino cherry

Stir and strain.

BOOTLEGGER MARTINI

2 oz. Gordon's Gin
½ oz. Southern Comfort
lemon twist

Stir and serve in a chilled
martini glass.

BOSTON COCKTAIL

1½ oz. gin
1½ oz. apricot brandy
2 dashes grenadine
1 tsp. lemon juice
twist of lemon peel

Shake and strain.

BRONX SILVER COCKTAIL

1½ oz. gin
½ oz. dry vermouth
½ oz. sweet vermouth
juice of ¼ orange
slice of orange

Shake and strain.

BULLDOG COCKTAIL

2 oz. gin
juice of 1 orange
3 oz. chilled ginger ale

Pour over ice.

THE BUMPY GRAPEFRUIT

Pour Seagram's Gin over ice
in a highball glass. Fill with
grapefruit juice. Garnish with
lemon.

GIN

THE BUMPY SUNSET

Start with Seagram's Gin over ice. Add orange juice to taste and a dash of grenadine. Garnish with lime.

CABARET COCKTAIL

1½ oz. gin
½ oz. dry vermouth
2 dashes Benedictine
1 dash Angostura Bitters
maraschino cherry

Stir and strain.

CAPE SAPPHIRE

1¼ oz. Bombay Saphire Gin
2½ oz. cranberry juice

Stir and serve over ice.

CLASSIC GIN MARTINI

1 oz. Gilbey's Gin
¼ oz. dry vermouth
lemon twist

Stir well with ice. Strain into martini glass. Garnish with lemon twist.

CLOVER CLUB COCKTAIL

1½ oz. gin
juice of ½ lime or lemon
2 tsp. grenadine
sprig of fresh mint

Shake and strain.

COPENHAGEN

1 oz. dry gin
1 oz. aquavit
½ oz. dry vermouth
green olive

COPPER ILLUSION MARTINI

1 part Gordon's Gin
1 part Grand Marnier
1 part Campari

Serve with an orange slice.

CORONET

2 oz. dry gin
¾ oz. port wine
twist of lemon peel

CRIMSON SUNSET

2 oz. gin
2 tsp. lemon juice
½ tsp. grenadine
½ oz. tawny port

Shake and strain.

DEMPSEY COCKTAIL

1 oz. gin
1 oz. Calvados or apple brandy
½ tsp. Pernod
2 dashes grenadine

Stir and strain.

DEPTH CHARGE

1¼ oz. dry gin
1¼ oz. Lillet
¼ oz. Pernod

orange peel

———— ❧ ————

DUBARRY COCKTAIL

1½ oz. gin
¾ oz. dry vermouth
½ tsp. Pernod
1 dash Angostura Bitters
thin slice orange

Stir and strain.

———— ❧ ————

DUBONNET COCKTAIL

1½ oz. dry gin
1½ oz. Dubonnet
tsp. lemon juice

Shake and strain.

———— ❧ ————

EARTHQUAKE

1 oz. rye or bourbon
1 oz. gin
1 oz. Pernod

Shake and strain.

———— ❧ ————

ELEGANT MARTINI

1¾ oz. Gordon's Gin
½ oz. dry vermouth
¼ oz. Grand Marnier

———— ❧ ————

ELEPHANT'S EAR

1 oz. dry gin
¾ oz. dry vermouth
¾ oz. Dubonnet

FALLEN ANGEL

1 oz. Bombay Saphire Gin
½ oz. apricot brandy
½ oz. brandy

Shake. Serve up.

———— ❧ ————

FAVORITE COCKTAIL

1 oz. gin
1 oz. apricot brandy
½ oz. dry vermouth
½ tsp. fresh lemon juice

Shake and strain.

———— ❧ ————

FIFTY-FIFTY COCKTAIL

1½ oz. gin
1½ oz. dry vermouth
green olive

Stir and strain.

———— ❧ ————

FINE-AND-DANDY COCKTAIL

1½ oz. gin
¾ oz. cointreau or triple sec
½ oz. lemon juice
1 dash Angostura Bitters
maraschino cherry

Stir and strain.

———— ❧ ————

FINO MARTINI

2½ oz. gin
1½ tsp. Fino Sherry
1 lemon twist

Stir and strain.

FLYING DUTCHMAN

2 oz. gin
½ oz. cointreau or triple sec

Stir.

———— ❧ ————

FOURTH DEGREE

¾ oz. dry gin
¾ oz. dry vermouth
¾ oz. sweet vermouth
¼ oz. Pernod

twist of lemon peel

———— ❧ ————

GIBSON

2½ oz. gin
1½ tsp. dry vermouth
3 cocktail onions

Stir and strain.

———— ❧ ————

GIBSON MARTINI

Gordon's Gin
dry vermouth
cured onion

GILBEY'S GIN RUMMY

1 oz. Gilbey's Gin
½ oz. dry vermouth
1 dash bitters
1 dash lemon juice

Shake well with ice. Strain into martini glass.

———— ❧ ————

GILBEY'S TRIO

1 oz. Gilbey's Gin
½ oz. Leroux Triple Sec
1 oz. pineapple juice

Fill shaker halfway with ice; add gin, pineapple juice, and lemon juice; shake well; pour into old-fashioned glass.

———— ❧ ————

GIN & SIN

1 oz. gin
1 oz. orange juice
1 oz. lemon juice
1 dash grenadine

Shake and strain.

———— ❧ ————

GIN & TONIC

3 oz. gin
4-6 oz. cold tonic (Quinine)
slice or wedge of lemon or lime

Mix and pour over ice; add lemon or lime garnish.

GIN BUCK

2 oz. gin
juice of ½ lemon
3 oz. chilled ginger ale

Pour over ice.

GIN DAISY

2 oz. gin
1 oz. lemon juice
½ tsp. sugar
1 tsp. raspberry syrup (or grenadine)

Shake and strain.

GIN FIZZ

2 oz. gin
1 tsp. sugar
1 oz. lemon juice
2 oz. chilled club soda

Shake and strain.

GIN GREYHOUND

1½ oz. gin
¾ oz. grapefruit juice

Shake and strain.

GIN RICKEY

2 oz. gin
juice of ½ lime
2 oz. chilled club soda
maraschino cherry

Stir.

GIN TART

1 oz. Gilbey's Gin
½ oz. lime juice
½ oz. lemon juice

Fill mixing glass with ice, add gin, lime and lemon juice, strain into cocktail glass, garnish with lime.

GLOOM RAISER

2½ oz. gin
½ oz. dry vermouth
2 dashes Pernod
2 dashes grenadine

Stir and strain.

GOLDEN DAWN

1½ oz. gin
¾ oz. apricot brandy
¾ oz. orange juice

Shake and strain.

GOLF COCKTAIL

2 oz. gin
1 oz. dry vermouth
2 dashes Angostura Bitters

Stir and strain.

GOLLY DOLLY

1½ oz. gin
1 oz. peach brandy
1 tsp. grenadine
½ oz. heavy cream

Shake.

GRAPEFRUIT COCKTAIL

2 oz. gin
1 oz. grapefruit juice

Shake and strain.

GREEN DEVIL

1½ oz. gin
2 tsp. green creme de menthe
½ oz. lime juice
fresh mint leaves

Shake and strain.

GYPSY LIFE

2 oz. gin
1 oz. Benedictine
1-2 dashes Angostura Bitters

Shake and strain.

HASTY COCKTAIL

1 ½ oz. gin
¾ oz. dry vermouth
¼ tsp. Pernod
3 dashes grenadine

Shake and strain.

HAWAIIAN COCKTAIL

2 oz. gin
½ oz. cointreau or triple sec
½ oz. pineapple juice

Shake and strain.

ITALIAN MARTINI

2 parts Bombay Saphire Gin
1 part Disaronno Amaretto

Stir on the rocks.

LAST TANGO

1½ oz. dry gin
1 oz. orange juice
½ oz. dry vermouth
½ oz. red vermouth
½ oz. cointreau

Shake and strain.

LEAVE-IT-TO-ME COCKTAIL

1 oz. gin
½ oz. apricot brandy
½ oz. dry vermouth
2 dashes lemon juice
1 dash grenadine

Shake and strain.

LITTLE DEVIL COCKTAIL

1 oz. gin
1 oz. light rum
¾ oz. cointreau or triple sec
juice of ¼ lemon

Shake and strain.

GIN

MAIDEN'S BLUSH COCKTAIL

1½ oz. gin
1 tsp. cointreau or triple sec
1 tsp. grenadine
2 dashes lemon juice

Shake and strain.

MAIDEN'S PRAYER

1½ oz. gin
1½ oz. cointreau or triple sec
½ oz. lemon juice

Shake and strain.

MANHASSET MAULER

2 oz. gin
1 oz. sloe gin
lemon zest

Shake and strain.

MIDNIGHT MARTINIS

Stir Seagram's Gin and dry vermouth over ice and strain into chilled glass. Garnish with black olive.

MOONSHOT

1¼ oz. Bombay Saphire Gin
3 oz. clam juice
dash red pepper sauce

Stir over ice cubes.

MORRO

1 oz. gin
½ oz. dark rum
½ oz. lime juice
½ oz. pineapple juice
½ tsp. sugar

Shake and strain.

NAPOLEON

1¼ oz. Bombay Saphire Gin
½ oz. Dubonnet Rouge
½ oz. Grand Marnier

In a mixing glass, combine all of the ingredients. Stir well. Strain into a cocktail glass.

NEGRONI

1½ oz. gin
1½ oz. Campari
1½ oz. sweet vermouth
twist of lemon peel

Stir.

NINETEENTH HOLE

1½ oz. dry gin
1 oz. dry vermouth
1 tsp. red vermouth
dash of Angostura

Stir and strain. Serve with impaled green olive.

NINETEEN-TWENTY

1 oz. dry gin
1 oz. dry vermouth
1 oz. kirsch
dash of Pernod

Shake and strain.

—⊗⊗⊗—

NUPTIAL BLISS

1½ oz. dry vermouth
½ oz. kirsch
1 tsp. each: cointreau, orange
 juice, lemon juice

Shake and strain.

—⊗⊗⊗—

ORANGE BLOSSOM COCKTAIL

2 oz. gin
1 oz. orange juice
¼ tsp. sugar (optional)

Shake and strain.

—⊗⊗⊗—

ORANGE OASIS

1½ oz. gin
½ oz. cherry brandy
4 oz. chilled orange juice
2 oz. chilled ginger ale

Pour over ice.

—⊗⊗⊗—

ORIENT EXPRESS

1 oz. gin
1 oz. bourbon
1 oz. brandy

Stir and strain.

PALL MALL

1½ oz. gin
½ oz. dry vermouth
½ oz. sweet vermouth
1 tsp. white creme de menthe
1 dash orange bitters (optional)

Stir and strain.

—⊗⊗⊗—

PARISIAN

1 oz. gin
1 oz. dry vermouth
1 oz. creme de cassis

Shake and strain.

—⊗⊗⊗—

PARK AVENUE

2 oz. gin
1 oz. sweet vermouth
1 oz. pineapple juice
1-2 dashes curacao (optional)

Shake and strain.

—⊗⊗⊗—

PARK WEST

2 oz. gin
2 oz. pineapple juice
2 oz. grapefruit juice

Shake.

—⊗⊗⊗—

PICCADILLY COCKTAIL

1½ oz. gin
¾ oz. dry vermouth
1 dash Pernod
1 dash grenadine

Stir and strain.

PINK LADY

1¼ oz. Bombay Saphire Gin
2 tsp. grenadine
3 oz. half & half

Shake with ice and strain into cocktail glass or serve on the rocks.

———⊗∞⊙———

PINK LADY COCKTAIL

2 oz. gin
1 tsp. grenadine
1 tsp. cream
1 egg white
1 tsp. lemon juice (optional)

Shake and strain.

———⊗∞⊙———

POLLYANNA COCKTAIL

2 oz. gin
⅔ oz. sweet vermouth
½ tsp. grenadine
3 slices of orange
3 slices of pineapple

Shake and strain.

———⊗∞⊙———

POLO

1¼ oz. Bombay Saphire Gin
2 oz. grapefruit juice
2 oz. orange juice

In a tall glass with ice, fill with half grapefruit juice and half orange juice.

POLO COCKTAIL

1½ oz. gin
¾ oz. orange juice
¾ oz. lemon juice

Shake and strain.

———⊗∞⊙———

RED RUBY

1½ oz. Bombay Saphire Gin
½ oz. grenadine
½ oz. dry vermouth

In a mixing glass half filled with ice cubes, combine all ingredients. Stir well. Strain into cocktail glass.

———⊗∞⊙———

SALTY DOG

1¼ oz. Bombay Saphire Gin
3 oz. grapefruit juice
salt

Wet rim of tall glass with juice or water and dip into salt to coat (optional). Pour Bombay over ice, fill with grapefruit juice, and stir.

———⊗∞⊙———

SAPPHIRE & SEVEN

1½ oz. Bombay Saphire Gin
7-Up

In a tall glass with ice fill with 7-Up. Garnish with lemon twist.

SAPPHIRE AND TONIC

1¼ oz. Bombay Saphire Gin
3 oz. tonic

In a tall glass filled with ice, add Bombay Sapphire and fill with tonic. Add squeeze of lime.

———— ⊗∞ ————

SAPPHIRE CASSIS

3 parts Bombay Saphire Gin
1 part creme de cassis

Stir on the rocks.

———— ⊗∞ ————

SAPPHIRE COCKTAIL

1 part Bombay Saphire Gin
2 parts Dubonnet

Stir on the rocks. Add lemon twist.

———— ⊗∞ ————

SAPPHIRE DAIQUIRI

2 oz. Bombay Saphire Gin
½ cup fresh lime juice
⅓ cup crushed ice

Blend well with ice and serve in a cocktail or rocks glass.

———— ⊗∞ ————

SAPPHIRE DRIVER

1¼ oz. Bombay Saphire Gin
4 oz. orange juice
2 oz. tonic water

In a tall glass filled with ice, add Bombay Sapphire and orange juice. Fill with tonic water.

SAPPHIRE GIMLET

3 parts Bombay Saphire Gin
1 part lime juice

Stir on the rocks. Add squeeze of lime.

———— ⊗∞ ————

SAPPHIRE JEWEL

1 part Bombay Saphire Gin
1 part Perle de Brillet

Stir on the rocks.

———— ⊗∞ ————

SAPPHIRE JULEP

1¼ oz. Bombay Saphire Gin
4 sprigs mint
1 tsp. sugar

In a highball glass filled with shaved ice, stir until glass is frosted. Garnish with fresh mint.

———— ⊗∞ ————

SAPPHIRE SCREWDRIVER

1¼ oz. Bombay Saphire Gin
3 oz. orange juice

In a tall glass filled with ice, add Bombay and fill with orange juice.

———— ⊗∞ ————

SAPPHIRE SLICE

1 oz. Bombay Saphire Gin
¼ oz. cointreau
1 oz. lemon juice

Shake, serve over ice. Garnish with orange slice.

SAPPHIRE STINGER
1 oz. Bombay Saphire Gin
¼ oz. white creme de menthe

Stir well on the rocks.

―――∞∞∞―――

SAPPHIRE SUNSET
1½ oz. Bombay Saphire Gin
½ oz. banana liqueur
1 oz. sweet & sour mix
1 oz. orange juice

Shake well with ice and serve on the rocks.

―――∞∞∞―――

SEAGRAM'S GIN GIMLET
1¼ oz. Seagram's Gin
¾ oz. lime juice

Pour over ice in a cocktail glass. Stir. Garnish with a slice of lime.

―――∞∞∞―――

SIDECAR IN BOMBAY
1 oz. Bombay Saphire Gin
¼ oz. Grand Marnier
¼ oz. lemon juice

Shake with ice and serve on the rocks or up in a sugar-rimmed glass.

SINGAPORE SLING I
1½ oz. gin
½ oz. lemon juice
1 tsp. grenadine
½ oz. cherry brandy
chilled club soda (do not shake or mix—top off)
slice of lemon or lime
maraschino cherry

Mix.

―――∞∞∞―――

SISTER SAPPHIRE
1½ oz. Bombay Saphire Gin
1 oz. white creme de menthe
1 oz. half & half

Shake with ice. Serve up or on the rocks.

―――∞∞∞―――

SLIM GIN
¼ oz. Bombay Saphire Gin

In a tall glass filled with ice and your favorite diet soda.

―――∞∞∞―――

SLING
2 oz. gin
1 oz. cherry brandy
juice of ½ lemon
1 tsp. sugar
1 tsp. water
twist of lemon peel

Shake and strain.

SMOOTH MELODY
1 oz. Gilbey's Gin
1 oz. orange juice
ginger ale

Fill glass with ice, add juice and gin, fill rest with ginger ale, stir, garnish with maraschino cherry.

SOUTHERN BOMBAY
1 oz. Bombay Saphire Gin
¼ oz. Southern Comfort
1¼ oz. grapefruit juice

Stir on the rocks.

STINGER
2½ oz. gin
¾ oz. white creme de menthe

Shake and strain.

TWISTED TONIC
1¼ oz. Seagram's Lime Twisted
 Gin
6 oz. Seagram's Tonic Water

Pour Seagram's Lime Twisted Gin over ice in a tall glass. Fill with tonic water. Stir to blend. If you wish, drop a slice of lime into glass.

UNION JACK
1½ oz. gin
½ oz. sloe gin
1 tsp. grenadine

Shake and strain.

THE YELLOW FELLOW
1 oz. Bombay Saphire Gin
¼ oz. yellow Chartreuse

Shake, strain into cocktail glass.

XANTHIA
1½ oz. dry gin
1 oz. dry vermouth
1 oz. cointreau

Mix and serve on the rocks.

GIN

Whiskey

ALLEGHENY
1 oz. Canadian Club
1 oz. Martini & Rossi Dry Vermouth
1½ tsp. blackberry-flavored brandy

Pour ingredients into ice filled mixing glass and stir. Strain into a chilled cocktail glass. Garnish with a twist of lemon.

BABY'S BOTTOM
1½ oz. Rittenhouse
½ oz. white creme de menthe
½ oz. white creme de cacao

Stir well. Strain into a cocktail glass.

BARNSTORMER
1½ oz. whiskey
½ oz. peppermint schnapps
splash dark creme de cacao
splash white creme de cacao
½ oz. lemon juice

Shake. Strain into an old-fashioned glass with ice.

BENT NAIL
1½ oz. Crown Royal
½ oz. Drambuie
3 oz. crushed ice

Shake. Strain into cocktail glass.

BLACK HAWK
2 oz. whiskey
1 oz. sloe gin

Pour ingredients into ice filled mixing glass and stir. Pour into a chilled cocktail glass. Garnish with a cherry.

BLACK HAWK COLLINS
1 oz. whiskey
½ oz. blackberry-flavored brandy
2 oz. sweet & sour mix

Pour ingredients into cocktail shaker with ice. Shake and strain into collins glass filled with ice cubes. Fill with soda, garnish with cherry and lime squeeze.

BLENDER
¼ oz. Black Velvet
¼ oz. white creme de cacao

Blend with crushed ice.

BLINKER
1¼ oz. rye whiskey
2½ oz. grapefruit juice
½ oz. grenadine

Shake well with ice. Strain into old-fashioned glass.

BOILERMAKER

1½ oz. American whiskey
8 oz. beer

Drink the whiskey, sip the beer, or drop the whiskey in the beer.

~

BOUNTY

2 oz. whiskey
¼ oz. Martini & Rossi Sweet
  Vermouth
¼ oz. Benedictine

Pour ingredients into ice filled mixing glass and stir vigorously. Strain into chilled cocktail glass. Lemon or orange twist is an optional garnish.

~

CANADIAN ALEXANDER

¾ oz. Canadian Club
¾ oz. Hiram Walker Dark Creme
  de Cacao
¾ oz. heavy cream

Shake all ingredients with cracked ice. Strain into a cocktail glass. Sprinkle with nutmeg.

~

CANADIAN ALGONQUIN

2 oz. Crown Royal
¼ oz. Martini & Rossi Dry
  Vermouth
¼ oz. pineapple juice

Pour ingredients into ice filled mixing glass. Stir and pour into chilled cocktail glass.

CANADIAN APPLE PIE

Into a highball glass filled with ice
  pour:
¾ oz. Canadian Club
¾ oz. Hiram Walker Cinnamon
  Schnapps
apple cider or apple juice

Stir and serve. Add orange slice garnish.

~

CANADIAN BEAUTY

½ oz. Canadian Club
½ oz. Martini & Rossi Dry
  Vermouth
¼ tsp. white creme de menthe
1 Tbsp. orange juice
1 Tbsp. grenadine
1 dash port

Shake first 5 ingredients with ice. Strain into a cocktail glass. Finish with a dash of port.

~

CANADIAN BOOMERANG

1½ oz. Canadian Club
1 oz. Martini & Rossi Dry
  Vermouth
1 dash Angostura Bitters
1 dash maraschino

Pour ingredients into ice filled mixing glass and stir. Strain into a chilled cocktail glass and top with a twist of lemon.

CANADIAN BOSTON

¾ oz. Canadian Club
¾ oz. apricot-flavored brandy
juice of ¼ lemon
1½ tsp. grenadine

Pour ingredients into ice filled mixing glass and stir. Strain into a chilled cocktail glass.

CANADIAN CITRUS SOUR

1¼ oz. Canadian Club
¾ oz. sweet & sour
¾ oz. orange juice
¾ oz. lime juice

Pour ingredients into cocktail shaker with ice. Shake and strain into sour glass. Garnish with lemon, orange, and/or lime slices.

CANADIAN CLUB AVRIL

2 oz. Canadian Club
½ oz. Cranberry Liqueur

Stir well. Strain into a cocktail glass.

CANADIAN CLUB COCKTAIL

2 oz. Canadian Club
1 tsp. sugar syrup
1 dash Angostura Bitters

Pour ingredients into ice filled mixing glass. Strain into a chilled cocktail glass. Top with a cherry.

CANADIAN CLUB ICED TEA

1 oz. Canadian Club
1 oz. Absolut Vodka
2 oz. sweet & sour mix
6 oz. cola

Pack a 12 oz. glass with ice. Add liquors and sweet & sour. Fill with cola. Garnish with lemon wheel or twist.

CANADIAN CLUB SOUR

1¼ oz. Canadian Club
2 oz. sweet & sour mix
or
2 oz. lemon juice & 1 tsp. superfine sugar

Pour ingredients into cocktail shaker with ice. Shake and strain into sour glass. Garnish with cherry and orange slice.

CANADIAN COCKTAIL

In an old-fashioned/rocks glass place:
2 dashes Angostura Bitters
¼ oz. cointreau
½ tsp. superfine sugar
1 oz. soda or water
1¼ oz. Canadian Club

Stir first three ingredients until sugar dissolves, then add soda and Canadian Club. Stir and add cherry and lemon peel garnish.

CANADIAN COLLINS

1 ¼ oz. Canadian Club
2 oz. sweet & sour mix

Pour ingredients into cocktail shaker with ice. Shake and strain into collins glass filled with ice cubes. Fill with soda, add cherry and orange slice garnish, insert long straws.

⌘

CANADIAN COOLER

1¼ oz. Canadian Club
½ oz. Major Peters' Sweet & Sour
½ oz. orange juice
½ oz. pineapple juice
½ oz. cranberry juice

Stir vigorously, fill with soda, and add lime squeeze as garnish. A dash of grenadine on top is optional.

⌘

THE CANADIAN DRY MANHATTAN

2 oz. Canadian Club
½ oz. Martini & Rossi Dry
  Vermouth

Pour ingredients into ice filled mixing glass and stir. Strain into chilled cocktail glass. Add olive and/or lemon twist as desired.

CANADIAN HOT TODDY

1½ oz. Canadian Club
2½ oz. hot water
1 tsp. granulated sugar

Over sugar, fill mug ⅔ full with hot water. Add Canadian Club. Stir. Top with a slice of lemon and a dusting of nutmeg.

⌘

CANADIAN OLD-FASHIONED

1 oz. soda or water
½ tsp. superfine sugar
2 dashes Angostura Bitters
1½ oz. Canadian Club

Place first three ingredients into an old-fashioned glass and stir. Then add ice cubes and the Canadian Club. Garnish with cherry, orange slice and lemon peel.

⌘

THE CANADIAN PERFECT MANHATTAN

2 oz. Canadian Club
¼ oz. Martini & Rossi Sweet
  Vermouth
¼ oz. dry vermouth

Pour ingredients into ice filled mixing glass and stir. Strain into chilled cocktail glass. Add cherry, olive, or lemon twist as desired.

WHISKEY

CANADIAN RAINBOW SOUR

½ oz. Canadian Club
½ oz. apricot-flavored brandy
½ oz. Hiram Walker Peach
  Schnapps
½ oz. Hiram Walker Triple Sec
2 oz. Major Peters' Sweet & Sour

Pour ingredients into cocktail shaker with ice. Shake and strain into double old-fashioned/rocks glass with ice cubes. Garnish with cherry, orange slice, and lime squeeze.

———— ∞ ————

CANADIAN SLING

1 oz. Canadian Club
½ oz. Hiram Walker Cherry-
  Flavored Brandy
2 oz. sweet & sour mix
dash Benedictine

Pour ingredients into cocktail shaker with ice. Shake and strain into collins glass filled with ice cubes. Fill with soda, add cherry & orange slice garnish, and insert long straws.

———— ∞ ————

CANADIAN STONE COLLINS

1¼ oz. Canadian Club
1 oz. sweet & sour mix
1 oz. orange juice

Pour ingredients into cocktail shaker with ice. Shake and strain into collins glass filled with ice cubes. Fill with soda, add cherry and orange slice garnish, and insert long straws.

CANADIAN STONE SOUR

1¼ oz. Canadian Club
1 oz. sweet & sour mix
1 oz. orange juice

Pour ingredients into cocktail shaker with ice. Shake and strain into sour glass. Garnish with cherry and orange slice.

———— ∞ ————

THE CANADIAN SWEET MANHATTAN

2 oz. Canadian Club
½ oz. Martini & Rossi Sweet
  Vermouth

Pour ingredients into ice filled mixing glass and stir. Strain into chilled cocktail glass. Add maraschino cherry as garnish or lemon twist if desired.

———— ∞ ————

CANADIAN WARD EIGHT

1¼ oz. Crown Royal
2 oz. sweet & sour mix
¼ oz. grenadine

Pour ingredients into cocktail shaker with ice. Shake and strain into sour glass. Garnish with cherry and orange slice.

———— ∞ ————

CC CIDER

1 oz. Canadian Club
½ oz. cinnamon schnapps
3 oz. apple cider
¼ unpeeled red apple

Blend. Pour unstrained.

COMMODORE COCKTAIL

1¼ oz. whiskey
2 dashes Angostura Bitters
1 oz. sweet & sour
dash Rose's Lime Juice (optional)

Pour ingredients into cocktail shaker with ice and shake. Strain into chilled glass.

DIXIE WHISKY

2 oz. Ritten House
½ tsp. white creme de menthe
¼ tsp. cointreau
½ oz. sugar syrup

Pour ingredients into an ice filled mixing glass and stir vigorously. Strain into a cocktail glass.

EARTHSHAKE

½ oz. Canadian Club
½ oz. Beefeater Gin
½ oz. Anisette

Shake well with ice. Strain into cocktail glass.

FOX RIVER

2 oz. whiskey
1 Tbsp. dark creme de cacao
4 dashes Angostura Bitters

Pour ingredients into ice filled mixing glass and stir. Strain into a cocktail glass.

FRENCH CANADIAN COLLINS

¾ oz. Canadian Club
¾ oz. Courvoisier Cognac
¼ oz. Benedictine
2 oz. sweet & sour mix

Pour ingredients into cocktail shaker with ice. Shake and strain into collins glass filled with ice cubes. Fill with soda, add cherry and orange slice garnish, and insert long straws.

FRISCO

1½ oz. Crown Royal
¾ oz. Benedictine

Stir ingredients with cracked ice. Strain into a cocktail glass and top with a twist of lemon.

GREATHEAD

1½ oz. American whiskey
½ oz. applejack

Stir well. Strain into a cocktail glass.

HOT BRICK TODDY

2 oz. whiskey
1½ oz. hot water
1 tsp. granulated sugar
1 tsp. butter
2-3 pinches cinnamon

In mug, dissolve sugar, butter and cinnamon with hot water. Add Canadian Club, stir and serve.

HOTEY TOTEY
½ oz. whiskey
½ oz. cinnamon schnapps
½ oz. dark creme de cacao

Fill with hot chocolate. Top with a half dozen mini-marshmallows.

IRISH CANADIAN
1½ oz. Black Velvet
½ oz. Irish Mist

Stir ingredients with ice until well mixed. Strain into a cocktail glass.

LADIES NIGHT OUT*
2 oz. Black Velvet
½ tsp. anisette
2 dashes Angostura Bitters

Stir all ingredients with ice. Strain into a cocktail glass. Top with a pineapple stick.
   * Originally called "Ladies Day."

LAWHILL
1½ oz. Canadian Mist
¾ oz. Martini & Rossi Dry
   Vermouth
¼ tsp. anisette
¼ tsp. maraschino
1 dash Angostura Bitters

Pour ingredients into ice filled mixing glass. Strain into a cocktail glass.

LINSTEAD
1½ oz. Seagrams V.O.
¾ oz. pineapple juice
¼ tsp. anisette
¼ tsp. lemon juice
½ tsp. granulated sugar

Shake all ingredients with ice (vigorously) and strain into a cocktail glass.

MAPLE LEAF
1 oz. Canadian Club
½ oz. Irish Mist
1 tsp. creme de cacao
1 oz. heavy cream

Shake all ingredients with ice (vigorously) and strain into a cocktail glass.

METS MANHATTAN
2 oz. Crown Royal
¼ oz. Martini & Rossi Dry
   Vermouth
¼ oz. strawberry schnapps

Pour ingredients into ice filled mixing glass and stir vigorously. Strain into a chilled cocktail glass. Optional strawberry garnish.

MILLIONAIRE MANHATTAN
1¼ oz. American whiskey
¼ oz. Harvey's Bristol Cream

Serve on the rocks or up.

MONTE CARLO

¾ oz. whiskey
¾ oz. Dubonnet
1 dash Angostura Bitters

Pour ingredients into ice filled mixing glass and stir vigorously. Strain into a chilled cocktail glass. Top with a twist of lemon.

MR. NEVINS

1½ oz. Canadian Club
1½ tsp. apricot-flavored brandy
1 Tbsp. grapefruit juice
1½ tsp. lemon juice
1 dash Angostura Bitters

Pour ingredients into ice filled mixing glass and stir vigorously. Strain into a chilled cocktail glass. Top with a twist of lemon.

NIAGARA FALLS

1½ oz. Canadian Club
½ oz. Irish Mist
½ oz. heavy cream

Shake all ingredients. Serve up.

OLD OLD-FASHIONED*

2 dashes Angostura Bitters
½ tsp. superfine sugar
1 oz. soda or water
1¼ oz. Canadian Club

Muddle sugar, bitters, and a cherry, a lemon peel and an orange slice in the bottom of the glass for ten seconds. Add ice cubes, soda or water, and Canadian Club. Stir and serve.

* At the turn of the century, this was the traditional method for preparing an old-fashioned and it most certainly resulted in more complex flavors.

PALMER COCKTAIL

1¼ oz. whiskey
2 dashes Angostura Bitters
1 oz. lemon juice

Pour ingredients into mixing glass filled with ice cubes. Stir and strain into chilled glass.

PREAKNESS

1¼ oz. Kentucky Fine Whiskey
¼ oz. Martini & Rossi Sweet
  Vermouth
¼ oz. Benedictine
1 dash Angostura Bitters

Stir and strain into chilled cocktail glass.

WHISKEY

QUEBEC

2 oz. Canadian Club
¼ oz. sweet vermouth
¼ oz. Campari or Amer Picon
¼ oz. maraschino cherry juice

Pour ingredients into cocktail shaker with ice. Shake and pour over ice cubes in a double old-fashioned/rocks glass. Garnish with cherry.

SHORT CUT OLD-FASHIONED

1¼ oz. Canadian Club
2 dashes Angostura Bitters
1 oz. 7-Up

Place the ingredients in an old-fashioned/rocks glass filled with ice cubes and stir. Garnish with cherry, orange slice, and lemon peel.

STILETTO SOUR

1 oz. whiskey
½ oz. Hiram Walker Amaretto
2 oz. Major Peters' Sweet & Sour

Pour ingredients into cocktail shaker with ice. Shake and strain into sour glass. Garnish with cherry and orange slice.

T.N.T. COCKTAIL

¾ oz. Canadian Club
¾ oz. anisette

Shake with cracked ice. Strain into cocktail glass.

THE TRADITIONAL CANADIAN MANHATTAN

2 oz. Canadian Club
½ oz. Martini & Rossi Sweet Vermouth
2 dashes Angostura Bitters

Pour ingredients into ice filled mixing glass and stir. Strain into chilled cocktail glass. Add maraschino cherry as garnish or lemon twist if desire

TWIN HILLS SOUR

(Also known as Frisco Sour)
1¼ oz. Canadian Club
½ oz. Benedictine
1½ oz. Major Peters' Sweet & Sour
½ oz. Major Peters' Lime Juice

Pour ingredients into cocktail shaker with ice. Shake and strain into sour glass. Garnish with lemon and lime slices.

WARD EIGHT COLLINS

1¼ oz. Crown Royal
2 oz. sweet & sour
¼ oz. grenadine

Pour ingredients into cocktail shaker with ice. Shake and strain into collins glass filled with ice cubes. Fill with soda, add lime squeeze garnish, and insert long straws.

WINDSOR COLLINS

1 oz. Windsor Canadian
½ oz. cointreau
½ oz. Peachtree Schnapps
2 oz. sweet & sour mix

Pour ingredients into cocktail shaker with ice. Shake and strain into a collins glass with ice cubes. Add lime squeeze garnish.

YES YES

1¼ oz. American whiskey
¼ oz. Opal Nera

Serve on the rocks.

YUKON COCKTAIL

1½ oz. Canadian Club
2 dashes Angostura Bitters
¼ oz. Hiram Walker Triple Sec
1 tsp. superfine sugar

Pour ingredients into cocktail shaker with ice and shake. Strain into chilled glass.

AFTER 8
½ oz. Baileys Irish Cream
½ oz. Kahlua
½ oz. green creme de menthe

Shake and serve in shot glass.

BAILEYS ALEXANDER
2 oz. Baileys Irish cream
½ oz. cognac

Shake and serve.

BAILEYS ALMOND CREAM
2 parts Baileys Irish Cream
2 parts light cream
dash pure almond extract

Shake and serve.

BAILEYS CUDDLER
1½ oz. Baileys Irish Cream
1½ oz. Disaronno Amaretto

Shake and serve.

BAILEYS DUBLIN DOUBLE
1 part Baileys Irish Cream
1 part Disaronno Amaretto

Shake and serve.

BAILEYS FIZZ
2 oz. Baileys Irish Cream
1 oz. club soda

Pour over crushed ice.

BAILEYS O'
Equal parts:
Baileys Irish Cream
Stolichnaya Ohranj

BAILEYS ROMA
1 part Baileys Irish Cream
1 part Romana Sambuca

BAILEYS SLIPPERY ELF
1 part Baileys Irish Cream
1 part Smirnoff Vodka

Serve in a shot glass.

BARNUMENTHE & BAILEYS
1½ oz. Baileys Irish Cream
½ oz. white creme de menthe

Serve over cracked ice or as a shot.

BLARNEY COCKTAIL
1½ oz. Jameson Irish Whiskey
1 oz. Italian vermouth
2 dashes green creme de menthe

Shake and serve.

BOILERMAKER
1¼ oz. Kilbeggan Irish Whiskey
10 oz. beer

Serve whiskey in a shot glass with a glass of beer.

BORU 007
2 oz. Boru Orange Vodka
1 oz. orange juice
1 oz. 7-Up (top off)

Stir with ice.

BORU CITRUS KAMIKAZE

Sugar coat the rim of a shot glass and add Boru Citrus and a splash of lime juice.

BUNGI JUMPER
1¼ oz. Irish Mist
4 oz. orange juice
½ oz. cream
splash amaretto

Mix all except amaretto. Float amaretto.

BUSHMILLS FUZZY VALENCIA
1½ oz. Bushmills Irish Whiskey
¾ oz. amaretto
5 oz. orange juice

Serve in tall glass over ice.

BUSHMILLS SURPRISE
1 oz. Bushmills
½ oz. triple sec
2 oz. lemon juice

Shake and serve.

BUSHMILLS TRIPLE TREAT
1½ oz. Bushmills
¾ oz. amaretto
5 oz. orange juice

Serve in a tall glass over ice.

CAROLARETTO
1 part Carolans Irish Cream
1 part amaretto

Shake or stir on the rocks.

CELTIC BERRY PATCH
½ oz. half & half
½ oz. Chambord
½ oz. Celtic Crossing
¾ oz. raspberry vodka

IRISH
COCKTAILS

CELTIC BULL

1½ oz. Jameson Irish Whiskey
2 oz. beef consommé or bouillon
2 oz. tomato juice
several dashes Worcestershire
 sauce
freshly ground pepper

Shake or blend. Pour into a chilled old-fashioned glass.

CELTIC CITRUS MARTINI

Boru Citrus Vodka with the "hint of honey" of Celtic Crossing.

CELTIC COCKTAIL

1 part Celtic Crossing
1 part vodka
splash of Midori Melon Liqueur

Shake and serve in a martini glass. Garnish with an orange slice.

CELTIC COSMO

1 oz. Celtic Crossing
1 oz. vodka
2 oz. cranberry juice
¼ oz. lime juice

CELTIC CROSSBONES

half Celtic Crossing
half Irish whiskey

CELTIC FROST

1½ oz. Celtic Crossing
½ oz. Frangelico
two scoops of vanilla ice cream
½ scoop of ice
½ oz. whipped cream
¼ tsp. nutmeg

Blend. Serve in a tall glass with whipped cream and nutmeg!

CELTIC GOLD

1 part Celtic Crossing
1 part Goldschlager

Combine. Shake and pour.

CELTIC KISS

Celtic Crossing with a splash of Irish Cream, served over ice.

CELTIC KISS ROYALE

1 oz. Celtic Crossing
4 oz. chilled champagne

CELTIC MARTINI

1 part Celtic Crossing
1 part lemon vodka

Mix and garnish with a lemon twist.

CEMENT MIXER

¾ shot Irish Cream
¼ shot lime juice

Combine in a shot glass.

CHIP SHOT

3/4 oz. Devonshire
3/4 oz. Tuaca
1 ½ oz. coffee

Serve on the rocks or in a shot glass.

———✸———

CORK COMFORT

1½ oz. Jameson Irish Whiskey
¾ oz. sweet vermouth
several dashes Angostura Bitters
several dashes Southern Comfort

Shake or blend.

———✸———

COUNTY CLARE COOLER

3 oz. Bunratty Meade
2 oz. 7-Up
4 ice cubes

Serve in a tall glass with a lemon slice.

———✸———

DANCING LEPRECHAUN

1½ oz. Jameson Irish Whiskey
1½ oz. lemon juice
1 oz. club soda
1½ oz. ginger ale

Stir.

———✸———

DUBLIN HANDSHAKE

½ oz. Baileys Irish Cream
½ oz. Irish whiskey
¾ oz. sloe gin

Shake and serve.

EMERALD ISLE

3/4 shot Tullamore Dew
3/4 shot green creme de menthe
2 scoops vanilla ice cream
2 oz. soda water

Blend first 3 ingredients, then add soda water. Stir after adding soda water.

———✸———

ERIE TOUR

⅓ Irish Mist
⅓ Carolans Irish Cream
⅓ Irish whiskey

Serve over ice.

———✸———

ERIN CROSS

½ oz. Celtic Crossing
½ oz. Irish Cream
½ oz. Irish whiskey

Serve layered in a shot glass.

———✸———

EXTRA NUTTY IRISHMAN

Equal parts:
Irish Mist
Frangelico
Carolans Irish Cream

Shake and serve topped with whipped cream.

———✸———

EYES R SMILIN

1 oz. Baileys Irish Cream
1 oz. vodka
½ oz. gin
½ oz. triple sec

Stir and serve.

FIFTH AVENUE

½ oz. Baileys Irish Cream
½ oz. apricot brandy
½ oz. white creme de cacao

Shake and serve.

—∞∞—

FRUITY IRISHMAN

2 parts Carolans Irish Cream
1 part Midori Melon Liqueur

Stir.

—∞∞—

GEORGE BUSH

1½ oz. Bushmills Irish Whiskey
1 strip lemon peel
3-4 oz. ginger ale, chilled

Serve over crushed ice.

—∞∞—

GINOLANS

2 parts Carolans Irish Cream
1 part Gordon's Gin

Stir.

—∞∞—

INTERNATIONAL COFFEE

½ oz. Devonshire
½ oz. Chambord
3 oz. hot coffee

Serve in a mug.

IRISH 2-O

½ oz. Boru Orange Vodka
½ oz. Irish Cream Liqueur
½ oz. hazelnut liqueur

Serve on the rocks or in a shot glass.

—∞∞—

IRISH ANGEL

¾ oz. Jameson Irish Whiskey
¼ oz. white creme de cacao
¼ oz. white creme de menthe
1 1/2 oz. heavy cream

Shake and serve.

—∞∞—

IRISH APPLE

2 parts Carolans Irish Cream
1 part Laird's AppleJack

Stir.

—∞∞—

IRISH CANADIAN

½ oz. Irish Mist
1½ oz. Canadian whiskey

Stir well and serve.

—∞∞—

IRISH CANDY

3 oz. Baileys Irish Cream
1¼ oz. chocolate raspberry liqueur
1 oz. white creme de cacao

Stir and serve.

IRISH CELEBRATION

1¼ oz. Bushmills
¼ oz. green creme de menthe
splash champagne

Shake; top with champagne.

IRISH COOLER

1¼ oz. Tullamore Dew
6 oz. club soda

Garnish with a lemon peel spiral.

IRISH COWBOY

1 part Baileys Irish Cream
1 part bourbon

Shake and serve.

IRISH DELIGHT

1½ oz. Bushmills Irish Whiskey
¾ oz. cream

Stir and serve.

IRISH DREAM

½ oz. Carolans Irish Cream
½ oz. hazelnut liqueur
½ oz. dark creme de cacao
1 scoop vanilla ice cream

Blend and serve.

IRISH EYES

1 oz. Kilbeggan Irish Whiskey
¼ oz. green creme de menthe
2 oz. heavy cream

Shake. Garnish with maraschino cherry.

IRISH FLAG SHOOTER

1 oz. green creme de menthe
1 oz. Carolans Irish Cream
1 oz. Grand Marnier

Pour ingredients in order.

IRISH FROG

¾ oz. Midori
¾ oz. Baileys Irish Cream
  (chilled)
1½ oz. cordial glass

Layer in above order.

IRISH FROST SHOOTER

1 shot Baileys Irish Cream
1 splash Coco Lopez Cream of
  Coconut
1 splash half & half

Blend.

IRISH HEADLOCK

¼ oz. Carolans Irish Cream
¼ oz. Irish whiskey
¼ oz. amaretto
¼ oz. brandy

Layer in above order.

IRISH KILT

1 oz. Kilbeggan Irish Whiskey
1 oz. scotch
1 oz. lemon juice
1½ oz. sugar syrup or to taste
several dashes orange bitters

Shake or blend.

IRISH KNIGHT

2 oz. Bushmills Irish Whiskey
2 dashes Noilly Prat Dry
  Vermouth
2 dashes Benedictine

In an old-fashioned glass, add twist of orange peel.

IRISH LACED

1 shot Irish Mist
2 splashes Coco Lopez Cream of
  Coconut
2 splashes half & half
3 splashes pineapple juice
2 scoops ice

Blend.

IRISH MAGIC

1 oz. Jameson Irish Whiskey
¼ oz. white creme de cacao
5 oz. orange juice

Stir and serve.

IRISH MARTINI

1 oz. Bushmills
1 oz. Baileys

Shake and serve.

IRISH NIGHT CAP

1 1/2 oz. Jameson Irish Whiskey
4 oz. hot milk
1 tsp. sugar

Stir.

IRISH PENANCE

1 part Carolans Irish Cream
1 part cointreau

Shake slowly and serve on the rocks.

IRISH PRINCE

1¼ oz. Jameson Irish Whiskey
3 oz. tonic water

Stir.

IRISH QUAALUDE

½ oz. Baileys Irish Cream
½ oz. Absolut
½ oz. Frangelico
½ oz. white creme de cacao

Shake and strain.

IRISH RASPBERRY

1 oz. Devonshire Irish Cream
½ oz. Chambord

Blend.

IRISH RICKEY

1½ oz. Tullamore Dew
1 cube ice
juice of ½ lime

Fill 8 oz. highball glass with carbonated water and stir. Leave lime in glass.

IRISH RUSSIAN

1 part Carolans Irish Cream
1 part vodka

Stir.

IRISH SLING

1 jigger Tullamore Dew
1 jigger gin

Crush one lump of sugar and two lumps of ice and add to glass.

IRISH SPRING

1 oz. Jameson Irish Whiskey
½ oz. peach schnapps
1 oz. orange juice
1 oz. sweet & sour mix

Stir and serve.

IRISH WHISKEY COOLER

1 jigger Tullamore Dew
1 pint club soda
1 dash Angostura Bitters
1 lemon rind

Serve in a tall glass.

LEPRECHAUN

2 oz. Tullamore Dew
3 oz. tonic water
3-4 ice cubes
twist lemon peel

Stir gently. Drop in lemon peel.

LEPRECHAUN'S CHOICE

1¼ oz. Baileys Irish Cream
¾ oz. Smirnoff Vodka
1 oz. club soda

Serve in tall glass. Top with club soda.

LIMP MOOSE

½ shot Carolans Irish Cream
½ shot Canadian Club

Serve as a shot.

MEADE SPRITZER

2 oz. Bunratty Meade
3 oz. club soda

Serve in tall glass with ice.

MEXICAROLANS

1 part Carolans Irish Cream
1 part tequila

Shake and serve.

MILK & HONEY

Equal parts:
Irish Mist
Carolans Irish Cream

Serve in a rocks glass.

MISTER MURPHY

1 part Irish Mist
1 part white rum
1 part orange juice

Serve in a rocks glass with a dash of Angostura Bitters.

MURPHY'S DREAM

1 part Irish Mist
1 part gin
1 part lemon juice
sugar

Shake. Serve up or on the rocks.

NELLIE JANE

1¼ oz. Irish Mist
¼ oz. Hiram Walker Peach Schnapps
3 oz. orange juice
1 oz. ginger ale

Mix all but ginger ale. Float ginger ale.

NUT N' HOLLI

¼ Irish Mist
¼ amaretto
¼ Carolans Irish Cream
¼ Frangelico

Shake. Serve as a shot.

NUTTY IRISHMAN

½ shot Carolans Irish Cream
½ shot Frangelico

Serve as a shot.

NUTTY PROFESSOR

⅓ shot Carolans Irish Cream
⅓ shot Frangelico
⅓ shot Grand Marnier

Serve as a shot.

O'CASEY'S SCOTCH TERRIER

1 part Baileys Irish Cream
1 part J&B Scotch

Stir.

PADDY COCKTAIL

1½ oz. Tullamore Dew
¾ oz. sweet vermouth
several dashes Angostura Bitters

Shake or blend.

PATTY'S PRIDE

1¼ oz. Bushmills Irish Whiskey
¼ oz. peppermint schnapps

Serve on the rocks.

ROAD KILL

⅓ shot Jameson Irish Whiskey
⅓ shot Wild Turkey
⅓ shot 151-proof rum

Serve as a shot.

SCOTCH IRISH

1 part Baileys Irish Cream
1 part J&B Scotch

Shake or stir on the rocks.

SCREAMING ORGASM

¼ shot Irish Cream
¼ shot Kahlua
¼ shot vodka
¼ shot amaretto

Serve as a shot.

ST. PATRICK'S DAY COCKTAIL

¾ oz. Bushmills Irish Whiskey
¾ oz. green creme de menthe
¾ oz. green Chartreuse
1 dash Angostura Bitters

Stir.

TERMINATOR

⅕ shot Irish Cream
⅕ shot Kahlua
⅕ shot Sambuca
⅕ shot Grand Marnier
⅕ shot vodka

Layer.

THREE-LEAF SHAMROCK SHAKER

1 oz. Bushmills Irish Whiskey
1 oz. light rum
1 oz. brandy
1 tsp. lemon juice
sugar syrup to taste

Shake. Strain into chilled glass.

TINKER'S TEA

1½ oz. Baileys Irish Cream
3 oz. hot tea

Pour Baileys in mug or cup. Fill with hot tea.

TIPPERARY

1 oz. Jameson Irish Whiskey
½ oz. Noilly Prat Sweet Vermouth
¼ oz. green Chartreuse

Stir.

TOASTED IRISHMAN

1 part Irish Mist
1 part Kahlua
1 part Disaronno Amaretto

Shake with ice and serve on the rocks.

WILD IRISH ROSE

1½ oz. Tullamore Dew
1½ tsp. grenadine
½ oz. lime juice
club soda

Stir; fill with club soda.

IRISH COCKTAILS

BACARDI & COLA

2 oz. Bacardi Light or Dark Rum
3 oz. cola

Pour rum into tall glass filled with ice. Fill with your favorite cola and garnish with a squeeze of a lemon.

BACARDI & TONIC

2 oz. Bacardi Light Rum
3 oz. tonic

Pour rum into a tall glass filled with ice. Fill with tonic.

BACARDI BLOSSOM

1¼ oz. Bacardi Light Rum
1 oz. orange juice
½ oz. lemon juice
½ tsp. sugar

Hamilton blend.*

BACARDI CHAMPAGNE COCKTAIL

1 oz. Bacardi Silver Rum
3 oz. champagne
1 tsp. sugar
dash bitters

In tall glass, mix rum, sugar and bitters. Fill with champagne.

BACARDI COCKTAIL*

1¼ oz. Bacardi Light Rum
1 oz. Rose's Lime Juice
½ tsp. sugar
½ oz. Rose's Grenadine

Mix in a shaker or Hamilton blend* with ice and strain into a chilled cocktail glass or serve on the rocks. *The NY Supreme Court ruled in 1936 that a Bacardi cocktail is not a Bacardi cocktail unless it's made with Bacardi rum.

BACARDI DAIQUIRI*

1¼ oz. Bacardi Light Rum
½ oz. lemon juice
½ tsp. sugar

Mix in shaker or Hamilton blend* with ice and strain into a chilled cocktail glass or serve on the rocks. *The original Daiquiri was made with Bacardi rum in 1896. You may add bananas, orange juice, peaches, etc.

BACARDI FIRESIDE

1¼ oz. Bacardi Light or Dark Rum
1 tsp. sugar
3 oz. hot tea

In a mug place sugar and rum. Fill with very hot tea and one cinnamon stick. Stir.

BACARDI FIZZ

1¼ oz. Bacardi Light Rum
¼ oz. lemon juice
¼ oz. Rose's Grenadine
3 oz. soda

Pour rum and lemon juice in a highball glass filled with ice. Add the grenadine and fill with soda.

BACARDI HEMINGWAY

1½ oz. Bacardi Light Rum
juice of ½ lime
¼ oz. grapefruit juice
¼ oz. maraschino liqueur

Mix.

BACARDI PINK SQUEEZE

Pour 1½ oz. Bacardi Light Rum into tall glass filled with ice. Fill with pink lemonade.

BACARDI SUNSET

1¼ oz. Bacardi Light Rum
2 oz. orange juice
squeeze of lime

Fill tall glass with crushed ice. Add a squeeze of lime. Garnish with orange wheel.

BANANA DAIQUIRI

1¼ oz. Bacardi Light Rum
¼ oz. lemon or Rose's Lime Juice
½ tsp. sugar
1 banana

Hamilton blend.*

BANANA MAN

1 oz. Bacardi Light Rum
¼ oz. Hiram Walker Banana Liqueur
½ oz. lemon or Rose's Lime Juice

Hamilton blend.*

BANANA RUM CREAM

1½ oz. Puerto Rican Dark Rum
½ oz. creme de bananes
1 oz. light cream

Shake well.

THE BARBADOS COCKTAIL

2 oz. Mount Gay Rum
½ oz. cointreau
½ oz. sweet & sour mix

Shake.

BAT BITE

1¼ oz. Bacardi Silver Rum
¾ cup cranberry juice

In a 10 oz. glass filled with ice, squeeze and drop in 1 lime or lemon wedge. Stir and serve.

BEACH PARTY

1¼ oz. Bacardi Light or Dark Rum
1 oz. pineapple juice
1 oz. orange juice
1 oz. Rose's Grenadine

Hamilton blend.*

BEACHCOMBER

¾ oz. Rose's Lime Juice
¼ oz. triple sec
dash maraschino liqueur
1½ oz. Puerto Rican White Rum

Shake.

BEE'S KISS

¾ oz. cream
2 barspoons honey
1 oz. Puerto Rican White Rum
¼ oz. Myers's Dark Rum

Shake.

THE BIGWOOD GIRLS

¾ oz. Puerto Rican Light Rum
½ oz. brandy
½ oz. cointreau or triple sec
½ oz. lemon juice.

Shake.

BLACK DEVIL

1½ oz. Puerto Rican Light Rum
½ oz. dry vermouth
1 pitted black olive

Stir well.

BLACK MARIA

1 oz. Myers's Dark Rum
¾ oz. Tia Maria
1 barspoon sugar
1 cup cold coffee
lemon peel

Stir.

BLIGHTER BOB

1 oz. Puerto Rican Light Rum
½ oz. Puerto Rican Dark Rum
½ oz. creme de cassis
1 oz. orange juice
2 dashes orange bitters
2 oz. ginger ale
1 lemon twist

Stir.

BOLERO

1½ oz. Rhum Barbancort
½ oz. Calvados
2 tsp. sweet vermouth
1 dash bitters

Stir. Serve up or on the rocks.

BONBINI

1 oz. Bacardi Light or Dark Rum
¼ oz. Hiram Walker Orange Curacao
dash bitters

Stir.

BONGO DRUM

1 oz. Bacardi Light Rum
¼ oz. Hiram Walker Blackberry-
   flavored Brandy
3 oz. pineapple juice

Pour rum into a tall glass half filled with ice. Fill with pineapple juice and float the blackberry-flavored brandy on top.

BROWN DERBY

1¼ oz. Puerto Rican Dark Rum
½ oz. lime juice
⅙ oz. maple syrup

Shake.

BUCK-A-ROO

1¼ oz. Bacardi Light or Dark
   Rum
3 oz. root beer

Pour rum into a highball glass filled with ice.

BUSHRANGER

1 oz. Dubonnet
1 oz. Puerto Rican White Rum
dashes of Angostura Bitters

Stir.

CAPTAIN MORGAN SOUR

1¼ oz. Captain Morgan Original
   Spiced Rum
1 oz. fresh squeezed lemon juice
1 tsp. sugar

Shake.

CARNIVAL COOLER

¾ oz. lime juice
2 oz. Fernandes "19" White Rum
2 dashes Angostura Bitters
3 oz. club soda

In collins glass mix first three ingredients with ice and stir. Fill with club soda.

CHERRIED CREAM RUM

1½ oz. Rhum Barbancort
½ oz. cherry brandy
½ oz. light cream

Shake.

CHICAGO STYLE

¾ oz. Bacardi Light Rum
¼ oz. Hiram Walker Triple Sec
¼ oz. Hiram Walker Anisette
¼ oz. lemon or Rose's Lime Juice

Hamilton blend.*

CLAM VOYAGE

1 oz. Bacardi Light or Dark Rum
¼ oz. apple-flavored brandy
1 oz. orange juice
dash orange bitters

Hamilton blend.*

RUM

COCOMOTION

4 oz. Coco Lopez Real Cream of
  Coconut
2 oz. lime juice
1½ oz. Puerto Rican Dark Rum
1½ cups ice

Hamilton blend.*

COFFEE CREAM COOLER

1¼ oz. Bacardi Light or Dark
  Rum
3 oz. cold coffee
½ oz. cream

Pour rum into a tall glass half
filled with ice. Fill with cold
coffee and cream to desired
proportions.

COLUMBUS COCKTAIL

1 scoop crushed ice
juice of ½ lime
¾ oz. apricot brandy
1½ oz. Puerto Rican Golden Rum

Mix.

CONTINENTAL

1 oz. Bacardi Light Rum
¼ oz. Hiram Walker Green Creme
  de Menthe
¾ oz. Rose's Lime Juice
¼ tsp sugar (optional)

Hamilton blend.*

CORKSCREW

¾ oz. Bacardi Light Rum
¼ oz. Asbach Uralt
¼ oz. port wine
½ oz. lemon or Rose's Lime Juice

Stir.

COW PUNCHER

1 oz. Bacardi Light or Dark Rum
1 oz. Hiram Walker White Creme
  de Cacao
3 oz. milk

Pour rum and creme de cacao
into a tall glass half filled with
ice. Fill with milk.

CRAN-RUM TWISTER

2 oz. Puerto Rican Light Rum
3 oz. cranberry juice
2 oz. lemon-lime soda
lime slice for garnish (optional)

In tall glass with ice.

CREOLE

3-4 ice cubes
2 splashes lemon juice
3½ oz. beef bouillon
1¼ oz. Puerto Rican White Rum
pepper, salt, Tabasco,
  Worcestershire sauce, to taste

Serve on the rocks.

CRICKET

¾ oz. Bacardi Light Rum
¼ oz. Hiram Walker White Creme
de Cacao
¼ oz. Hiram Walker Green Creme
de Menthe
1 oz. cream

Hamilton blend.*

―――☙☙☙―――

CUBA LIBRE

3-4 ice cubes
1¾ oz. Bacardi Rum
cola to taste
¼ lime

Mix with ice; add lime, stir.

―――☙☙☙―――

THE ECLIPSE

1½ oz. Mount Gay Rum
1 oz. pineapple juice
1 oz. orange juice

Shake.

―――☙☙☙―――

FLAMINGO

Juice of a quarter lime
dashes grenadine
1 oz. pineapple juice
1½ oz. Rhum Barbancort

Shake.

―――☙☙☙―――

FLIRTING WITH THE SANDPIPER

1½ oz. Puerto Rican Light Rum
½ oz. cherry brandy
3 oz. orange juice
2 dashes orange bitter

Stir well.

FLYING KANGAROO

½ oz. cream
¾ oz. coconut cream
1½ oz. pineapple juice
¾ oz. orange juice
¼ oz. Galliano
1 oz. vodka
1 oz. Rhum Barbancort

Shake.

―――☙☙☙―――

FRENCH COLADA

1 scoop crushed ice
¾ oz. sweet cream
¾ oz. Coco Lopez Real Cream of
Coconut
1½ oz. pineapple juice
splash of cassis
¾ oz. cognac
1½ oz. Puerto Rican White Rum

Hamilton blend.*

―――☙☙☙―――

FROZEN WHITE-CAP

1½ oz. Appleton Estate V/X
2 oz. pineapple juice
1 Tbsp. lime juice
1 scoop crushed ice

Hamilton blend.*

―――☙☙☙―――

GINGER COLADA

1½ oz. Coco Lopez Real Cream of
Coconut
1 oz. Canton Delicate Ginger
Liqueur
½ oz. rum
1 cup ice

Hamilton blend.*

RUM

GRAPE PUNCH

1¼ oz. Bacardi Light Rum
grape juice
lime or lemon wedge

Pour rum into a tall glass filled with ice. Fill with grape juice and garnish with a squeeze of lime or lemon.

GRASSHOPPER

2 oz. Bacardi Light Rum
¼ oz. Hiram Walker Green Creme de Menthe
½ oz. cream

Stir or blend.

GREEN PARROT

1½ oz. Appleton Estate V/X
4 oz. orange juice
1 oz. blue curacao

Pour ingredients, one at a time in the order listed above, into large stemmed glass over ice. Do not mix. Garnish with orange slice.

HARD HAT

1¼ oz. Bacardi Silver Rum
1¼ oz. fresh lime juice
1 tsp. sugar
¼ oz. Rose's Grenadine
club soda

In a shaker with ice, all but club soda. Strain into 10 oz. glass. Fill with club soda.

HAVANA SIDECAR

3-4 ice cubes
¾ oz. lemon juice
¾ oz. triple sec
1½ oz. Puerto Rican Golden Rum

Mix.

HAWAIIAN NIGHT

1 oz. Bacardi Light Rum
¼ oz. Hiram Walker Cherry-flavored Brandy
pineapple juice

Pour rum into a tall glass half filled with ice. Fill with pineapple juice and float cherry flavored brandy on top.

HEAT WAVE

1¼ oz. Bacardi Light Rum
4 oz. orange juice

Hamilton blend.*

ICE BREAKER

½ oz. Myers's Original Dark Rum
¼ oz. creme de noyeaux
¼ oz. Cognac
¼ oz. gin
2 oz. lemon juice
1 oz. orange juice

Shake.

RUM

ISLA GRANDE ICED TEA

1½ oz. Puerto Rican Dark Rum
3 oz. pineapple juice
unsweetened brewed iced tea
pineapple, lemon or lime slice
  for garnish (optional)

In tall glass with ice.

―――❀❀❀―――

ITALIAN COLADA

1 scooped crushed ice
¾ oz. sweet cream
¼ oz. Coco Lopez Real Cream of
  Coconut
2 oz. pineapple juice
¼ oz. amaretto
1½ oz. Puerto Rican White Rum

Hamilton blend.*

―――❀❀❀―――

JADE

1½ oz. Puerto Rican White Rum
¾ oz. lime juice
1 barspoon sugar
dash triple sec
dash green creme de menthe

Shake.

―――❀❀❀―――

THE KAHLUA COLADA

1 oz. Coco Lopez Real Cream of
  Coconut
2 oz. pineapple juice
1 oz. Kahlua
½ oz. rum
1 cup ice

Hamilton blend.*

THE LIMBO DRINK (PARTY IN A PITCHER)

6 oz. Coruba Jamaica Rum
3 oz. peach schnapps
3 oz. sour mix
6 oz. cranberry juice
6 oz. pineapple juice
3 tsp. sugar
1 oz. lime juice

Hamilton blend.* Makes 6 drinks.

―――❀❀❀―――

LUCKY LADY

¾ oz. Bacardi Light Rum
¼ oz. Hiram Walker Anisette
¼ oz. Hiram Walker White Creme
  de Cacao
¾ oz. cream

Hamilton blend.*

―――❀❀❀―――

MALIBU BAY BREEZE

1½ oz. Malibu
2 oz. cranberry juice
2 oz. pineapple juice

Serve over ice.

―――❀❀❀―――

MALIBU BEACH

1½ oz. Malibu
1 oz. Smirnoff Vodka
4 oz. orange juice

Serve over ice.

MALIBU ORANGE COLADA
1½ oz. Malibu
1 oz. triple sec
4 oz. Coco Lopez Real Cream of Coconut

Hamilton blend.*

MALIBU SUNTAN
1½ oz. Malibu
5 oz. iced tea
squeeze of lemon

Serve over ice.

MARY PICKFORD
1 scoop crushed ice
1½ oz. pineapple juice
1 splash grenadine
1½ oz. Puerto Rican White Rum

Shake.

MIAMI SPECIAL
1 oz. Bacardi Light Rum
¼ oz. Hiram Walker White Creme de Menthe
¾ oz. lemon or Rose's Lime Juice

Hamilton blend.*

MONTEGO MARGARITA
1½ oz. Appleton Estate V/X
½ oz. triple sec
1 oz. lemon or lime juice
1 scoop crushed ice

Hamilton blend.*

THE MORGAN CANNONBALL
1 ¼ oz. Captain Morgan Original Spiced Rum
3 oz. pineapple juice
float of White Creme de Menthe

Hamilton blend.*

MORGAN'S JOLLY ROGER

In a shot glass, pour equal parts (¾ oz.) Captain Morgan Original Spiced Rum and cinnamon schnapps.

MORGAN'S RED ROUGE
1 oz. Captain Morgan Original Spiced Rum
½ oz. blackberry brandy
2 oz. pineapple juice
½ oz. lemon juice. Stir.

MORGAN'S SPICED RUM ALEXANDER
1 oz. Captain Morgan Original Spiced Rum
½ oz. creme de cacao
1 oz. heavy cream

Shake and strain. Dust with nutmeg.

MORGAN'S WENCH

In a shot glass, pour equal parts (¾ oz.) Captain Morgan Original Spiced Rum and amaretto. Add a float of dark creme de cacao.

THE MOUNT GAY GRINDER

1½ oz. Mount Gay Rum
cranberry juice
splash of 7-Up

Serve in a tall glass.

MYERS'S HEATWAVE

¾ oz. Myers's Original Dark Rum
½ oz. peach schnapps
6 oz. pineapple juice
1 splash grenadine

Pour rum and schnapps over ice. Fill with juice and splash of grenadine.

PEACH BANANA DAIQUIRI

1½ oz. Puerto Rican Light Rum
½ medium banana, diced
1 oz. fresh lime juice
¼ cup sliced peaches (fresh, frozen or canned)
1 cup crushed ice

Hamilton blend.*

PEACH MELBA

½ oz. Captain Morgan Original Spiced Rum
¾ oz. raspberry liqueur
2 oz. peach cocktail mix
1 oz. heavy cream
2 peach halves
8 oz. crushed ice

Hamilton blend.* Top with raspberry syrup.

PINA COLADA

1¼ oz. Bacardi Light or Dark Rum
2 oz. unsweetened pineapple juice
2 oz. Coco Lopez Real Cream of Coconut

Mix in a shaker or Hamilton blend* with crushed ice, or stir and serve on the rocks.

PINEAPPLE TWIST

1½ oz. Appleton Estate V/X
6 oz. pineapple juice
splash of lemon juice (½ tsp.)

Shake and pour into tall glass over ice.

PINK PANTHER

1¼ oz. Bacardi Light Rum
¾ oz. lemon juice
¾ oz. cream
½ oz. Rose's Grenadine

Hamilton blend.*

RUM

PIRATES PUNCH

1¾ oz. Rhum Barbancort
¼ oz. sweet vermouth
dash of Angostura Bitters

Shake.

PORT ROYAL

1½ oz. Appleton Estate V/X
½ oz. sweet vermouth
juice of ¼ orange
juice of ¼ lime

Shake with ice and strain into large rocks glass over ice cubes. Garnish with orange or lime wedge.

PRESIDENTE

6-8 ice cubes
¼ oz. dry vermouth
¾ oz. sweet vermouth
1½ oz. Puerto Rican White Rum
1 splash grenadine

Mix.

PUERTO RICAN RUM CAPPUCCINO

1½ oz. Puerto Rican Dark Rum
1 tsp. sugar
3 oz. hot strong coffee
¼ oz. steamed milk
½ oz. whipped cream
dash ground cinnamon

Combine and stir in a hot mug.

QUARTER DECK

1 oz. Puerto Rican Light Rum
½ oz. Puerto Rican Dark Rum
½ oz. cream sherry
½ oz. lime juice

Shake.

R & B

1¼ oz. Captain Morgan Original Spiced Rum
2 oz. orange juice
2 oz. pineapple juice
1 splash grenadine

Pour over ice.

RACER'S EDGE

1 oz. Bacardi Light Rum
¼ oz. Hiram Walker Green Creme de Menthe
grapefruit juice

Pour rum into a tall glass half filled with ice. Fill with grapefruit juice and float creme de menthe.

RED HOT MAMA

1¼ oz. Bacardi Silver Rum
4 oz. cranberry juice
2 oz. chilled club soda

Over ice.

SECRET PLACE

1½ oz. Puerto Rican Dark Rum
½ oz. cherry brandy
2 tsp. dark creme de cacao
4 oz. cold coffee
crushed ice

Stir.

SPANISH TOWN COCKTAIL

2 oz. Rhum Barbancort
1 tsp. triple sec

Stir and strain.

———∞∞———

SUNSPLASH

¾ oz. Coco Lopez Real Cream of
 Coconut
1¼ oz. Frangelico Liqueur
¾ oz. Captain Morgan Orginal
 Spiced Rum
5 oz. orange juice

Shake.

———∞∞———

TOP TEN

1¼ oz. Captain Morgan Original
 Spiced Rum
2 oz. cola
1 oz. Coco Lopez Real Cream of
 Coconut
1 oz. heavy cream
1 scoop crushed ice

Hamilton blend.

———∞∞———

TRIP TO THE BEACH

½ oz. Malibu
½ oz. peach schnapps
½ oz. Smirnoff Vodka
3 oz. orange juice

Serve over ice.

VICIOUS SID

1½ oz. Puerto Rican Light Rum
½ oz. Southern Comfort
½ oz. cointreau or triple sec
1 oz. lemon juice
1 dash bitters

Shake.

———∞∞———

THE WAVE CUTTER

1½ oz. Mount Gay Rum
1 oz. cranberry juice
1 oz. orange juice

Shake.

———∞∞———

YELLOW BIRD

¾ oz. Bacardi Rum
¼ oz. Liquore Galliano
¼ oz. Hiram Walker Creme de
 Banana
2 oz. pineapple juice
2 oz. orange juice

Shake.

Scotch

ABERDEEN SOUR
2 oz. Cutty Sark
1 oz. orange juice
1 oz. lemon juice
½ oz. cointreau
1 scoop crushed ice

Shake or blend. Pour into an old-fashioned glass.

AFFINITY
1½ oz. scotch
1 oz. Martini & Rossi Sweet
  Vermouth
1 oz. Martini & Rossi Dry
  Vermouth
2 dashes orange bitters

Stir well. Strain into a cocktail glass.

BARBARY COAST
½ oz. scotch
½ oz. Beefeater Gin
½ oz. white creme de cacao
½ oz. heavy cream

Blend. Pour into cocktail glass.

BLACK JACK
1½ oz. scotch
1 oz. Kahlua
½ oz. cointreau
½ oz. lemon juice

In a shaker half-filled with ice, combine all ingredients. Shake well. Strain into a cocktail glass.

BLINDER
1½ oz. scotch
4 oz. grapefruit juice
dash grenadine

Pour the scotch and grapefruit juice into a highball glass filled with ice. Drop the grenadine into the drink.

BOBBY BURNS
1 oz. scotch
¼ oz. Martini & Rossi Sweet
  Vermouth
3 dashes Benedictine

Stir and serve.

CELTIC MIX COCKTAIL
1½ oz. scotch
1 oz. Tullamore Dew
½ oz. lemon juice
1 dash bitters

Shake. Strain into a cocktail glass.

CUTTY CARIBBEAN

1 oz. scotch
½ oz. Bacardi Coco
½ oz. blue curacao

Shake. Pour into cocktail glass. Garnish with lemon slice.

CUTTY CLIPPER

An exotic mix of:
1¼ oz. scotch
¼ oz. creme d'almond
2 oz. pineapple juice
2 oz. orange juice

Mix in a tall glass with ice.

DERBY FIZZ

1¼ oz. scotch
½ oz. sweet & sour mix
¼ oz. cointreau
2 oz. soda

Blend. Pour into tall glass. Fill with soda.

DUDE

1 oz. scotch
dash grenadine
½ oz. Harvey's Bristol Cream

Build in rocks glass with ice. Float Harvey's.

GODFATHER

2 parts scotch
2 parts amaretto

Stir on the rocks.

GRAND MASTER

2 oz. scotch
½ oz. peppermint schnapps
3 oz. club soda
1 lemon twist

Stir well. Garnish with the lemon twist.

HEATHCLIFF

1 oz. scotch
1 oz. Calvados
½ oz. Beefeater Gin
1 tsp. heather honey or sugar syrup
1 scoop crushed ice

Shake. Strain into cocktail glass.

HIGHLAND FLING

2 oz. scotch
½ oz. Martini & Rossi Sweet Vermouth
2 dashes orange bitters
1 maraschino cherry

Stir. Strain into cocktail glass. Garnish with cherry.

LASER DISK

½ oz. scotch
½ oz. Drambuie
½ oz. lemonade

Shake. Serve in shot glass.

MAMIE TAYLOR

1¼ oz. scotch
¼ oz. fresh lime juice
ginger ale

Build in tall glass with ice. Top with ginger ale.

OLD ROB ROY

2 oz. scotch
⅛ oz. Martini & Rossi Sweet Vermouth
¼ tsp. sugar
dash Angostura Bitters

Stir. Serve over rocks.

PERFECT ROB ROY

2 oz. scotch
¼ oz. Martini & Rossi Sweet Vermouth
¼ oz. Martini & Rossi Dry Vermouth

Serve in rocks glass with ice. Garnish with lemon twist.

RUSTY NAIL

1 oz. scotch
1 oz. Drambuie

Stir with ice.

SCARLET SCHOONER

2 oz. scotch
1 oz. Peachtree Schnapps
2 oz. cranberry juice

Stir in tall glass with ice.

SCOTCH COLLINS

1¼ oz. scotch
1½ oz. sweet & sour mix
2 oz. 7-Up

Serve in tall glass with ice. Garnish with red cherry.

SCOTCH OLD-FASHIONED

1¼ oz. scotch
½ tsp. sugar
2 dashes Angostura Bitters
splash soda

Put in sugar, bitters, red cherry, lemon twist, orange slice, and muddle. Add ice and top with club soda.

SCOTTY DOG

1¼ oz. scotch
1½ oz. lime juice

Shake. Garnish with a slice of lime.

STAIRCASE

1 oz. scotch
¼ oz. Martini & Rossi Dry Vermouth
¼ oz. Martini & Rossi Sweet Vermouth
¼ oz. Drambuie

Serve in rocks glass with ice.

STARBOARD

1 oz. scotch
1 oz. grapefruit juice
1 oz. Martini & Rossi Dry
  Vermouth
1 scoop crushed ice

Shake. Serve in a chilled old-fashioned glass.

———⋙⋘———

TASTE OF HONEY

1 oz. scotch
½ oz. honey
1 oz. heavy cream

Blend with ice. Serve in cocktail glass.

———⋙⋘———

TARTANTULA

1½ oz. scotch
1 oz. Martini & Rossi Sweet
  Vermouth
½ oz. Benedictine
1 lemon twist

Stir. Strain into a cocktail glass.

———⋙⋘———

ULTIMATE SOUR

1 oz. scotch
4 oz. sweet & sour mix
splash orange juice

Shake. Serve in an old-fashioned glass with ice.

SCOTCH

Tequila

1800 BITE THE BERRY

1¼ oz. Jose Cuervo 1800 Tequila
½ oz. triple sec
¼ oz. raspberry liqueur
2½ oz. sweet & sour mix
2 oz. cranberry juice

In a rocks glass. Garnish: orange slice.

1800 LEMON DROP

1¼ oz. Jose Cuervo 1800 Tequila
½ oz. triple sec
1 oz. sweet & sour mix
1 oz. lemon-lime soda

In a rocks glass and mix. Add a fresh lemon juice float.Garnish with fresh lemon.

1800 PINK CAD

1 oz. Jose Cuervo 1800 Tequila
½ oz. triple sec
2½ oz. sweet & sour mix
½ oz. fresh lime juice
splash cranberry cocktail
premier orange liqueur float

Garnish with lime slice.

43 AMIGOS

3 oz. Jose Cuervo Gold Tequila
½ oz. Licor 43
½ oz. triple sec
½ oz. lime juice

Shake. Strain into chilled martini glass. Garnish with lime wedge.

ACAPULCO GOLD

1¼ oz. Jose Cuervo Especial Tequila
⅝ oz. Grand Marnier
10 oz. sweet & sour mix

Blend.

AGAVALADA

1½ oz. Agavero Liqueur
1 oz. Rhum Barbancourt
4 oz. pineapple juice
¾ oz. cream of coconut
pineapple stick
maraschino cherry

Shake or blend and pour into a chilled collins glass. Garnish: pineapple stick and cherry.

THE ALAMO SPLASH

1½ oz. Jose Cuervo Gold Tequila
1 oz. orange juice
½ oz. pineapple juice
splash 7-Up

Mix well with cracked ice, strain and serve from a porron in a thin, well-aimed stream. No glasses required.

ALBUQUERQUE REAL

1½ oz. Jose Cuervo Especial Tequila
½ oz. triple sec
½ oz. sweet & sour mix
¼ oz. cranberry juice
float Grand Marnier

Blend.

APPLE KIR

1 oz. Jose Cuervo Gold Tequila
½ oz. creme de cassis
1 oz. apple juice
1 tsp. fresh lemon juice

Mix in rocks glass over ice. Garnish with lemon wedge.

BLUE SHARK

1 oz. Herradura Tequila
1 oz. Crown Russe Vodka
dash blue curacao

Mix ingredients in cocktail shaker with shaved ice. Strain into cocktail glass.

CAMINO REAL

1½ oz. Gran Centenario Plata or Reposado Tequila
½ oz. banana liqueur
1 oz. orange juice
dash lime juice
dash coconut milk
lime slice

Shake or blend. Garnish: lime slice.

CAN-CAN

1 jigger Tequila
½ jigger French vermouth
2 jiggers grapefruit juice
1 tsp. sugar
ice
orange twist

Shake together over ice and service with twist.

THE CATALINA MARGARITA

1¼ oz. Jose Cuervo Gold Tequila
1 oz. peach schnapps
1 oz. blue curacao
4 oz. sweet & sour mix

Blend.

CAVALIER

1½ oz. Sauza Tequila
½ oz. Galliano
1½ oz. orange juice
½ oz. cream

Blend with crushed ice and strain into cocktail glass.

TEQUILA

THE CHIMAYO COCKTAIL
ice
1¼ oz. Herradura Silver Tequila
¼ oz. creme de cassis
1 oz. fresh apple cider or apple juice
¼ oz. freshly squeezed lemon juice
1 red apple wedge

Fill a double old-fashioned glass with ice. Pour the ingredients over ice, and stir. Garnish: apple wedge.

⎯⎯⎯∞⎯⎯⎯

COCO LOCO (CRAZY COCONUT)
1½ oz. Herradura Tequila
3 oz. pineapple juice
2 oz. coconut syrup mix
grated coconut

Blend. Garnish with pineapple spear.

⎯⎯⎯∞⎯⎯⎯

COCO MARGARITA
1¼ oz. Jose Cuervo 1800 Tequila
1 oz. sweet & sour mix
1½ oz. pineapple juice
½ oz. fresh lime juice
½ oz. cream of coconut

Shake. Garnish with fresh pineapple.

COCOMISTICO
½ oz. Jose Cuervo Mistico
½ oz. Baileys Irish Cream
½ oz. Godiva Liqueur
1 oz. half & half

Shake, strain into rocks glass.

⎯⎯⎯∞⎯⎯⎯

COCONUT ALMOND MARGARITA
1¼ oz. Jose Cuervo 1800 Tequila
2½ oz. sweet & sour mix
½ oz. cream of coconut
¼ oz. amaretto liqueur
½ oz. fresh lime juice

Shake. Garnish with lime.

⎯⎯⎯∞⎯⎯⎯

COINTREAU SANTA FE MARGARITA
1½ oz. Jose Cuervo Gold Tequila
¾ oz. cointreau
2 oz. sweet & sour mix
2 oz. cranberry juice

Blend.

⎯⎯⎯∞⎯⎯⎯

COINTREAU STRAWBERRY MARGARITA
1¼ oz. Jose Cuervo Gold Tequila
¾ oz. cointreau
2 oz. sweet & sour mix
3 oz. frozen strawberries

Blend.

COSMORITA

1½ oz. Gran Centenario Plata
  Tequila
½ oz. triple sec
½ oz. fresh lime juice
½ oz. cranberry juice
1 Tbsp. Agavero Liqueur

Mix all ingredients, except Agavero and lime slice; shake or blend. Serve in a chilled cocktail glass. Float Agavero. Garnish: lime slice.

CRAN RAZZ

2 oz. Two Fingers Tequila
2 oz. cranberry juice
1 oz. raspberry liqueur

In a shaker, mix all ingredients. Serve over rocks.

CRIPPLE CREEK

½ oz. Herradura Tequila
½ oz. Benchmark Bourbon
1 oz. orange juice

Shake and strain. Float 1/2 oz. Galliano.

CUERVO ALEXANDER

1 oz. Jose Cuervo Gold Tequila
1 oz. coffee-flavored liqueur
1 oz. wild cherry brandy
2 large scoops vanilla ice cream

Blend until smooth. Serve in stemmed glass.

CUERVO BRAVE BULL

1½ oz. Jose Cuervo White Tequila
1½ oz. coffee liqueur

Garnish with lemon twist.

CUERVO CARAMBA

1½ oz. Jose Cuervo Gold Tequila
3 oz. grapefruit juice
1 Tbsp. sugar
club soda

Shake, fill with club soda.

CUERVO COLA

1 oz. Jose Cuervo Gold Tequila
3 oz. cola
1 oz. fresh lemon juice

Pour into a tall glass with ice.

CUERVO CRANBERRY TODDY

1¼ oz. Jose Cuervo Gold Tequila
5 oz. cranberry juice cocktail,
  heated
1 oz. triple sec
½ oz. apple schnapps

In mug, garnish with orange slice.

CUERVO CRUSH

1½ oz. Jose Cuervo Gold Tequila
4 oz. freshly squeezed orange
  juice

In a tall glass. Stir.

TEQUILA

CUERVO GOLD MARGARITA

1½ oz. Jose Cuervo Gold Tequila
1 oz. triple sec
2 oz. lime juice
2 oz. sweet & sour mix
squeeze fresh lime

Blend. Garnish with a lime wheel.

CUERVO GOLDEN BREEZE

1½ oz. Jose Cuervo Gold Tequila
4 oz. grapefruit juice
2 oz. cranberry juice
squeeze lime

Garnish: lime wheel.

CUERVO MEXICALI ROSE

1 oz. Jose Cuervo White Tequila
4 oz. cranberry juice cocktail
½ oz. lime juice

Garnish with lime slice.

CUERVO MEXICAN COFFEE

1 oz. Jose Cuervo Gold Tequila
¾ oz. Kahlua Coffee Liqueur
fresh hot coffee to fill

Top with whipped cream.

CUERVO MOCHA MELT

1 oz. Jose Cuervo Gold Tequila
5 oz. freshly brewed, strong, hot coffee
1 single serving envelope hot cocoa mix
½ oz. coffee brandy

Top with whipped cream.

CUERVO MOCKINGBIRD

1½ oz. Jose Cuervo Gold Tequila
¾ oz. creme de menthe
fresh lime squeezed

Shake and strain.

CUERVO MOONLIGHT MARGARITA

1½ oz. Jose Cuervo Gold Tequila
1 oz. blue curacao
1 oz. lime juice
squeeze fresh lime

Rub rim of cocktail glass with lime rind, dip into salt. Blend. Garnish: lime slice.

CUERVO MOUNTAIN MELTER

1 oz. Jose Cuervo Gold Tequila
½ oz. triple sec
5 oz. hot water
1 single serving envelope hot cocoa mix

Top with whipped cream and ground cinnamon.

CUERVO NATION COCKTAIL

1½ oz. Jose Cuervo Gold Tequila
1½ oz. pineapple juice
1½ oz. orange juice
float blue curacao

CUERVO ORANGE MARGARITA

1½ oz. Jose Cuervo Gold Tequila
½ oz. triple sec
3 oz. orange juice
½ oz. sweet & sour mix

Blend. Garnish with strawberries.

CUERVO PEACH MARGARITA

1½ oz. Jose Cuervo Gold Tequila
1 oz. triple sec
1 oz. lime juice
½ cup peaches (canned)

Blend. Garnish with peach slices.

CUERVO PINATA

1½ oz. Jose Cuervo Gold Tequila
5 oz. pineapple juice

Garnish with fresh pineapple.

CUERVO RASPBERRY MARGARITA

1½ oz. Jose Cuervo Gold Tequila
1 oz. triple sec
1 oz. lime juice
½ cup raspberries (frozen)

Blend. Garnish with fresh raspberries.

CUERVO SANTA FE MAGGIE

1¼ oz. Jose Cuervo Gold Tequila
1/2 oz. triple sec
2 oz. sweet & sour mix
2 oz. cranberry juice

Garnish with lime wedge, drop into glass.

CUERVO SIDE-OUT

1½ oz. Jose Cuervo Gold Tequila
1 oz. triple sec
2 oz. cranberry juice
1½ oz. lime juice

Blend.

CUERVO SPIKE

1 1/2 oz. Jose Cuervo Gold Tequila
grapefruit juice to fill

Stir and serve.

CUERVO STRAWBERRY MARGARITA

1½ oz. Jose Cuervo Gold Tequila
1 oz. triple sec
1 oz. lime juice
½ cup frozen strawberries

Blend. Garnish with strawberries.

TEQUILA

CUERVO SUNRISE

1½ oz. Jose Cuervo Gold Tequila
3 oz. cranberry juice
½ oz. lime juice
½ oz. grenadine

Shake. Garnish with lime.

———

CUERVO TRADITIONAL AZTEC RUIN

½ oz. Jose Cuervo Traditional
  Tequila
½ oz. Rose's Lime Juice

Serve as a shot.

———

CUERVO TRADITIONAL AZTEC SKY

¾ oz. Jose Cuervo Traditional
  Tequila
¾ oz. blue curacao

———

CUERVO TROPICAL

1½ oz. Jose Cuervo Gold Tequila
3 oz. orange juice
1 tsp. lemon juice
½ oz. grenadine

Mix in high ball glass filled with cracked ice. Garnish with half an orange slice and a cherry.

———

DISARITA MARGARITA

1 oz. Jose Cuervo 1800 Tequila
½ oz. Disaronno Amaretto
3 oz. margarita mix
½ cup crushed ice

Blend. Garnish with lime.

DOUBLE GOLD

½ oz. Jose Cuervo Gold Tequila
½ oz. Goldschlager

Serve in a shot glass.

———

FREDDIE FUDPUCKER

1 oz. Herradura Tequila
4 oz. orange juice
½ oz. Galliano
½ oz. Kahlua

Shake and serve.

———

FUZZY RITA

1½ oz. Jose Cuervo Gold Tequila
½ oz. peach liqueur
½ oz. cointreau
1½ oz. lime juice

Serve on the rocks.

———

GENTLE BULL

1½ oz. Two Fingers Tequila
1 oz. heavy cream
¾ oz. coffee liqueur
1 scoop crushed ice

Shake. Garnish: whipped cream and a cherry.

———

GRAND MARGARITA

1 oz. Sauza Conmemorativo
  Anejo
¾ oz. Grand Marnier
1 part fresh lime juice

Fill martini glass with ice. Pour Sauza and add Grand Marnier. Fill with fresh lime juice and sugar to taste. Shake. Garnish: lime wedge.

HOT BOMB

¾ oz. Two Fingers Tequila
¼ oz. Du Bouchett Hot
  Cinnamon Schnapps
shaker can
⅓ cup ice

Put ingredients in can. Shake.
Strain into shot glass.

IGUANA

½ oz. Herradura Tequila
¾ oz. Nikolai Vodka
¾ oz. coffee liqueur

Serve on the rocks.

INNOCULATION SHOT

¾ oz. Jose Cuervo Gold Tequila
¼ oz. blue curacao

Combine in a shot glass.

JALAPENORITA

1¼ oz. Gold Tequila
⅔ oz. Grand Marnier
juice of half lime
½ tsp. Tabasco Jalapeno Pepper
  Sauce
slice lime for garnish

Rub rim of goblet with cut side
of lime, then dip rim into a
saucer of salt. Fill glass with ice.
Pour first three ingredients into
an ice-filled cocktail shaker or
pitcher, and shake or stir vigorously. Strain into ice-filled glass.
Shake in Tabasco and stir.
Garnish: lime slice.

LA BOMBA

1¼ oz. Jose Cuervo 1800 Tequila
¾ oz. cointreau
1½ oz. pineapple juice
1½ oz. orange juice
2 dashes grenadine

Shake ingredients, except
grenadine. Pour into glass,
add grenadine. Garnish: lime
wheel.

LA JOLLARITA

1½ oz. Jose Cuervo Traditional
  Tequila
½ oz. cointreau
½ oz. Chambord

Shake, strain and serve.

LATIN LOVER

1 oz. Herradura Tequila
½ oz. amaretto

In an old-fashioned glass.

LEMON-GINGER MARGARITA

1¼ oz. Jose Cuervo 1800 Tequila
½ oz. triple sec
2½ oz. sweet & sour mix
½ oz. fresh lemon juice

Garnish with lemon wedge.

LIZARD SLIME

1½ oz. Jose Cuervo
¼ oz. Midori Melon Liqueur

In a shot glass, float Midori.

MACARENA

1 oz. Jose Cuervo Especial
 Tequila
½ oz. Malibu Coconut Rum
3 oz. sweet & sour mix
1 oz. orange juice
1 oz. pineapple juice
splash cranberry juice

Shake and pour over ice into a
16 oz. tumbler. Garnish with
pineapple, orange, and a cherry.

MARGARITA MADRES

1¼ oz. Jose Cuervo Gold Tequila
½ oz. cointreau
1½ oz. sweet & sour mix
1½ oz. orange juice
1½ oz. cranberry juice

Blend.

MARGAVERO

3 oz. Agavero Liqueur
1 oz. fresh lime juice
1 dash Stolichnaya Ohranj
1 dash coarse salt
lime wedge

Shake or blend and strain into
a chilled cocktail glass, the
rim of which has been moistened with lime juice and
dipped in salt. Garnish: lime
wedge.

MEXICAN BANANA

1½ oz. Sauza Tequila
¾ oz. creme de banana

Pour ingredients into an old-
fashioned glass filled with ice.

MEXICAN GOLD

1½ oz. Sauza Tequila
¾ oz. Galliano

In an old-fashioned glass
filled with ice pour Sauza
Tequila and float Galliano.

MEXICO MARTINI

1½ oz. Gran Centenario Plata
 Tequila
1 Tbsp. extra dry vermouth
2-3 drops vanilla extract

Shake and strain into iced
glass.

MEXICO ROSE

1½ oz. Sauza Tequila
1 oz. lime juice
½ oz. grenadine (or creme de cassis)

In an old-fashioned glass filled
with ice, pour Sauza Tequila,
lime juice and grenadine.

MISTIC BEACH

1¼ oz. Jose Cuervo Mistico
¾ oz. cointreau
3 oz. cranberry juice

Stir. Garnish: lemon wedge.

MISTIC CHOCKLIC
¾ oz. Jose Cuervo Mistico
¾ oz. Kahlua Coffee Liqueur
1 oz. orange juice

Shake, strain into a rocks glass.

MISTIC MERLIN
¾ oz. Jose Cuervo Mistico
¾ oz. orange liqueur
½ oz. lime juice

Shake with ice and strain.

MISTIC SHANDY
1¼ oz. Jose Cuervo Mistico
7 oz. draft beer

Combine Jose Cuervo and beer in a chilled mug.

MISTICAL MAYAN
1¼ oz. Jose Cuervo Mistico
3 oz. orange juice
7-Up to fill

Stir. Garnish: lime wedge.

MISTICO BANDITO
1 oz. Jose Cuervo Mistico
1 oz. cranberry juice
1 oz. blackberry juice

Shake, serve in shot glass.

MISTICO BERRY
1 oz. Jose Cuervo Mistico
1 oz. cabernet wine
splash triple sec
splash lime juice
splash 7-Up
sweet & sour mix to fill

Serve in a tall glass with a lemon wedge.

MISTICO CALIENTE
shot Jose Cuervo Mistico
splash Tabasco

Combine in shot glass and drop into a draft beer.

MISTICO CARIBBEAN SEA
1¼ oz. Jose Cuervo
¾ oz. blue curacao
½ oz. Peachtree Schnapps
sweet & sour mix to fill

Serve in a tall glass over ice.

MISTICO DESERT BERRY
1½ oz. Jose Cuervo Mistico
dash Chambord

Strain into a shot glass.

MISTICO LEMONADE
1 oz. Jose Cuervo Mistico
1 oz. orange curacao
1 oz. club soda
1 oz. cranberry juice
juice from ½ lemon

Garnish: lemon wedge.

TEQUILA

MISTICO MARTINI
1 oz. Jose Cuervo Mistico
1 oz. Chambord
1 oz. sweet & sour mix

Strain into martini glass.

———∞———

MISTICO MIRAGE
1½ oz. Jose Cuervo Mistico
1½ oz. orange juice
1 ½ oz. tonic water

Stir. Garnish: lime wedge.

———∞———

MISTICO MISSILE
1 oz. Jose Cuervo Mistico
½ oz. peach schnapps
splash grapefruit juice

Shake and strain. Serve in shot glass.

———∞———

MISTICO MORNING
1 oz. Jose Cuervo Mistico
1 oz. pineapple juice
1 oz. orange juice
splash triple sec
grenadine

Float grenadine on top. Garnish: lime.

———∞———

MISTICO MYSTERY
1 oz. Jose Cuervo Mistico
1 oz. triple sec
1 oz. pineapple juice

Shake, strain into shot glass.

MISTICO SLIDE
½ oz. Kahlua Coffee Liqueur
½ oz. Baileys Irish Cream
½ oz. Jose Cuervo

Layer ingredients in order listed in a shot glass.

———∞———

MISTICO SPIKE
1½ oz. Jose Cuervo Mistico
3 oz. ruby red grapefruit juice
dash bitters

Stir. Garnish with orange wedge.

———∞———

MISTICO VERTIGO
1¼ oz. Jose Cuervo Mistico
2 oz. sweet & sour mix
1 oz. cranberry juice
juice from ½ lemon

Stir. Garnish: orange wheel.

———∞———

MONSTER MASH
½ oz. Two Fingers Tequila
½ oz. Du Bouchett Tequila Monster
½ oz. Du Bouchett Blue Curacao
¼ oz. Du Bouchett Melon Liqueur

Shake. Strain into shot glass.

———∞———

MONSTER ON THE BEACH
1½ oz. Du Bouchett Tequila Monster
2 oz. cranberry juice
splash of lime juice
splash of grenadine

Serve over ice.

NEON TEQUILA MONSTER

3 oz. orange juice
1 oz. Burnett's Vodka
1 oz. Tequila Monster

———∞∞∞———

NEW LIFE

1½ oz. Sauza Tequila
1 lump sugar
3 dashes Angostura Bitters
lemon twist

Muddle sugar and bitters in an old-fashioned glass and fill with crushed ice. Add 1½ oz. Sauza Tequila. Garnish: lemon twist.

———∞∞∞———

PINK CAD WITH HAWAIIAN PLATES

1¼ oz. Jose Cuervo 1800 Tequila
2 oz. pineapple juice
2 oz. cranberry juice
½ oz. sweet & sour mix

Serve in a rocks glass. Garnish: lime wedge.

———∞∞∞———

PINK PANTHER

1½ oz. Sauza Tequila
½ oz. grenadine
2 oz. cream or half & half

Blend with ice and strain. Pour into chilled cocktail glass.

PULCO

2 oz. Jose Cuervo 1800 Tequila
½ oz. cointreau
1½ oz. lime juice

Serve on the rocks.

———∞∞∞———

PURPLE GECKO

1½ oz. Jose Cuervo Especial
 Tequila
½ oz. blue curacao
½ oz. Bols Red Curacao
1 oz. cranberry juice
1 oz. sweet & sour mix
½ oz. lime concentrate

Shake. Pour into a large salt-rimmed margarita glass. Garnish with lime wedge.

———∞∞∞———

RED CACTUS

1½ oz. Jose Cuervo Especial
 Tequila
4 oz. oregon raspberry puree
1½ oz. Sunkist sweet & sour mix
4 oz. ice

Blend. Garnish with lime wheel.

———∞∞∞———

RED MONSTER

⅓ Du Bouchett Tequila Monster
⅓ orange juice
⅓ tomato juice

———∞∞∞———

SHADY LADY

1 oz. Two Fingers Tequila
1 oz. melon liqueur
3 oz. grapefruit juice

Combine all ingredients in a shaker. Serve over rocks.

TEQUILA

SIESTA

1½ oz. Sauza Tequila
¾ oz. lime juice
½ oz. sloe gin

Blend or shake with ice and strain. Pour into chilled cocktail glass.

SOL-A-RITA

1¼ oz. Jose Cuervo Gold Tequila
¾ oz. cointreau
1½ oz. orange juice
2 dashes grenadine

Serve on the rocks.

SOUTHERN TRADITIONAL MARGARITA

1½ oz. Jose Cuervo Gold Tequila
⅝ oz. Southern Comfort
5 oz. sweet & sour mix
½ oz. fresh lime juice

Combine in tall glass over ice. Drop a lime wedge in glass.

SPANISH MOSS

½ oz. Herradura Tequila
¾ oz. Kahlua
½ oz. green creme de menthe

Shake and strain.

TEQUADOR

1½ oz. Herradura Tequila
2 oz. pineapple juice
1 dash Rose's Lime Juice
3 drops grenadine

Shake. Add a few drops of grenadine. Over crushed ice.

TEQUILA GIMLET

1½ oz. Sauza Tequila
1½ oz. Rose's Lime Juice
lime wheel or green cherry

Blend Sauza Tequila and Rose's Lime Juice with crushed ice and strain into a cocktail glass. Garnish: lime wheel or green cherry.

TEQUILA JULEP

1¼ oz. Gran Centenario Reposado Tequila
1 tsp. superfine sugar
2 springs fresh mint
club soda

Crush 3 mint leaves with sugar in a chilled highball glass and fill with ice. Add Gran Centenario and top with club soda. Garnish with sprig of mint.

TEQUILA TEASER

1½ oz. Sauza Tequila
½ oz. DeKuyper Triple Sec
1½ oz. orange juice
½ oz. grapefruit juice

Pour ingredients into tall glass filled with ice.

TEQUINA

2 oz. Sauza Tequila
½ oz. dry vermouth
lemon twist

Stir Sauza Tequila and dry vermouth with ice in a mixing glass until chilled. Strain into a chilled cocktail glass and garnish with a lemon twist.

———⚭———

THUNDERBOLT

2 parts Herradura Tequila
1 part Dr. McGillicuddy's
Imported Mentholmint
Schnapps

Stir on the rocks.

———⚭———

TIJUANA TEA

¾ oz. Jose Cuervo 1800 Tequila
¾ oz. Jose Cuervo Gold Tequila
½ oz. triple sec
1 oz. sweet & sour mix
3 oz. cola

Stir. Garnish with lime slice and maraschino cherry.

———⚭———

TRES MARTINI

Rinse a chilled martini with splash of cointreau and discard. Place 1½ oz. Tres Generaciones in a shaker. Fill with ice, shake and strain. Garnish: orange zest.

TEQUILA

Vodka

A-BOMB
½ oz. vodka
½ oz. coffee liqueur
½ oz. Irish Cream
½ oz. orange liqueur

Shake with ice, strain and serve in 7 oz. rocks glass.

ADIOS MOTHER
½ oz. vodka
½ oz. blue curacao
½ oz. gin
½ oz. rum
2 oz. sweet & sour mix

Build over ice in 12 oz. snifter glass and fill with soda water.

ALICE-BE-BANANALESS
¾ oz. vodka
¾ oz. amaretto
¾ oz. Midori
1 oz. cream

Build over ice in shaker. Shake and strain into 7 oz. rocks glass with ice.

ANTI-FREEZE
1½ oz. vodka
½ oz. Midori

Shake with ice, strain and serve.

BEACH BUM
1 oz. vodka
1½ oz. Midori
1 oz. cranberry juice

Combine with ice and shake. Strain into cocktail glass and serve straight up.

BLACK MAGIC
1½ oz. vodka
¾ oz. coffee liqueur

Mix both ingredients with cracked ice in a shaker or blender. Pour into a chilled old-fashioned glass. Add several dashes lemon juice.

BLACK ORCHID
1 oz. vodka
½ oz. blue curacao
1½ oz. cranberry juice

Build over ice in a 7 oz. rocks glass.

BLACK RUSSIAN
1½ oz. vodka
¾ oz. coffee liqueur

Add, in order, to glass filled with cubed ice; stir briskly. Garnish with swizzle stick.

BLOODY CAESAR

1¼ oz. vodka
Clamato Juice

Pour vodka into glass with ice and fill with Clamato Juice. Add dash of Tabasco, Worcestershire, pepper, salt and garnish with celery stalk or lime wheel.

———— ∞ ————

BLOODY MARY

1¼ oz. Absolut Peppar
3 oz. tomato juice
3 drops Worcestershire sauce
3 drops Tabasco sauce

Pour Peppar over ice in a tall glass. Fill with tomato juice. Add a dash or two of Worcestershire sauce. Stir. Garnish with a celery stalk. For those who enjoy their Bloody Marys extremely spicy, add a dash of Tabasco to taste.

———— ∞ ————

BLUE BLOCKER

1 oz. Ohranj
½ oz. blue curacao

Serve on the rocks.

———— ∞ ————

BROWN BEAR

1 oz. vodka
1½ oz. coffee liqueur

In a cocktail shaker, mix together. Strain, leaving out ice, and pour into stemmed glass.

BUBBLE GUM

1 oz. cranberry vodka
¼ oz. peach schnapps
¼ oz. creme de banana
1 oz. orange juice

Shake. Serve on the rocks.

———— ∞ ————

BUTTERSCOTCH BOMBER

½ oz. vodka
½ oz. Baileys Irish Cream
½ oz. schnapps

Shake with ice.

———— ∞ ————

CAJUN MARTINI

1¼ oz. Peppar
dash extra dry vermouth

Pour Peppar and vermouth over ice. Shake or stir well. Strain and serve in a cocktail glass straight-up or over ice. Garnish with a twist or an olive.

———— ∞ ————

CAPE CODDER

1½ oz. vodka
4 oz. cranberry juice
club soda to fill
orange slice

Add in order to collins glass filled with cubed ice, vodka, and cranberry juice cocktail. Fill glass with club soda and stir. Garnish with orange slices on right side of glass and two 9-inch straws.

VODKA

CHOCOLATE MARTINI

1¼ oz. Kurant
dash white creme de cacao

Pour Kurant and creme de cacao over ice. Shake or stir well. Strain and serve in a chocolate-rimmed cocktail glass straight-up or over ice. Garnish with an orange peel. (Hint: to rim the glass, first rub a piece of orange around the top of the glass, then gently place the glass upside down in a plate of unsweetened chocolate powder.

CITRON COOLER

1¼ oz. Citron
½ oz. fresh lime juice
2 oz. tonic

Pour Citron and lime juice over ice in a tall glass. Fill with tonic. Garnish with a wedge of lime.

CITRON KAMIKAZE

¾ oz. Citron
¾ oz. triple sec
splash lime juice

Pour Citron, triple sec and lime juice over ice in a glass. Shake well and strain into a cocktail glass. Serve straight-up or on the rocks. Garnish with a wedge of lime.

CITRON MARTINI

1¼ oz. Citron
dash extra dry vermouth

Pour Citron and vermouth over ice. Shake or stir well. Strain and serve in a cocktail glass straight-up or over ice. Garnish with a twist or an olive.

COSMO KAZI

4 parts vodka
1 part triple sec
dash lime juice
splash cranberry juice

Combine ingredients and pour over ice.

COSSACK CHARGE

1½ oz. vodka
½ oz. cognac
½ oz. cherry brandy

Mix all ingredients with cracked ice in a shaker or blender and pour into a chilled cocktail glass.

CRANPEPPAR

1¼ oz. Peppar
3 oz. cranberry juice

Pour Peppar over ice in a tall glass. Fill with cranberry juice.

CREAMSICLE

1½ oz. Ohranj
½ oz. Irish Cream

On the rocks.

———⟨∞⟩———

CUTTHROAT

1¼ chilled cranberry vodka
3 oz. orange juice

In a tall glass with ice; fill with
orange juice.

———⟨∞⟩———

ELECTRIC
LEMONADE

1¼ oz. vodka
½ oz. blue curacao
2 oz. sweet & sour mix
splash 7-Up
lemon slice

Combine ingredients, flash
blend. Pour over ice in a tall
glass and garnish with lemon
slice.

———⟨∞⟩———

ELECTRIC PEACH

2 oz. vodka, chilled
¼ oz. peach schnapps
½ oz. cranberry juice cocktail
¼ oz. orange juice

Shake with ice. Serve over ice.

———⟨∞⟩———

FIRE

1¼ oz. Ohranj
¼ oz. Cinnamon Schnapps

Over ice.

FUDGSICLE

2 oz. vodka, chilled
½ oz. creme de cacao
¼ oz. chocolate syrup

Shake with ice. Serve over ice.

———⟨∞⟩———

GIMLET

1¼ oz. vodka
½ oz. fresh lime juice

Mix vodka and lime juice in a
glass with ice. Strain and serve
in cocktail glass. Garnish with
twist of lime.

———⟨∞⟩———

GRAPE CRUSH

1 oz. vodka
1 oz. black raspberry liqueur
2 oz. sour mix
1 oz. 7-Up
orange or cherry garnish

Serve over ice in collins glass.
Garnish with an orange or
cherry.

———⟨∞⟩———

GREEN HORNET

2 oz. vodka, chilled
¼ oz. Midori
½ oz. sweet & sour mix

Shake with ice. Serve up or
over ice.

GREEN SNEAKER

1 oz. vodka
½ oz. Midori
½ oz. triple sec
2 oz. orange juice

Stir with ice, strain and serve straight up.

———— ✸ ————

GREMLIN #2

1½ oz. vodka
¾ oz. blue curacao
¾ oz. rum
½ oz. orange juice

Shake with ice, strain and serve straight up.

———— ✸ ————

GREYHOUND

1½ oz. vodka
grapefruit juice to fill

Combine ingredients over crushed ice in a tall glass. Serve with a straw.

———— ✸ ————

HAWAII FIVE-O

1½ oz. pineapple vodka, chilled
¼ oz. blue curacao

Shake. Serve in a hurricane glass with ice. Garnish with pineapple spear, cherry and umbrella.

———— ✸ ————

HAWAIIAN PIPELINE

1½ oz. pineapple vodka, chilled
2 oz. orange juice
1 oz. cranberry juice

Shake. Serve over ice.

HEARTTHROB

1¼ oz. cranberry vodka, chilled
¼ oz. peach schnapps
¼ oz. grapefruit juice

Shake. Serve in a tall glass with ice.

———— ✸ ————

HOLLYWOOD

1 oz. vodka
1 oz. black raspberry liqueur

Combine ingredients in a tall glass with ice. Fill with cranberry juice.

———— ✸ ————

HOT LIPS

2 oz. cranberry vodka, chilled
¼ oz. Goldschlager

Serve up or over ice.

———— ✸ ————

HULA-HOOP

2 oz. vodka, chilled
1 oz. pineapple juice
½ oz. orange juice

———— ✸ ————

IRISH QUAALUDE #1

½ oz. vodka
½ oz. Irish Cream
½ oz. coffee liqueur
½ oz. hazelnut liqueur

Strain and serve straight up.

IRON BUTTERFLY
¾ oz. vodka
¾ oz. coffee liqueur
¾ oz. Irish Cream

Combine with ice, shake, strain and serve straight up.

ISLAND TEA
1½ oz. vodka
1 oz. grenadine
1 tsp. lemon juice

Combine with ice and shake. Strain over ice in an old-fashioned glass and garnish with mint sprig.

KAYTUSHA ROCKET
1 oz. vodka
½ oz. coffee liqueur
1 dash cream
1 oz. pineapple juice

Combine with ice, shake, strain and serve straight up.

KOOL-AID
1 oz. vodka
1 oz. honeydew melon liqueur
2 oz. cranberry juice

Combine ingredients over ice in a rocks glass.

KRETCHMA
1 oz. vodka
1 oz. creme de cacao
½ oz. lemon juice
½ tsp. grenadine

Mix all ingredients with cracked ice in a shaker or blender. Strain into a chilled cocktail glass.

KURANT AFFAIR
1¼ oz. Kurant
3 oz. cranberry juice
1 oz. club soda

Pour Kurant over ice in a tall glass. Fill most of the way with cranberry juice. Top with a splash of soda. Garnish with a wedge of lime.

KURANT AND 7-UP
1¼ oz. Kurant
2 oz. 7-Up

Pour Kurant over ice in a tall glass. Fill with 7-Up. Garnish with a slice of lemon and a slice of lime.

KURANT BON BON
1 oz. Kurant
½ oz. Godiva Liqueur

Combine Kurant and Godiva in a brandy snifter.

KURANT COSMOPOLITAN

1¼ oz. Kurant
3 oz. cranberry juice
¼ oz. lime juice

Pour chilled Kurant into a cocktail glass. Add a splash of cranberry juice and splash of lime juice.

KURANT MARTINI

1¼ oz. Kurant
dash extra dry vermouth

Pour Kurant and vermouth over ice. Shake or stir well. Strain and serve in a cocktail glass straight-up or over ice. Garnish with a twist or an olive.

LEMON CHI CHI

1½ oz. vodka
1½ oz. sweet & sour mix
2-3 oz. pina colada mix
1½ oz. pineapple juice

Blend with crushed ice and serve in 15 oz. glass.

LEMON CHIFFON

2 oz. vodka, chilled
¼ oz. triple sec
1 oz. sweet & sour mix

Squeeze and drop in a fresh lemon wedge.

LEMON DROP

1¼ oz. vodka
2 oz. sweet and sour mix
splash 7-Up
splash club soda
lemon wedge or lemon slice
  sprinkled with sugar

Combine ingredients over ice. Squeeze lemon wedge and drop in as a garnish, or garnish with a lemon slice sprinkled with sugar.

LEMON ICE

1¼ oz. vodka
½ oz. triple sec
1½ oz. sweet & sour mix
½ oz. lemon juice

Build over iced and fill with 7-Up in a 15 oz. glass. Garnish with lemon slice.

MADRAS

1¼ oz. vodka
2 oz. cranberry juice
2 oz. orange juice

Pour vodka over ice in a tall glass. Fill halfway with orange juice and top it off with cranberry juice.

MALIBU RAIN

2 oz. vodka, chilled
1½ oz. pineapple juice
½ oz. Malibu
splash orange juice

MARGARITA

1¼ oz. Kurant
½ oz. orange liqueur
juice of small lime

Mix Kurant, orange liqueur
and lime juice with ice. Strain
and serve in a cocktail glass.
Garnish with a slice of lime.

MARTINI

1¼ oz. vodka
Dash extra dry vermouth

Pour vodka and vermouth
over ice. Shake or stir well.
Strain and serve in a cocktail
glass straight up or over ice.
Garnish with a twist or an
olive.

MELON BALL

½ oz. vodka
1 oz. honeydew melon liqueur

Combine ingredients in a
glass with ice. Fill with equal
parts orange juice and
pineapple juice.

MIAMI SHADES

1 oz. Ohranj
¼ oz. peach schnapps
2 oz. grapefruit juice

Serve over ice.

MIDNIGHT ORCHID

1½ oz. cranberry vodka, chilled
¼ oz. Chambord
2 oz. pineapple juice
½ oz. half & half

Shake. Serve over crushed ice
or blend with ice.

MIND ERASER

1 oz. vodka
1 oz. coffee liqueur
soda water to fill

Combine ingredients over ice.
Fill with soda water and serve
with a straw.

MONSOON

¼ oz. vodka
¼ oz. coffee liqueur
¼ oz. amaretto
¼ oz. Irish Cream
¼ oz. hazelnut liqueur

MOSCOW CHILL

1½ oz. vodka
4 oz. Dr. Pepper
wedge lime

Pour vodka over shaved ice in
champagne glass. Fill with Dr.
Pepper. Garnish with wedge
of lime.

MUDSLIDE

⅔ oz. vodka
⅔ oz. Irish Cream
⅔ oz. coffee liqueur

Shake with ice.

VODKA

NEVA

1½ oz. vodka
½ oz. tomato juice
½ oz. orange juice

In cocktail shaker, mix all ingredients. Pour over ice into stemmed glass.

—⟨∞⟩—

NUT HOUSE

2 oz. cranberry vodka, chilled
¼ oz. amaretto

—⟨∞⟩—

NUTS & BERRIES

½ oz. vodka
½ oz. hazelnut liqueur
½ oz. coffee liqueur
¼ oz. cream

Combine with ice, shake, strain and serve straight up in 4 oz. rocks glass.

—⟨∞⟩—

OHRANJ JULIUS

Fill glass with crushed ice.
½ shot Ohranj Vodka
½ shot cointreau

Mix with ½ oz. Mr. & Mrs. T's Sweet & Sour Mix and ½ oz. orange juice. Garnish with orange slice.

—⟨∞⟩—

ORANGE CRUSH #1

1¼ oz. vodka
¾ oz. triple sec
2 oz. orange juice

Shake with ice, strain and serve.

OUTRIGGER

1 oz. vodka
½ oz. peach schnapps
1 dash lime juice
2 oz. pineapple juice

Combine with ice, shake and strain over ice into an old-fashioned glass.

—⟨∞⟩—

OYSTER SHOOTER

1 oz. vodka
1 raw oyster
spoonful cocktail sauce
squeeze lemon

Served in a small rocks glass, it calls for a dash of horseradish too, for those who dare. Take a deep breath, down the hatch.

—⟨∞⟩—

PEPPAR SALTY DOG

1¼ oz. Peppar
3 oz. grapefruit juice

Salt the rim of a rocks glass. Fill with ice. Pour in Peppar and fill with grapefruit juice.

—⟨∞⟩—

PEPPER MANHATTAN

1½ oz. vodka
½ oz. sweet vermouth
cherry

Mix vodka and sweet vermouth in cocktail shaker over ice; stir. Strain, leaving out ice, and pour into stemmed glass. Add cherry for garnish.

PEPPERTINI
1½ oz. vodka
½ oz. vermouth
olive

Mix vodka and dry vermouth in cocktail shaker over ice; stir, and pour into rocks glass. Add olive for garnish.

———

PINEAPPLE PIE
1¼ oz. pineapple vodka, chilled
¼ oz. white creme de cacao

Shake with ice. Strain into rocks glass with dollop of whipped cream.

———

PINK LEMONADE
1¼ oz. vodka
1 oz. cranberry juice
1¼ oz. sweet & sour mix
½ tsp. sugar
soda to fill
lime wedge garnish

Combine vodka, sugar, sweet and sour mix, and cranberry juice in tall 12 oz. glass. Stir to dissolve sugar. Add ice and top with soda. Add squeeze of lime from wedge.

———

PINK MUSTANG
1 part cranberry vodka, chilled
1 part Rumple Minze Peppermint Schnapps

On the rocks.

PURPLE HOOTER
½ oz. vodka
½ oz. black raspberry liqueur
½ oz. cranberry juice
splash club soda

Shake and strain vodka, black raspberry, and cranberry juice. Top with splash of club soda.

———

RAZZ-MA-TAZZ
2 oz. vodka, chilled
½ oz. Chambord
1½ oz. club soda

———

RUBY SLIPPERS
1 part cranberry vodka, chilled
1 part Goldschlager

Shake. Serve on the rocks.

———

S.O.S.
1 part Ohranj
1 part Sambuca

On the rocks.

———

SALT AND PEPPAR
1¼ oz. Peppar

Pour chilled Peppar into a salt-rimmed cocktail glass. Garnish with a cucumber spear.

———

SCREWDRIVER
1 1/2 oz. vodka
orange juice to fill

VODKA

SEABREEZE

1¼ oz. vodka
2 oz. cranberry juice
2 oz. grapefruit juice

Pour vodka over ice in a tall glass. Fill halfway with grapefruit juice and top it off with cranberry juice.

SEX ON THE BEACH #2

¾ oz. vodka
¾ oz. Midori
1 oz. pineapple juice
1 oz. cranberry juice

Build in mixing glass, shake or stir, and strain into a 5 oz. glass.

SIBERIAN SUNRISE

1½ oz. vodka
4 oz. grapefruit juice
½ oz. triple sec

Mix all ingredients with cracked ice in a shaker or blender and pour into highball glass.

SOVIET COCKTAIL

1½ oz. vodka
½ oz. dry vermouth
½ oz. dry sherry
lemon peel

Mix all ingredients, except lemon peel, with cracked ice in a shaker or blender and strain into a chilled cocktail glass. Twist lemon peel over drink and drop into glass.

ST. PETERSBURG

2 oz. vodka
¼ tsp. orange bitters
1 orange wedge

Pour vodka and bitters into mixing glass with several ice cubes. Stir until very cold and pour into a chilled old-fashioned glass. Score peel of orange wedge with tines of fork and drop into drink.

SUNSHINE FROSTY PUNCH

1¼ oz. vodka
2 scoops vanilla ice cream

Blend until smooth and serve in a 12 oz. brandy snifter.

SUNSTROKE

1½ oz. vodka
3 oz. grapefruit juice
splash triple sec

Pour vodka and grapefruit juice into short glass filled with ice. Add a little triple sec and stir. Sugar may be substituted for triple sec.

TABOO

1½ oz. pineapple vodka, chilled
½ oz. cranberry juice
½ oz. sour mix
splash triple sec

Blend with crushed ice. Serve in a tall glass. Garnish with pineapple wedge and cherry.

TANGERINE
1¼ oz. Ohranj Vodka
2 oz. orange juice
dash grenadine

Shake on the rocks.

———∞∞∞———

TAXI
1 part Ohranj Vodka
1 part coffee liqueur

On the rocks.

———∞∞∞———

TROPICAL ICEBERG
1½ oz. pineapple vodka, chilled
½ oz. banana liqueur or ½ banana
½ oz. cream of coconut
dash cream or half & half

———∞∞∞———

WATERMELON
1 oz. vodka
1 oz. honeydew melon liqueur
2 oz. orange juice
2 oz. cranberry juice

Fill with equal parts orange and cranberry juices, over ice.

———∞∞∞———

WHITE RUSSIAN
1 oz. vodka
½ oz. Godiva Liqueur
1 oz. heavy cream

Pour vodka, Godiva Liqueur and cream over ice in a rocks glass. Shake and serve.

WOO WOO
1 oz. vodka
½ oz. peach schnapps
2 oz. cranberry juice

Combine ingredients over ice.

VODKA

ABSOLUTION

1 part Absolut Vodka
5 parts champagne

In a fluted champagne glass, add ingredients. Cut a lemon peel in the form of a ring to represent a halo. The lemon peel can be either wrapped around the top of the glass or floated on top of the champagne. (Created by Jimmy Caulfield at the River Cafe, New York, NY)

ALFONSO

1 oz. Dubonnet
1 dash Angostura Bitters
1 sugar cube
3 oz. chilled champagne

Place sugar in a champagne saucer glass and sprinkle with bitters. Add one ice cube, fill with champagne and garnish with a lemon twist.

AMBROSIA

1 oz. apple jack
1 oz. brandy
¼ oz. cointreau
½ oz. lemon juice
2 oz. champagne

Shake the first four ingredients over ice and strain into a champagne flute. Fill with champagne.

AMERICANA

1 tsp. bourbon
1 dash Angostura Bitters
4 oz. champagne
fresh peach slice

Pour the bourbon and bitters into a flute. Add champagne and garnish with the peach slice.

AMERICAN FLYER

1½ oz. light rum
1 Tbsp. lime juice
½ tsp. simple sugar syrup
2 oz. champagne or sparkling wine

Shake first three ingredients together. Strain into chilled white wine goblet. Top with champagne.

AMERICAN ROSE

¼ oz. brandy
¼ oz. Pernod
splash grenadine
¼ oz. peach schnapps
2 oz. champagne

Stir gently.

APRICOT SMOOTHIE
¼ oz. apricot brandy
¼ oz. vodka
2½ oz. champagne
2 oz. orange juice

Stir gently.

———∞∞———

ARISE MY LOVE
3 oz. champagne
¼ oz. green creme de menthe

Stir gently.

———∞∞———

BACARDI CHAMPAGNE COCKTAIL
1 oz. Bacardi Silver Rum
3 oz. champagne
1 tsp. sugar
dash bitters

In a tall glass mix rum, sugar, and bitters. Fill with champagne.

———∞∞———

BARRACUDA
1¼ oz. Ron Rico Dark Rum
1 oz. pineapple juice
½ oz. Rose's Lime Juice
¼ tsp. sugar

Shake everything but the champagne. Fill to the top with champagne.

BELLINI
1 peach half
2 oz. champagne
¼ oz. simple syrup

Muddle peach in a champagne glass with simple syrup. Fill the glass with champagne.

———∞∞———

BETELGEUSE
1 oz. Stoli Vanilla Vodka
1 Tbs. vanilla liqueur
1 Tbs. Rose's Lime Juice
1 oz. white zinfandel wine
2 oz. champagne in a flute

(Pops for Champagne, Chicago, IL)

———∞∞———

BLACK VELVET (A.K.A. BISMARCK OR CHAMPAGNE VELVET)
1 part Guinness Stout
1 part champagne

Layer the champagne over the Guinness in a champagne flute.

———∞∞———

BLUE BUBBLES
¼ oz. blueberry schnapps
splash of blue curacao
3 oz. champagne

———∞∞———

BLUE VELVET
1 splash blue curacao
3 oz. champagne in a flute

BOLLI-STOLLI

1 oz. Stolichnaya Vodka in a flute

Gradually add 3 oz. Bollinger Champagne.

―∞∞―

BOOM BOOM PUNCH

1 oz. dark rum
1 Tbsp. orange juice
1 oz. sweet vermouth
3 oz. champagne in a flute

Garnish with banana slices.

―∞∞―

BUZZ BOMB

splash lime juice
splash cointreau
¼ oz. cognac
¼ oz. Benedictine
¼ oz. vodka
3 oz. champagne

―∞∞―

CALIFORNIA SUNSHINE

3 oz. champagne
1 oz. orange juice
¼ oz. creme de cassis

―∞∞―

CARIBBEAN CONTESSA

1 splash each:
cointreau
cranberry juice
orange juice
vodka

Add 4 oz. champagne in a flute.
(The Bubble Lounge, New York, NY)

CARIBOU MARTINI

1 oz. Stolichnaya Kafya Vodka
3 oz. champagne

―∞∞―

CELESTIAL FIZZ

1 oz. cognac
1 Tbs. Grand Marnier
2 oz. cranberry juice
2 oz. champagne in a flute garnished with a lemon twist

(Pops for Champagne, Chicago, IL)

―∞∞―

CHAMBORD AND CHAMPAGNE (CHAMPAGNE ROYALE)

Pour a splash of Chambord into a champagne glass. Fill with champagne.
(Four Seasons Restaurant, New York, NY)

―∞∞―

CHAMBORD ROYALE SPRITZER

1½ oz. Chambord
3 oz. champagne
club soda

Pour Chambord into wine glass. Fill with champagne. Top with club soda.

―∞∞―

CHAMPAGNE BAYOU

2 oz. dry gin
1 tsp. lemon juice
1 tsp. superfine sugar
3 oz. champagne in a flute

CHAMPAGNE BLITZ

3 oz. champagne
¼ oz. white creme de menthe

CHAMPAGNE BUCK

1 oz. dry gin
1 splash cherry brandy

1 splash orange juice in a shaker filled with ice. Strain into a cocktail glass and slowly add 2 oz. champagne.

CHAMPAGNE CASSIS

3 oz. champagne
¼ oz. creme de cassis

CHAMPAGNE COCKTAIL

3 oz. champagne, chilled
1 cube sugar
dash Angostura Bitters

Stir ingredients slowly. Garnish with a lemon twist.

CHAMPAGNE COCKTAIL NO.2

1 oz. Southern Comfort
dash Angostura Bitters
4 oz. chilled champagne
twist lemon peel

CHAMPAGNE COCKTAIL NO.3

1 oz. brandy
4 oz. chilled champagne
twist orange peel

Pour brandy into champagne glass, fill with champagne.

CHAMPAGNE COCKTAIL NO.4

2 small sugar cubes
1 oz. Benedictine
1 oz. creme de cacao
4 oz. champagne

Fill with chilled champagne.

CHAMPAGNE CORNUCOPIA

2 oz. cranberry juice
½ oz. rainbow sherbet
½ oz. vodka
½ oz. peach schnapps
champagne

CHAMPAGNE FIZZ

1½ oz. gin
1 oz. lemon juice
1 tsp. superfine sugar
3 oz. chilled champagne

In a shaker half-filled with ice cubes, combine the gin, lemon juice and sugar. Shake well. Strain into a champagne flute. Add the champagne.

CHAMPAGNE

CHAMPAGNE NORMANDY

1 oz. Calvados
1 tsp. sugar
dash Angostura Bitters
chilled champagne

In a champagne glass; add an orange slice.

CHAMPAGNE RITA

1 oz. tequila
½ oz. cointreau
splash limeade or Rose's Lime Juice
3 oz. champagne

CHAMPAGNE SIDECAR

1 oz. brandy
½ oz. cointreau
½ oz. lemon juice
chilled champagne

Shake first three ingredients over ice. Strain into a champagne glass and top with champagne.

CHICAGO

1 oz. brandy
1 dash curacao
2 dashes Angostura Bitters
4 oz. champagne

Frost the rim of the flute with lemon juice and sugar before pouring.

CILVER CITRON

1¼ oz. Absolut Citron
3 oz. chilled champagne

Combine in a champagne glass.

CITRUS CENTAURI

1½ oz. lemon-flavored vodka
1 splash Rose's Lime Juice
1 splash blue curacao
3 oz. champagne

Garnish with a lemon twist. (Pops for Champagne, Chicago, IL).

CULLODEN

1 oz. Drambuie
4 oz. champagne

DAWN

3 oz. champagne
1 oz. Fino Sherry
splash fresh lime juice

Stir and serve in a cocktail glass.

DEATH IN THE AFTERNOON

1½ oz. Pernod
3 oz. champagne

Pour Pernod into a chilled champagne glass. Fill the glass with champagne.

DIAMOND FIZZ

1 oz. gin
1 tsp. lemon juice
3 oz. champagne

—∞—

EIFFEL VIEW

1 oz. citrus vodka
1 splash grenadine syrup
4 oz. champagne in a flute

—∞—

FIRST LOVE

3 oz. champagne
1 oz. gin
1 tsp. sugar
½ oz. Cherry Herring

—∞—

FRAMBOISE ROYALE

1 splash Framboise and 5 oz. champagne in a flute.

—∞—

FRENCH 75

1½ oz. cognac
½ tsp. lemon juice
½ tsp. powdered sugar
champagne

Combine everything but champagne. Shake and pour in a champagne glass. Fill with champagne. Garnish with a lemon twist.

—∞—

FRENCH KISS

1 oz. vodka
1 Tbs. Lillet Blanc
3 oz. champagne

Garnish with an orange twist. (Oliver's, Seattle, WA)

FRENCH REVOLUTION

1 oz. brandy
2 oz. Framboise
3 oz. champagne

In a flute, garnished with a lemon twist.

—∞—

FROBISHER

2 oz. gin
3 dashes Angostura Bitters
3 oz. champagne

Fill a highball glass with ice, add gin and bitters. Stir. Fill with champagne. Garnish with a lemon twist.

—∞—

FROZEN BIKINI

2 oz. vodka
1 oz. peach schnapps
3 oz. peach nectar
2 oz. orange juice
splash fresh lemon juice
1 oz. champagne

—∞—

GOLDEN KISS

1 oz. Goldenbaar Chocolate
 Vodka
4 oz. champagne in a flute

—∞—

GOLDEN PASSION

1 oz. Goldenbaar Chocolate
 Vodka
4 oz. champagne
1 splash Alize Passion Fruit
 Liqueur

HOLIDAY CHEER

3 oz. champagne
¼ oz. cranberry juice

Serve in a tall glass and garnish with lime.

───◦◦◦───

IMPERIAL FIZZ

1 oz. bourbon
½ oz. lemon juice
½ tsp. sugar
chilled champagne

Add bourbon, lemon juice and sugar to mixing glass. Shake. Strain into a chilled glass. Fill with champagne.

───◦◦◦───

IRISH CELEBRATION

1¼ oz. Bushmills Irish Whiskey
¼ oz. green creme de menthe
splash champagne

Shake the first two ingredients well with ice and strain. Top with champagne.

───◦◦◦───

KING'S PEG

1 oz. brandy
4 oz. champagne in a flute

───◦◦◦───

KIR OR KIR ROYALE

3 oz. champagne
splash creme de cassis

Fill the glass with champagne and add a splash of creme de cassis.

LUXURY COCKTAIL

1 oz. brandy
2 dashes orange bitters
3 oz. champagne in a flute

───◦◦◦───

MAMBO KING

1 oz. Stoli Razberi Vodka
4 oz. champagne

Frost the rim with grenadine syrup and raw sugar. (Asia de Cuba, New York, NY)

───◦◦◦───

MANDRIN COCKTAIL

1 oz. Absolut Mandrin Vodka
4 oz. champagne in a flute

───◦◦◦───

MARTINI ROYALE

3 oz. vodka or gin
1 oz. champagne in a martini glass (stir gently)

Garnish with a lemon twist.

───◦◦◦───

METRO

1 splash cranberry juice
1 dash Rose's Lime Juice
1 dash cointreau
1 oz. vodka
4 oz. champagne in a flute

───◦◦◦───

MIDORI COCKTAIL

3 oz. champagne
1 oz. Midori

MIMI-"BUBBLE" ZAZA

Combine 1 splash each: cointreau, vodka, orange juice. Add 4 oz. champagne. Garnish with an orange twist. (The Bubble Lounge, New York, NY)

❦

MIMOSA

3 oz. champagne
2 oz. orange juice

Combine in a champagne flute and stir.

❦

MONTE CARLO IMPERIAL HIGHBALL

1 oz. gin
½ oz. white creme de cacao
3 oz. champagne

Garnish with a lemon twist.

❦

NELSON'S BLOOD

3 oz. champagne
½ oz. tawny port

Stir slowly but well.

PANACEA

1 Tbsp. creme de cassis
1 oz. Finlandia Arctic Cranberry Vodka
1 Tbsp. fresh lime juice (sweetened to taste)
1 splash cointreau

Shake and strain into a flute. Add 3 oz. champagne and garnish with a whole cranberry and a lime twist. (Oliver's Seattle, WA)

❦

PASSIONE

1½ oz. Alize Passion Brandy
½ oz. Chambord
6 oz. champagne
4 oz. freshly squeezed orange juice
10 raspberries

Fill a large goblet with ice cubes. Pour in the brandy, Chambord, champagne and orange juice. Stir to blend well. Add the raspberries and stir again.

❦

PASSION MIMOSA

1 oz. Alize
3 oz. champagne

Garnish with strawberry.

❦

PINK CALIFORNIA SUNSHINE

4 oz. pink champagne
4 oz. chilled orange juice
dash creme de cassis

CHAMPAGNE

PINK PASSION

1 splash each: vodka, cherry
brandy, creme de cassis, grapefruit juice
3 oz. champagne.

───⊗⊗⊗───

POINSETTIA

1 oz. cranberry juice
4 oz. champagne

Garnish with an orange.

───⊗⊗⊗───

PURPLE PASSION

2 oz. Finlandia Arctic Cranberry
Vodka
splash cassis in champagne flute

Top with champagne.

───⊗⊗⊗───

QUEEN'S PEG

1 oz. gin
4 oz. champagne

In a flute.

───⊗⊗⊗───

RASPBERRY TRUFFLE

1 oz. Stoli Razberi Vodka
1 splash Godiva Chocolate
Liqueur
4 oz. champagne

In a flute.

RED PASSIONE

1 oz. chilled fresh orange juice
¾ oz. Alize Red Passion
¼ oz. Chambord
3 oz. chilled champagne
lemon slice and fresh maraschino cherry for garnish

Combine orange juice, Alize,
Chambord in chilled cham-
pagne flute; stir. Top with
champagne. Garnish with
lemon slice and cherry.

───⊗⊗⊗───

REMBRANDT

½ cup fresh strawberries
3 oz. chilled champagne

Puree strawberries in an electric blender, pour into champagne flute and slowly top off
with champagne.

───⊗⊗⊗───

RUBY RED

1 oz. Stoli Razberi Vodka
1 splash creme de cassis
4 oz. champagne

In a flute. (The Bubble
Lounge, New York, NY)

───⊗⊗⊗───

RUE DE LA PAIX

1 oz. cognac
2 oz. Framboise
3 oz. champagne in a flute, garnished with a lemon twist.

Russian Brunch
1½ oz. vodka
1 oz. orange juice
2 oz. champagne

———— ∞ ————

Sante
1½ oz. pear brandy
½ oz. cointreau
2½ oz. champagne (Pops,
   Chicago, IL)

———— ∞ ————

Scotch Fizz
1 oz. scotch
3 oz. pink champagne

———— ∞ ————

Scotch Royale
1½ oz. scotch
1 tsp. fine sugar
dash Angostura Bitters
3 oz. champagne

Dissolve sugar in bitters and scotch in a champagne flute. Fill with champagne. Stir gently.

———— ∞ ————

Southern Belle
1 Tbs. amaretto
1 Tbs. apricot brandy
4 oz. champagne

In a flute.

———— ∞ ————

Sparkling Strawberry Mimosa
2 oz. champagne
2 oz. orange juice
¼ oz. strawberry syrup
strawberries

Sparks
1 oz. Absolut Peppar Vodka
3 oz. champagne

Combine in a champagne glass.

———— ∞ ————

Sputnik
1 oz. Stolichnaya Ohranj Vodka
1 oz. fresh orange juice
1 splash grenadine syrup
3 oz. champagne

———— ∞ ————

Stratosphere Cocktail
1 oz. Creme Yvette
4 oz. champagne

———— ∞ ————

Thug Passion
2 oz. Alize
3 oz. champagne

———— ∞ ————

Typhoon
3 oz. champagne
1 oz. gin
½ oz. anisette
splash lime juice

———— ∞ ————

Velvet Swing
1 splash Armagnac
2 oz. ruby port
3 oz. champagne

In a flute.

———— ∞ ————

VODKA CHAMPAGNE PUNCH

1 oz. vodka
1 Tbsp. white rum
1 tsp. fresh lime juice
1 tsp. strawberry liqueur
3 oz. champagne

Combine in a flute. Garnish
with a fresh strawberry.

———∽∾∽———

WITCHES' BREW

3 oz. champagne
1 oz. Strega

Shooters

24 KARAT NIGHTMARE
1 oz. Goldschlager
1 oz. Rumple Minze

Serve straight up in shot glass.

AFTERBURNER
1 oz. Rumple Minze
1 oz. Tia Maria

Serve straight up in shot glass.

AFTER FIVE
1 oz. Baileys Irish Cream
1 oz. Rumple Minze

Serve straight up in shot glass.

ALABAMA SLAMMER
½ oz. Southern Comfort
½ oz. Absolut
¼ oz. sloe gin
¼ oz. Disaronno Amaretto
½ oz. orange juice

Serve straight up in shot glass.

ALICE IN WONDERLAND
1 oz. Herradura Tequila
½ oz. Tia Maria
½ oz. Grand Marnier

Serve straight up in shot glass.

APPLE PIE
½ oz. Hiram Walker Apple
  Schnapps
1 oz. Stolichnaya
½ oz. pineapple juice
dash powdered cinnamon

Serve straight up in shot glass.

B-52
½ oz. Kahlua
1/2 oz. Baileys Irish Cream
½ oz. Grand Marnier

Serve straight up in shot glass.

B-52 WITH BOMBAY DOOR
½ oz. Kahlua
½ oz. Baileys Irish Cream
½ oz. Grand Marnier
½ oz. Bombay Gin

Serve straight up in shot glass.

BANANA BOAT
½ oz. Malibu Rum
½ oz. banana liqueur
1 oz. pineapple juice

Serve straight up in shot glass.

BANANA BOOMER

1 oz. Puerto Rican Rum
½ oz. banana liqueur
½ oz. orange & pineapple juice

Serve straight up in shot glass.

BEAM ME UP SCOTTY

½ oz. Kahlua
1 oz. Baileys Irish Cream
½ oz. Hiram Walker Creme de
 Banana

Serve straight up in shot glass.

BLUE KAMAKAZI

1 oz. Absolut
splash Rose's Lime Juice
½ oz. blue curacao

Serve straight up in shot glass.

BLUE WHALE

½ oz. blue curacao
1 oz. Puerto Rican Rum
¼ oz. pineapple juice

Serve straight up in shot glass.

BOCCI BALL

½ oz. Disaronno Amaretto
1 oz. Stolichnaya
½ oz. orange juice

Serve straight up in shot glass.

BOURBON STREET

1 oz. bourbon
1 oz. DiSaronno Amaretto

Serve straight up in shot glass.

BRAIN

1 oz. Baileys Irish Cream
1 oz. Peachtree or strawberry
 schnapps

Serve straight up in shot glass.

BRAVE BULL

1 oz. Cuervo Tequila
1 oz. Kahlua

Serve straight up in shot glass.

BUBBLEGUM

½ oz. Midori
1 oz. Absolut
½ oz. creme de banana
½ oz. orange juice
splash Rose's Grenadine

Serve straight up in shot glass.

CANDY APPLE

1 oz. apple schnapps
½ oz. cinnamon schnapps
¾ oz. apple juice

Serve straight up in shot glass.

CANDY ASS

1 oz. Chambord
½ oz. Kahlua
½ oz. Baileys Irish Cream

Serve straight up in shot glass.

CEMENT MIXER

1 oz. Baileys Irish Cream
½ oz. Rose's Lime Juice

Serve straight up in shot glass.

CHERRY BOMB

½ oz. cherry brandy
1 oz. Bacardi Rum
½ oz. sour mix

Serve straight up in shot glass.

CHINESE TORTURE

1 oz. Canton Liqueur
1 oz. Bacardi 151 Rum

Serve straight up in shot glass.

COOL-AID

½ oz. Midori
½ oz. DiSaronno Amaretto
1 oz. pineapple juice

Serve straight up in shot glass.

CREATURE FROM THE BLACK LAGOON

1 oz. Jagermeister
1 oz. Della Notte

Serve straight up in shot glass.

CREMESICLE

1 oz. Galliano
½ oz. white creme de cacao
½ oz. orange juice
½ oz. cream

Serve straight up in shot glass.

DIRTY HARRY

1 oz. Grand Marnier
1 oz. Tia Maria

Serve straight up in shot glass.

DREAM SHAKE

1 oz. Baileys Irish Cream
1 oz. Tia Maria

Serve straight up in shot glass.

DUCK PIN

½ oz. Chambord
1 oz. Southern Comfort
½ oz. pineapple juice

Serve straight up in shot glass.

EYE DROP

½ oz Rumple Minze
½ oz. ouzo
1 oz. Stolichnaya

Serve straight up in shot glass.

FIREBALL

1 oz. cinnamon schnapps
½ oz. Tabasco

Serve straight up in shot glass.

SHOOTERS

FOOLS GOLD

1 oz. Absolut
1 oz. Galliano

Serve straight up in shot glass.

———⊗⊗⊗———

FRENCH CONNECTION

1 oz. Courvoisier
1 oz. Grand Marnier

Serve straight up in shot glass.

———⊗⊗⊗———

FRENCH KISS

1 oz. Martini & Rossi Sweet and 1 oz. Dry Vermouth

Serve straight up in shot glass.

———⊗⊗⊗———

FRENCH TICKLER

1 oz. Goldschlager
1 oz. Grand Marnier

Serve straight up in shot glass.

———⊗⊗⊗———

FRU-FRU

1 oz. 99 Bananas
1 oz. Peachtree Schnapps
½ oz. Rose's Lime Juice
½ oz. pineapple juice

Serve straight up in shot glass.

———⊗⊗⊗———

G. & C.

1 oz. Galliano
1 oz. Remy Martin Cognac

Serve straight up in shot glass.

GALLIANO HOT SHOT

1½ oz. Galliano
½ oz. hot coffee
whipped cream

Serve straight up in shot glass.

———⊗⊗⊗———

GOLD FURNACE

2 oz. Goldschlager
two dashes Tabasco

Serve straight up in shot glass.

———⊗⊗⊗———

GOLD RUSH

1 oz. Goldschlager
1 oz. Cuervo Gold

Serve straight up in shot glass.

———⊗⊗⊗———

GOOD AND PLENTY

1 oz. anisette
1 oz. 99 Blackberries

Serve straight up in shot glass.

———⊗⊗⊗———

GRAND AM

1 oz. Grand Marnier
1 oz. DiSaronno Amaretto

Serve straight up in shot glass.

———⊗⊗⊗———

GREEN CHILI

1 oz. Peachtree Schnapps
½ oz. Midori
3 dashes Tabasco

Serve straight up in shot glass.

GREEN DEVIL

1 oz. Beefeater Gin
1 oz. Hiram Walker Creme de
 Menthe
splash Rose's Lime Juice

Serve straight up in shot glass.

GREEN LIZARD

1 oz. Chartreuse (green)
1 oz. Bacardi 151 Rum
splash Rose's Lime Juice

Serve straight up in shot glass.

HARBOR LIGHT

1 oz. Galliano
1 oz. Remy Martin Cognac

Serve straight up in shot glass.

HARBOR LIGHTS

½ oz. Chambord
1 oz. Puerto Rican Rum
½ oz. orange juice

Serve straight up in shot glass.

HAWAIIAN PUNCH

1 oz. Southern Comfort
½ oz. Hiram Walker Sloe Gin
½ oz. cointreau
½ oz. pineapple juice

HOLLYWOOD

1 oz vodka
½ oz. Chambord
½ oz. pineapple juice

Serve straight up in shot glass.

IRON CROSS

1 oz. Rumple Minze
1 oz. Hiram Walker Apricot
 Brandy

Serve straight up in shot glass.

JAMAICAN DUST

1 oz. Puerto Rican Rum
½ oz. Tia Maria
½ oz. pineapple juice

Serve straight up in shot glass.

JELLY BEAN

1 oz. 99 Blackberries
1 oz. Sambuca Romana
½ oz. brandy

Serve straight up in shot glass.

JOLLY RANCHER

½ oz. Midori
1 oz. Peachtree Schnapps
½ oz. cranberry juice

Serve straight up in shot glass.

JUICY FRUIT

1 oz. Absolut
½ oz. Peachtree Schnapps
½ oz. Midori
½ oz. pineapple juice

Serve straight up in shot glass.

SHOOTERS

KAMIKAZE

1 oz. Stolichnaya
1 oz. cointreau
splash Rose's Lime Juice

Serve straight up in shot glass.

KANDY KANE

1 oz. Rumple Minze
1 oz. Hiram Walker Creme de
 Noya

Serve straight up in shot glass.

KOOL-AID

1 oz. Absolut
½ oz. Midori
½ oz. Disaronno Amaretto
½ oz. cranberry juice

Serve straight up in shot glass.

LAZER BEAM

1 oz. bourbon
½ oz. Rumple Minze
½ oz. Drambuie

Serve straight up in shot glass.

LEMON DROP

1 oz. Absolut Citron
squeeze lemon
½ oz. 7-Up

Serve straight up in shot glass.

LICORICE STICK

1 oz. Stolichnaya
½ oz. Hiram Walker Anisette
½ oz. cointreau

Serve straight up in shot glass.

LIFESAVER

½ oz. Malibu Rum
1 oz. Absolut
½ oz. Midori
splash 7-Up

Serve straight up in shot glass.

M&M

1 oz. Kahlua
1 oz. Disaronno Amaretto

Serve straight up in shot glass.

MEXICAN BERRY

1 oz. Chambord
1 oz. Jose Cuervo

Serve straight up in shot glass.

MIND ERASER

1 oz. Stolichnaya
1 oz. Kahlua
splash club soda

Serve straight up in shot glass.

Morgan's Jolly Roger

1 oz. Captain Morgan Original Spiced Rum
1 oz. Hiram Walker Cinnamon Schnapps

Serve straight up in shot glass.

Morgan's Wench

1 oz. Captain Morgan Original Spiced Rum
½ oz. Disaronno Amaretto
½ oz. Hiram Walker Dark Creme de Cacao float

Serve straight up in shot glass.

Mudslide

1 oz. Baileys Irish Cream
½ oz. Kahlua
½ oz. Absolut

Serve straight up in shot glass.

Oil Slick

1 oz. Rumple Minze
1 oz. bourbon

Serve straight up in shot glass.

Orgasm

½ oz Disaronno Amaretto
½ oz. Kahlua
1 oz. Baileys Irish Cream
1/4 oz. cream

Serve straight up in shot glass.

Peppermint Patty

1 oz. Rumple Minze Kahlua
1 oz. Hiram Walker Dark Creme de Cacao
¼ oz. cream

Serve straight up in shot glass.

Pineapple Bomb

1 oz. Malibu Rum
½ oz. Bacardi Black
½ oz. pineapple juice

Serve straight up in shot glass.

Pot O' Gold

1 oz. Goldschlager
1 oz. Baileys Irish Cream

Serve straight up in shot glass.

Prairie Fire

1½ oz. Herradura
3 dashes Tabasco

Serve straight up in shot glass.

Purple Haze

½ oz. Chambord
1 oz. Stolichnaya
½ oz. cranberry or sour mix

Serve straight up in shot glass.

Purple Orchid

½ oz. white creme de cacao
½ oz. 99Blackberries
½ oz. cream

Serve straight up in shot glass.

SHOOTERS

REAL GOLD

1 oz. Stolichnaya Cristall
1 oz. Goldschlager

Serve straight up in shot glass.

ROCKET FUEL

1 oz. Rumple Minze
1 oz. Bacardi 151 Rum

Serve straight up in shot glass.

ROOT BEER

½ oz. Kahlua
½ oz. Galliano
½ oz. cola
½ oz. beer

Serve straight up in shot glass.

SCORPION

1 oz Stolichnaya
1 oz. 99 Blackberries
splash Rose's Grenadine

Serve straight up in shot glass.

SEX ON THE BEACH

½ oz. Chambord
½ oz. Midori
½ oz. Absolut
½ oz. pineapple juice

Serve straight up in shot glass.

SICILIAN KISS

1 oz. Southern Comfort
1 oz. Disaronno Amaretto

Serve straight up in shot glass.

SILK PANTIES

1 oz. Stolichnaya
1 oz. Peachtree Schnapps

Serve straight up in shot glass.

SIMPLY BONKERS

½ oz. Chambord
1 oz. Puerto Rican Rum
½ oz. cream

Serve straight up in shot glass.

SLIPPERY NIPPLE

1 oz. Sambuca Romana
1 oz. Baileys Irish Cream

Serve straight up in shot glass.

SNOWSHOE

1 oz. Rumple Minze
1 oz. brandy

Serve straight up in shot glass.

SWEET TART

1 oz. Chambord
1 oz. Absolut
¼ oz. Rose's Lime Juice
¼ oz. pineapple juice

Serve straight up in shot glass.

TERMINATOR

2 oz. Bacardi 151 Rum
¼ oz. Hiram Walker Blackberry
Brandy
¼ oz. cranberry juice

Serve straight up in shot glass.

THUNDER AND LIGHTNING
1 oz. Rumple Minze
1 oz. Bacardi 151 Rum

Serve straight up in shot glass.

TIDY BOWL
1 oz. ouzo
1 oz. Hiram Walker Blue Curacao

Serve straight up in shot glass.

TOASTED ALMOND
1 oz. Disaronno Amaretto
1 oz. Kahlua
½ oz. cream

Serve straight up in shot glass.
Top with cream.

TOOTSIE ROLL
1 oz. Kahlua
1 oz. Stolichnaya
½ oz. orange juice

Serve straight up in shot glass.

TURBO
1 oz. Stolichnaya
½ oz. Hiram Walker Peach
   Schnapps
½ oz. Hiram Walker Apple
   Schnapps
½ oz. cranberry juice

Serve straight up in shot glass.

TWILIGHT ZONE
1 oz. Puerto Rican Light Rum
1 oz. Myers's Rum
⅛ oz. Rose's Grenadine

Serve straight up in shot glass.

VIKING
2 oz. Galliano
½ oz. akvavit

Serve straight up in shot glass.

VULCAN MIND PROBE
1 oz. ouzo
1 oz. Bacardi 151 Rum

Serve straight up in shot glass.

WATERMELON
1 oz. Midori
1 oz. Absolut
½ oz. cranberry juice

Serve straight up in shot glass.

WET SPOT
1 oz. Cuervo
1 oz. Baileys Irish Cream

Serve straight up in shot glass.

WHITE SPIDER
1 oz. Stolichnaya
1 oz. Rumple Minze

Serve straight up in shot glass.

Woo Woo

1 oz. Hiram Walker Peach
 Schnapps
1 oz. Absolut
½ oz. cranberry juice

Serve straight up in shot glass.

———∞∞∞———

Zipperhead

1 oz. Stolichnaya
½ oz. Chambord
½ oz. club soda top

Serve straight up in shot glass.

Blended Cocktails

ABERDEEN SOUR

1½ oz. Cutty Sark
1 oz. orange juice
1 oz. lemon juice
½ oz. triple sec
1 scoop crushed ice

Shake or blend. Pour into an old-fashioned glass.

———

ABSOLUT CITRON COLADA

1½ oz. Absolut Citron
1 oz. creme de banana
3 oz. pineapple juice
3 oz. pina colada mix
⅛ oz. lime juice
2 Tbs. sugar

Combine ingredients in a blender with 1 cup of ice. Garnish with pineapple and coconut slices.

———

ABSOLUT CRANBERRY CHILL

1½ oz. Absolut Citron
5 oz. lemonade
¼ oz. grenadine
3 oz. cranberry juice

Combine ingredients in a blender with 1 cup of ice. Garnish with cranberries and lemon zest.

ABSOLUT KURANT FREEZE

1½ oz. Absolut Kurant
1 oz. creme de banana
fresh raspberries
fresh bananas
2 Tbsp. sugar

Combine ingredients in a blender with 1 cup of ice.

———

ACAPULCO GOLD

1¼ oz. Jose Cuervo Especial
  Tequila
⅝ oz. Grand Marnier
1 oz. sweet & sour mix

Blend with ice.

———

AFTER-GLOW

1 part DeKuyper Melon Liqueur
2 parts vodka
1 part orange juice

Served very cold with a dash of lemon.

———

ALI-COLADA

2 oz. Alize
dash Bacardi Rum
colada mix

Mix Alize, rum, and pina colada mix in a blender with ice. Blend until smooth. Pour into pina colada glass. Garnish with a pineapple wedge.

BLENDED
COCKTAILS

ALIZE DREAMSICLE

1½ oz. Alize
½ oz. Absolut Vodka
2 oz. pineapple juice
2 oz. orange juice
½ oz. Coco Lopez
1 Tbs. Major Peters' Grenadine

Blend with ice.

※

AN ALTERNATE ROOT

1½ oz. Old Fashioned Root Beer
Schnapps

Fill with orange juice. Combine in blender with ice until smooth.

※

AMBROSIA PUNCH

20 oz. can crushed pineapple,
undrained
15 oz. Coco Lopez Cream of
Coconut
2 cups apricot nectar, chilled
2 cups orange juice, chilled
1½ cups light rum, optional
1 liter club soda, chilled

In a blender, puree the pineapple and cream of coconut until smooth. In a punch bowl, combine the pureed mixture, nectar, juice, and rum (if desired). Mix well. Just before serving, add club soda and serve over ice. Serves about 24.

ANGOSTURA SUNDAE

1 oz. gold rum
2 scoops vanilla ice cream
½ tsp. Angostura Bitters

Combine all ingredients in blender for 30 seconds. Pour into dessert glass.

※

APPLE DAIQUIRI

1 oz. Cider Mill Apple Schnapps
1 oz. light rum
½ oz. sweet & sour mix
¼ peeled apple

Combine in blender with 3 cracked ice cubes.

※

BACARDI BLACK COLADA

8 oz. Bacardi Black Rum
1 10-oz. can of Bacardi tropical
fruit mixer-pina colada mix

Mix ingredients in a blender with 2 cups of ice. Serve in a hurricane glass. Makes 5 servings.

※

BACARDI BLACK RUM RUNNER

1¼ oz. Bacardi Black Rum
⅞ oz. blackberry brandy
⅞ oz. banana liqueur
⅝ oz. grenadine
½ oz. lime juice

Mix all ingredients in blender with 2 cups of ice. Serve in iced champagne glasses with a swirl of Bacardi Black on top. Serves two.

BACARDI BLOSSOM

1¼ oz. Bacardi Light Rum
1 oz. orange juice
½ oz. lemon juice
½ tsp. sugar

Blend with crushed ice and pour.

BACARDI GRASSHOPPER

1 oz. Bacardi Light-Dry Rum
¼ oz. green creme de menthe
½ oz. cream

Mix in shaker or blender with ice and strain into a cocktail glass.

BACARDI PINA COLADA

1¼ oz. Bacardi Light-Dry or Gold Rum
2 oz. unsweetened pineapple juice
1 oz. Coco Lopez Cream of Coconut

Mix in a shaker or blender with crushed ice, or stir and serve on the rocks. Garnish with a pineapple spear, if desired. For best results, blend.

BAHAMA MAMA

½ oz. light rum
2 oz. apple juice
½ oz. cream of coconut
1 oz. orange juice
dash Angostura Grenadine
dash DJ Dotson Triple Sec

Blend and strain over crushed ice in collins glass.

BAILEYS ALEXANDER

½ oz. Baileys Irish Cream
½ oz. white creme de cacao
½ oz. cognac

Blend with ice until smooth, serve straight up.

BAILEYS BANANA BUSTER

1 oz. Baileys Irish Cream
1 oz. Malibu
½ oz. banana liqueur or ½ banana

Blend with ice until smooth.

BAILEYS BLIZZARD

1 oz. Baileys Irish Cream
½ oz. Rumple Minze
½ oz. Metaxa Brandy

Blend with ice and 3 oz. cream until smooth; serve straight up.

BAILEYS COCONUT FRAPPE

½ oz. Baileys Irish Cream
½ oz. Malibu
4 oz. milk

Blend until frothy, then pour over ice and garnish with toasted coconut.

BLENDED COCKTAILS

BAILEYS CREAM DREAM

2 oz. Baileys Irish Cream
2 oz. half & half
4 oz. ice cubes

Blend for 30 seconds and serve.

BAILEYS FLOAT

2 oz. Baileys Irish Cream
2 scoops softened ice cream

Blend ingredients until frothy. Top with one more scoop of ice cream.

BAILEYS FRENCH DREAM

1½ oz. Baileys Irish Cream
½ oz. raspberry liqueur
2 oz. half & half
4 oz. ice cubes

Blend for 30 seconds.

BAILEYS ICED CAPPUCCINO

Brew a pot of double-strength coffee and set aside to cool. In a blender combine:
½ cup ice
2 oz. Baileys Irish Cream
5 oz. double-strength coffee
1 oz. half & half
2 tsp. sugar

Blend for 10 seconds and pour into a 10 oz. glass filled with ice. Top with a dollop of whipped cream and a sprinkle of cinnamon if desired.

BAILEYS ITALIAN DREAM

1½ oz. Baileys Irish Cream
½ oz. Disaronno Amaretto
2 oz. half & half
4 oz. ice cubes

Blend for 30 seconds and serve.

THE BAILEYS LIGHT SHAKE

2 oz. Baileys Light
2 oz. softened vanilla frozen yogurt

Blend with 2 large scoops of softened vanilla frozen yogurt until frothy.

BAILEYS MALIBU SLIDE

1 part Baileys Irish Cream
1 part Kahlua
1 part Malibu

Blend with ice and serve in a rocks or margarita glass.

BAILEYS RUM YUM

1 oz. Baileys Irish Cream
1 oz. Malibu Rum
1 oz. cream or milk

Blend with ice.

BAILEYS SHAKE

2 oz. Baileys Irish Cream
2 oz. softened vanilla ice cream

Blend Baileys with 2 large scoops of softened vanilla ice cream until frothy. Top with whipped cream and a straw and serve.

———⊗⊗⊗———

BALLSBRIDGE BRACER

¾ oz. Irish Mist
1 oz. Tullamore Dew Irish Whiskey
3 oz. orange juice
1 egg white (for two drinks)

Mix all ingredients with cracked ice in a shaker o blender. Shake or blend. Strain into a chilled whiskey sour glass.

———⊗⊗⊗———

BANANA BANSHEE

1½ oz. creme de banana
½ oz. white creme de cacao
1 scoop vanilla ice cream

Blend until smooth and garnish with pineapple.

———⊗⊗⊗———

BANANA BOAT

½ oz. Kahlua
¼ oz. Tia Maria
¼ oz. peppermint schnapps
¼ oz. Carolans Irish Cream

Blend with crushed ice.

BANANA COLADA

5 oz. light rum
6 oz. cream of coconut
3 bananas
1 oz. Angostura Lime Juice
3 cups ice cubes

Blend for 10 seconds on high. Yields 32 oz.

———⊗⊗⊗———

BANANA DAIQUIRI

1½ oz. rum
½ oz. creme de banana
½ ripe banana (sliced)
juice of 1 lime

Blend all ingredients together until smooth and pour unstrained into a tall chilled glass.

———⊗⊗⊗———

BANANA DAIQUIRI

1½ oz. light rum
1 Tbs. DJ Dotson Triple Sec
½ oz. Angostura Lime Juice
½ banana
1 cup crushed ice

Blend for 30 seconds. Serve unstrained in cocktail glass.

———⊗⊗⊗———

BANANA LOPEZ

2 oz. Coco Lopez Cream of Coconut
1 medium banana
1 tsp. lemon juice
1 cup ice

Mix in blender until smooth.

BANANA MAN

1½ oz. Bacardi Light Rum
¼ oz. Hiram Walker Banana
Liqueur
⅛ oz. lemon juice or Rose's Lime
Juice

Blend with ice and serve.

BANILLA BOAT

1 oz. Drambuie Liqueur
½ oz. creme de banana
4 oz. vanilla ice cream

Blend until smooth. Serve in a champagne glass. Pour Raspberry Framboise over top. Garnish with a banana slice and a filbert.

BARBARY COAST

½ oz. Cutty Sark
½ oz. Beefeater Dry Gin
½ oz. white creme de cacao
½ oz. heavy cream

Blend. Pour into cocktail glass.

BEACH PARTY

1¼ oz. Bacardi Light or Dark
Rum
1 oz. pineapple juice
1 oz. orange juice
1 oz. Rose's grenadine

Blend with ice.

BEEFEATER BLUE DEVIL

1 oz. Beefeater Dry Gin
¼ oz. lemon juice
dash maraschino liqueur
dash blue curacao
a little powdered sugar

Mix well with ice in a shaker and strain into tumbler.

BELLINI 2000

1 oz. Cruzan Pineapple Rum
2 oz. sparkling wine
2 oz. peach daiquiri mix
spoonful of cream of coconut
blend with crushed ice

Serve in a tulip glass and float with Alize.
(Lisa Haines, El Torito Grill, Brea, CA.)

BIT O' HONEY

1 oz. Baileys Irish Cream
1 oz. white creme de menthe

Blend with 2 scoops vanilla ice cream until smooth and frothy.

BLACKTHORN #1

1½ oz. Irish whiskey
1½ oz. dry vermouth
3-4 dashes Pernod
3-4 dashes Angostura Bitters

Shake or blend with ice. Pour into a chilled rocks glass. Note: Sloe gin can be used in place of Irish whiskey.

BLIZZARD

1 scoop crushed ice
1½ oz. bourbon
1½ oz. cranberry juice
½ oz. Angostura lime juice
½ oz. Angostura grenadine
1 tsp. sugar

Place the crushed ice in a blender and add ingredients in the order listed. Blend on a slow speed for 15 to 30 seconds until frozen stiff. Pour into a chilled highball glass.

BLUE BAYOU

1 oz. Malibu
½ oz. DeKuyper Blueberry Schnapps
½ oz. blue curacao
3 oz. sweet & sour mix

Blend with crushed ice until frothy, garnish with orange wedge.

BLUE HAWAIIAN

1½ oz. Malibu
½ oz. blue curacao
4 oz. pineapple juice
splash sweet & sour mix

Blend with crushed ice a few seconds, garnish with pineapple wedge.

BLUE SKY

1½ oz. Canadian Mist
¾ oz. light rum
¾ oz. blue curacao
8 oz. pineapple juice
10 oz. ice
orange slice for garnish

Blend all ingredients until frozen. Use hurricane glass and garnish with orange slice and umbrella.

BOARSENBERRY

1½ oz. Gordon's Wildberry Vodka
¾ oz. Chambord
½ oz. Frangelico
¼ oz. white creme de cacao
¼ oz. creme de noyeaux
half & half or vanilla ice cream
nutmeg
handful blackberries

Start with a blender and ice. Add ingredients in order. Blend well until smooth and pour into 20 oz. dessert glass. Garnish: float blackberries and sprinkle nutmeg. (Mac Gregory, Gordon's)

BOSTON BREEZE

1¼ oz. rum
1 oz. Coco Lopez Cream of Coconut
3 oz. cranberry juice
1 cup ice

Blend and serve in a margarita glass.

BOW STREET SPECIAL

1½ oz. Tullamore Dew
½ oz. triple sec
1 oz. lemon juice

Mix with cracked ice in a shaker or blender and strain into a chilled cocktail glass.

―――∞∞∞―――

BROWN COW

1½ oz. Old Fashioned Root Beer Schnapps
3 oz. vanilla ice cream

Combine in blender with ice until smooth. Top with root beer.

―――∞∞∞―――

BUSHWACKER

1 oz. Kahlua
½ oz. dark creme de cacao
½ oz. dark rum
2 oz. Coco Lopez Cream of Coconut
4 oz. half & half

Add ice and blend until smooth.

―――∞∞∞―――

BUTTERNIP

1 oz. Carolans Irish Cream
½ oz. butterscotch schnapps
3 oz. cream/milk

Blend with ½ cup crushed ice. Serve in a chilled glass.

CALIFORNIA COASTLINE

1 oz. Malibu
1 oz. peach schnapps
½ oz. blue curacao
2 oz. sweet & sour mix
2 oz. pineapple juice

Blend for 30 seconds, pour over crushed ice, garnish with pineapple wedge.

―――∞∞∞―――

CALM VOYAGE

1 oz. Bacardi Light-Dry or Gold Rum
¼ oz. apple-flavored brandy
1 oz. orange juice, dash orange bitters

Mix in a shaker or blender with ice and strain into a cocktail glass.

―――∞∞∞―――

CALYPSO COLADA

1½ oz. creme de banana
4 oz. pineapple juice
1½ oz. cream of coconut

Blend together with cracked ice until smooth and garnish with a pineapple spear.

CALYPSO COOL-AID

1¼ oz. Rhum Barbancourt
1 oz. pineapple juice
½ oz. lemon or lime juice
¼ tsp. sugar
soda

Mix rum, juices and sugar in a shaker or blender with ice and pour into a tall glass. Fill with soda and garnish with pineapple spear and lime wheel.

CAMINO REAL

1½ oz. Gran Centenario Plata or Reposado Tequila
½ oz. banana liqueur
1 oz. orange juice
dash lime juice
dash coconut milk

Shake or blend. Garnish with a lime slice.

CAPTAIN'S BERRY DAIQUIRI

1¼ oz. Captain Morgan Spiced Rum
½ cup strawberries or raspberries
1 tsp. lime juice
½ tsp. sugar
½ cup crushed ice

Blend. Garnish with berries.

CAPTAIN'S COLADA

1¼ oz. Captain Morgan Spiced Rum
1 oz. cream of coconut
3 oz. pineapple juice (unsweetened)
½ cup crushed ice

Blend. Garnish with a pineapple spear.

CAPTAIN'S DAIQUIRI

1¼ oz. Captain Morgan Spiced Rum
2 tsp. lime juice
½ tsp. sugar

Shake or blend with ice. Garnish with a lime wedge.

CAPTAIN'S MORGARITA

1 oz. Captain Morgan Spiced Rum
½ oz. triple sec
16 oz. frozen limeade

1 cup ice cube. Blend until smooth.

CARIBBEAN COLADA

1½ oz. Rhum Grandier
4 oz. pineapple juice
1½ oz. cream of coconut

Blend together with cracked ice until smooth. Garnish with pineapple spear.

THE CATALINE MARGARITA

1¼ oz. Jose Cuervo Gold Tequila
1 oz. peach schnapps
1 oz. blue curacao
4 oz. sweet & sour mix

Blend with crushed ice.

CAVALIER

1½ oz. Sauza Tequila
½ oz. Galliano
1½ oz. orange juice
½ oz. cream

Blend with crushed ice and strain into a cocktail glass.

CC CIDER

1 oz. Canadian Club
½ oz. cinnamon schnapps
3 oz. apple cider
¼ unpeeled red apple

Blend. Pour unstrained.

CHAMBORD COLADA

1½ oz. Chambord
1½ oz. Bacardi Rum
2 oz. pineapple juice
½ oz. Coco Lopez Cream of Coconut
¾ oz. ice

Place all ingredients in a blender; process on high until smooth.

CHAMBORD DAIQUIRI

¾ oz. Chambord
¾ oz. Bacardi Light Rum
juice of ½ lime
1 tsp. powdered sugar
3-4 black raspberries (optional)

Add 1 cup crushed ice and mix in a blender for 30 seconds; strain into a champagne glass.

CHAMBORD FROST

1½ oz. Chambord
juice of ¼ lemon
1 cup crushed ice

Mix in a blender or shaker for 20 seconds. Pour into a cocktail glass with ice.

CHAMBORD MARGARITA

¼ oz. Chambord
¾ oz. Jose Cuervo Tequila
½ oz. triple sec
juice of ½ lime

Blend with ice.

CHAMBORLADA

1 oz. Chambord
½ oz. Bacardi Light Rum
½ oz. Bacardi Dark Rum
3 oz. pineapple juice
2 oz. Coco Lopez Cream of
  Coconut

Combine all ingredients, except Chambord with cracked ice in a blender. Blend. Pour the Chambord into the bottom of a wine glass. Pour the pina colada mixture on top. Top off with a little more Chambord.

CHERRY COLADA

1½ oz. cherry brandy
4 oz. pineapple juice
1½ oz. cream of coconut

Blend together with cracked ice until smooth. Garnish with a pineapple spear.

CHI CHI

1½ oz. Absolut Vodka
¾ oz. pineapple juice
1½ oz. cream of coconut

Blend with ice to slush. Add cherry.

CHICAGO STYLE

¾ oz. Bacardi Light-Dry Rum
¼ oz. triple sec
¼ oz. Romana Sambuca
½ oz. lemon or Major Peters'
  Lime Juice

Mix in a shaker or blender with ice and strain into a cocktail glass.

CHICAGO STYLE

¾ oz. Bacardi Light Rum
¼ oz. Hiram Walker Triple Sec
¼ oz. Hiram Walker Anisette
¼ oz. lemon or lime juice

Blend with ice.

CHI-CHI

1½ oz. vodka
1 oz. Coco Lopez Cream of
  Coconut
2 oz. pineapple juice
1 cup ice

Blend until smooth.

CHOCOLADA

2 oz. Bacardi Light
1½ oz. creme de coconut
1½ oz. milk
1 oz. dark creme de cacao
1 cup ice

Mix in blender. Garnish with whipped cream and chocolate chips. (Hennessey's)

BLENDED COCKTAILS

CHOCOLATE BANANA COLADA SHAKE

⅓ cup Coco Lopez Cream of
  Coconut
½ cup milk
1 Tbsp. chocolate syrup
1½ cups chocolate or vanilla ice
  cream
½ cup sliced bananas

Mix in a blender until smooth. Serve immediately.

CHOCOLATE COLADA SHAKE

⅓ cup Coco Lopez Cream of
  Coconut
½ cup milk
1 Tbs. chocolate syrup
1½ cups chocolate or vanilla ice
  cream

Mix in a blender until smooth. Serve immediately.

CHOCOLATE CREAM

¾ oz. Bacardi Gold Rum
¼ oz. dark creme de cacao
¼ oz. white creme de menthe
1 oz. cream

Mix in a shaker or blender with ice and strain into a cocktail glass.

CITRICE

equal parts:
Bacardi Limon
melon liqueur
pineapple juice
splash of Chambord

Serve in a martini glass straight up. (Chris Adams, Oddfellows Restaurant)

CITRUS MIST COLADA

1½ oz. Canadian Mist
4½ oz. pina colada mix
2 oz. lemon-lime soda
cherry and lime for garnish

Pour all ingredients into a blender with ice cubes. Blend until thick. Serve in old-fashioned glass. Garnish with cherry and lime. Multiply by six for a party pitcher!

CITRUS SUPREME

2 shots Gordon's Citrus Vodka
1 shot triple sec
1 12 oz. can frozen lemonade
2 cups lime or lemon-flavored
  water

Pour all into blender. Fill with ice. Mix until slushy. Pour into frozen long-stemmed bowl glass. Place a slice of lemon over rim and serve. (Norma Goodreau, Gordon's)

Clam Voyage

1 oz. Bacardi Light or Dark Rum
¼ oz. apple-flavored brandy
1 oz. orange juice
dash orange bitters

Blend with ice and serve in a margarita glass.

Classic Apricot Sour

1 oz. Snappy Apricot Schnapps
1½ oz. sweet & sour mix
½ oz. triple sec

Combine in blender with cracked ice.

Classic Peach Daiquiri

1½ oz. Jubilee Peach Schnapps
1/2 oz. triple sec
1/2 oz. sweet & sour
1 oz. rum

Combine in blender with ice until smooth. Optional: add ¼ canned peach with juice.

Clover Cooler

½ oz. Baileys Irish Cream
½ oz. Malibu
½ oz. blue curacao
4 oz. pineapple juice

Blend until smooth, serve in tall glass with club soda.

Coco Colada

1½ oz. dark creme de cacao
4 oz. pineapple juice
1½ oz. cream of coconut

Blend together with cracked ice until smooth and garnish with a pineapple spear.

Coco Loco (Crazy Coconut)

1½ oz. Herradura Tequila
3 oz. pineapple juice
2 oz. Coco Lopez Cream of Coconut

Blend. Garnish with a pineapple spear.

Coco Lopez Shake

2½ oz. Coco Lopez Cream of Coconut
1 scoop vanilla ice cream
1 cup ice

Mix in blender until smooth.

Coco Mocha Lopez

4 oz. Coco Lopez Cream of Coconut
2 oz. cold black coffee
1/2 tsp. brandy flavor
1½ cups ice

Mix in blender until smooth. Sprinkle with nutmeg.

BLENDED COCKTAILS

COCOBANA

1 part Bacardi Light
1 banana
1 part coconut milk
ice cubes, crushed

Blend & serve. (Susan McGowan, Oddfellows Restaurant)

COCONOTION

1½ oz. Puerto Rican Dark Rum
4 oz. Coco Lopez Cream of
  Coconut
2 oz. lime juice
1½ cups ice

Blend and serve in a margarita glass.

COCONUT BELLINI

3 oz. champagne
½ oz. peach schnapps
2 oz. Coco Lopez Cream of
  Coconut
2 oz. peach puree
1 cup ice

Blend until smooth.

COCONUT PUNCH

1¼ oz. Bacardi Light-Dry or Gold
  Rum
2 oz. Coco Lopez Cream of
  Coconut
½ oz. lemon juice
3-4 Tbsp. vanilla ice cream

Mix all ingredients in a shaker or blender with crushed ice and pour into a tall glass.

COCONUT/CRANBERRY SMOOTHIE

3 oz. Angostura Lime Juice
18 oz. cranberry juice
6 oz. cream of coconut

Blend for 10 seconds on high speed. Yields 32 oz.

COINTREAU COLADA

2 oz. cointreau
2 oz. Coco Lopez
pineapple juice to taste

Blend ingredients with ice in a blender. Pour into a large cocktail glass. Garnish with fresh pineapple and cherry on a toothpick.

COINTREAU ORANGE FREEZE

2 oz. cointreau
4 oz. orange soda
big scoop of vanilla ice cream

Blend ingredients in blender. Pour into balloon glass and serve with an orange slice.

COINTREAU SANTA FE MARGARITA

1½ oz. Jose Cuervo Gold Tequila
¾ oz. cointreau
2 oz. sweet & sour mix
2 oz. cranberry juice

Blend ingredients and serve in a margarita glass.

COINTREAU STRAWBERRY MARGARITA

1¼ oz. Jose Cuervo Gold Tequila
¾ oz. cointreau
2 oz. sweet & sour mix
3 oz. frozen strawberries

Blend ingredients and serve in a margarita glass.

COLADA

1 part Licor 43
1 part cream of coconut
2 parts pineapple juice

Mix in blender with ice and pour into a tall glass. Decorate with pineapple slice.

COLD GOLD

1 oz. Orchard Orange Schnapps
1 oz. vodka
2 oz. orange juice

Combine over ice.

COMFORT COLADA

1½ oz. Southern Comfort
1 oz. cream of coconut
2 oz. pineapple juice
1 or 2 ice cubes, crushed

Blend all ingredients until ice is completely broken up and liquid is frothy. Serve in tall glasses over ice. Garnish with cherries.

CONTINENTAL

1 oz. Bacardi Light Rum
¼ oz. green creme de menthe
¾ oz. Rose's Lime Juice
¼ tsp. sugar (optional)

Blend with ice.

CRICKET

¾ oz. Bacardi Light Rum
¼ oz. white creme de cacao
¼ oz. green creme de menthe
1 oz. cream

Blend ingredients with ice.

CUERVO ACAPULCO FIZZ

1½ oz. Cuervo Gold
1½ oz. cream
2 oz. orange juice
3 ice cubes
2 tsp. granulated sugar
2 dashes orange bitters
1 whole egg

Blend all ingredients together. Pour into a highball glass. Garnish with orange slice.

CUERVO ALEXANDER

1 oz. Jose Cuervo Gold Tequila
1 oz. coffee-flavored liqueur
1 oz. wild cherry brandy
2 scoops vanilla ice cream

Blend until smooth.

BLENDED COCKTAILS

CUERVO BAJA GOLD

2 oz. Cuervo Gold
1½ oz. simple syrup
¾ oz. fresh lime juice
¾ cup ice
4 oz. chilled beer

Blend in blender until smooth. Pour into chilled mug. Top with beer, lime garnish.

CUERVO GOLD MARGARITA

1½ oz. Cuervo Gold
1 oz. triple sec
2 oz. Major Peters' Lime Juice
2 oz. Major Peters' Sweet & Sour Mix

Blend ingredients with ice and pour into a margarita glass over ice or frozen.

CUERVO RASPBERRY MARGARITA

1 ½ oz. Cuervo Gold
1 oz. triple sec
1 oz. Major Peters' Lime Juice
½ cup raspberries (frozen)
fresh raspberries for garnish

In blender combine 1/2 cup ice with ingredients. Blend until frothy.

CUERVO SANTA FE MAGGIE

1¼ oz. Cuervo Gold
½ oz. triple sec
2 oz. Major Peters' Sweet & Sour Mix
2 oz. cranberry juice

Blend ingredients briefly with ice and pour into unsalted margarita glass. Squeeze in lime wedge and drop in glass.

CUERVO SIDE-OUT

1½ oz. Jose Cuervo Gold Tequila
1 oz. triple sec
2 oz. cranberry juice
1½ oz. lime juice

Blend.

CUERVO STRAWBERRY MARGARITA

1½ oz. Cuervo Gold Tequila
1 oz. DJ Dotson Triple Sec
1 oz. Angostura Lime Juice
½ cup frozen strawberries

In blender combine 1/2 cup ice with above ingredients. Blend wildly until icy. Serve in margarita glass & garnish with a fresh strawberry.

DAIQUIRI

1¼ oz. light rum
½ oz. sweetened lemon juice

Shake or blend with ice.

DE-MINTED DE-LIGHT

1¼ oz. Smirnoff Vodka
1 oz. Dotson Triple Sec
2½ oz. Angostura Lime Juice
a pack Sugar in the Raw
10 small mint leaves

Blend all ingredients with ice in a blender. Garnish with a mint sprig.

DISARONNO CREAMSICLE

1½ oz. Disaronno Amaretto
2 oz. orange juice
2 oz. cream

Blend to milkshake consistency, then serve in a large wine or balloon glass.

DISARONNO SHORTCAKE

1 oz. Disaronno Amaretto
1 oz. Tuaca
2 oz. strawberries
3 oz. cream

Blend to milkshake consistency.

DISARONNO SMOOTHIE

2 oz. Disaronno Amaretto
1 oz. sour mix
1 cup ice
4 or 5 large strawberries
whipped cream
mint leaf

Blend and serve in 4 oz. martini glass. Garnish with squirt of whipped cream and mint leaf.

DISARITA MARGARITA

1 oz. Jose Cuervo 1800 Tequila
1/2 oz. Disaronno Amaretto
3 oz. margarita mix
1/2 cup crushed ice

Blend. Garnish with lime.

DISCO-TEQ

1½ oz. Sauza Tequila
2 oz. orange juice
½ oz. cream or half & half
½ oz. grenadine

Blend all ingredients with crushed ice and pour into a tall glass.

BLENDED COCKTAILS

DOUBLE BERRY COCO PUNCH

20 oz. frozen strawberries in syrup, thawed
15 oz. Coco Lopez Cream of Coconut
48 oz. cranberry juice cocktail, chilled
2 cups light rum, optional
1 liter club soda, chilled

In a blender, puree the strawberries and cream of coconut until smooth. In a large punch bowl, combine the pureed mixture, cranberry juice, and rum (if desired). Just before serving, add club soda and serve over ice.

———— ∞ ————

DREAMCICLE

1½ oz. Orchard Orange Schnapps
3 oz. vanilla ice cream

Combine in blender until smooth.

———— ∞ ————

ELECTRIC LEMONADE

1¼ oz. vodka
½ oz. blue curacao
2 oz. sweet & sour mix
splash 7-Up

Blend. Pour over ice in a tall glass and garnish with a lemon slice.

ELECTRIC PEACH

1 oz. vodka
¼ oz. peach schnapps
½ oz. cranberry juice cocktail
¼ oz. orange juice

Blend. Pour over ice in a tall glass and garnish with a lemon slice.

———— ∞ ————

EMERALD ISLE

¾ shot Tullamore Dew
¾ shot green creme de menthe
2 scoops vanilla ice cream
soda water

Blend first 3 ingredients, then add soda water. Stir after adding soda water.

———— ∞ ————

EMERALD ISLE

¾ shot Tullamore Dew
¾ oz. green creme de menthe
2 scoops vanilla ice cream
soda water

Blend first three ingredients, then add soda water. Stir after adding soda water.

EVE'S APPLE

1 oz. apple-infused vodka
¼ oz. Hot Damn Cinnamon
  Schnapps
⅓ oz. blue curacao
1½ oz. apple juice
⅓ oz. Angostura Lime Juice
1 cup vanilla ice cream
1 cup crushed ice

Blend all and pour into large
balloon snifter. Garnish with
parfait apple & small orchid.

———⊗⊗⊗———

FINLANDIA CRANBERRY COOLER

2 oz. each Finlandia Cranberry
½ oz. Chambord
2 oz. cranberry juice

Mix in a blender with a handful of ice. Pour into a martini
glass and garnish with a lime.

———⊗⊗⊗———

FINLANDIA SEA GODDESS

4 oz. Finlandia Classic
1 oz. Alize Passion Liqueur
splash blue curacao liqueur

Mix in a blender with a handful of ice. Pour into a martini
glass.

FLAMINGO

1 oz. Beefeater Gin
2 oz. pineapple juice
1 oz. cream of coconut
1 oz. sweet & sour mix

Blend together with cracked
ice until smooth. Strain and
serve in chilled glass.

———⊗⊗⊗———

FLORIDA BANANA LOPEZ

2 oz. Coco Lopez Cream of
  Coconut
4 oz. orange juice
1 medium banana
1 cup ice

Mix in blender until smooth.

———⊗⊗⊗———

FLYING KANGAROO

1 oz. vodka, ¼ oz. Galliano
1 oz. Rhum Barbancort
1½ oz. pineapple juice
¾ oz. orange juice
¾ oz. coconut cream
½ oz. cream

Shake or blend with ice.

———⊗⊗⊗———

FRANGELICO FREEZE

1½ oz. Frangelico Liqueur
4 oz. vanilla ice cream
3-4 ice cubes
3 oz. milk or half & half

Blend until smooth and
creamy, top with a dollop of
whipped cream and a cherry.

BLENDED COCKTAILS

FRENCH COLADA

1½ oz. Puerto Rican White Rum
¾ oz. Cognac
1 scoop crushed ice
¾ oz. sweet cream
¾ oz. Coco Lopez Cream of
  Coconut
1½ oz. pineapple juice
splash creme de cassis

Blend with ice.

———— ✲ ————

FRENCH DREAM

½ oz. Chambord
1½ oz. Carolans Irish Cream
2 oz. half & half
4 oz. ice cubes

Blend.

———— ✲ ————

FREZSA DORADO

1½ oz. Sauza Conmemorativo

Blend with peach puree, raspberry mix, sweet & sour and ice. Serve in wide-rimmed glass.

———— ✲ ————

FRIS MADRAS

2 oz. Fris Vodka
2 oz. orange juice
2 oz. cranberry juice

Blend together in a tall glass over ice. Garnish with orange slice.

FROZEN APRICOT ORANGE LOPEZ

2 oz. Coco Lopez Cream of
  Coconut
1½ oz. orange juice
2 oz. apricot nectar
1½ cups ice

Mix in blender until smooth.

———— ✲ ————

FROZEN MATADOR

1½ oz. Sauza Tequila
2 oz. pineapple juice
½ oz. lime juice
½ oz. grenadine

Blend all ingredients with lots of crushed ice and build into a snow cone in a large cocktail glass.

———— ✲ ————

FROZEN PINE

1 oz. Canadian Mist
2 oz. pineapple juice
1 oz. grenadine
cherry for garnish

Place ingredients and ice in a blender. Blend until frozen. Pour into stemmed tulip glasses and garnish with a cherry. Multiply by six for a party pitcher!

FRUIT SALAD

1½ oz. DeKuyper Cheri-Beri
Pucker
½ oz. DeKuyper Grape Pucker
½ oz. DeKuyper Peachtree
Schnapps
splash of orange juice

Combine and serve as a shot
or mixed drink.

FUZZLESS SCREWDRIVER

1½ oz. Jubilee Peach Schnapps
1 oz. Vodka
2 oz. orange juice

Combine in blender with ice
until smooth.

GINGER COLADA

1 oz. Canton Delicate Ginger
Liqueur
½ oz. rum
1½ oz. Coco Lopez Cream of
Coconut

Blend with ice.

GRAPE CRUSH

1½ oz. DeKuyper Grape Pucker
2 oz. club soda
dash of lime juice

Pour Grape Pucker over ice.
Add club soda and lime juice.

GRAPE LOPEZ

3 oz. Coco Lopez Cream of
Coconut
4 oz. grape juice
1½ cups ice

Mix in blender until smooth.

GRASSHOPPER

½ oz. green creme de menthe
½ oz. white creme de cacao
½ oz. cream

Combine in a blender with ice
and blend until smooth.
Strain into a margarita glass.

HARVEYS BEE STING

1½ oz. Harveys Bristol Cream
3 oz. orange juice
1 Tbs. honey
1 Tbs. lemon juice
orange slices (optional)

Combine Harveys Bristol
Cream, orange juice, honey
and lemon juice in container
of electric blender. Cover and
blend until smooth. Serve over
ice. Garnish with orange slice,
if desired. Makes 1 serving.

BLENDED COCKTAILS

HARVEYS HAWAIIAN LEI

2½ oz. Harveys Bristol Cream
2½ oz. pineapple juice
1 oz. coconut cream
½ oz. lime juice
2 ice cubes, lime slice (optional)
pineapple wedge (optional)

Combine Harveys Bristol Cream, pineapple juice, coconut cream, lime juice and ice cubes in container of electric blender. Cover and blend until smooth. Pour into tall glass. Garnish with lime slice and pineapple wedge, if desired. Makes 1 serving.

HARVEYS PINEAPPLE GLACIER

1½ oz. Harveys Bristol Cream
1½ oz. Harveys Bristol Cream
2 oz. pineapple juice
2 oz. ice cream

Cover and blend until smooth. Pour into rocks glass. Garnish with pineapple wedge and nutmeg, if desired. Serve immediately. Makes 1 serving.

HAWAIIAN MINT LIMEADE

1½ oz. Fris Vodka
3 oz. limeade
2 oz. pineapple juice
1 tsp. green creme de menthe

Blend together with crushed ice. Strain and serve in a tall glass. Garnish with pineapple spear.

HEATHER'S DREAM

1½ oz. Romana Sambuca
1½ oz. cream
½ oz. fresh or canned peaches

Blend with ice in blender until smooth, serve in chilled wine glass.

HIBISCUS (THREE COCKTAILS)

¼ cup brandy or cognac
¾ cup Grand Marnier
¼ cup lemon juice
¼ cup lime juice
¼ cup orange juice

Combine all ingredients in blender with 2 cups ice cubes. Blend until ice is partially broken up. Pour unstrained into 8-oz. stemmed cocktail glasses.

HO HO AND A BARREL OF RUM

1½ oz. Old Fashioned Root Beer Schnapps
1 oz. Rum
1 oz. milk or cream

Combine in blender with ice until smooth.

ICY BRENDAN'S

3 oz. Saint Brendan's Superior Irish Cream
2 scoops vanilla ice cream

Blend until frothy.

INTERNATIONAL CREAM

½ shot Carolans Irish Cream
½ shot coffee-flavored liqueur
 (Kahlua)
splash Grand Marnier
2 scoops vanilla ice cream
splash milk

Blend.

INTERNATIONAL MAI TAI

½ oz. Malibu
½ oz. Myers's Dark Rum
½ oz. Stubbs Australian Rum
1 tsp. orgeat syrup
2 oz. pineapple juice
2 oz. sweet & sour mix

Blend a few seconds with ice,
garnish with pineapple wedge.

IRISH ANGEL

1 oz. Bushmills Irish Whiskey
¼ oz. creme de cacao
¼ oz. white creme de menthe
½ oz. cream

Mix with ice in a cocktail shaker
or blender. Strain into a cocktail glass.

IRISH DREAM

½ oz. Carolans Irish Cream
½ oz. hazelnut liqueur
½ oz. dark creme de cacao
1 scoop vanilla ice cream

Combine ingredients in a
blender with ice. Blend thoroughly. Pour into a collins or
parfait glass. Serve with a
straw.

IRISH EYES

1 oz. Irish whiskey
¼ oz. green creme de menthe
2 oz. heavy cream

Blend. Serve in chilled cocktail
glass. Garnish with maraschino
cherry.

IRISH KILT

1 oz. Irish whiskey
1 oz. scotch
1 oz. lemon juice
1½ oz. sugar syrup or to taste
3-4 dashes orange bitters

Mix all ingredients with
cracked ice in a shaker or
blender and strain into a
chilled glass.

BLENDED
COCKTAILS

IRISH LACE

2 oz. Irish Mist
2 splashes Coco Lopez Cream of
 Coconut
2 splashes half & half
3 splashes pineapple juice
2 scoops ice

Blend and serve in a margarita glass. Garnish with an orange flag.

———∞∞∞———

IRISH RAINBOW

1½ oz. Irish whiskey
3-4 dashes Pernod
3-4 dashes orange curacao
3-4 dashes maraschino liqueur
3-4 dashes Angostura Bitters

Mix all ingredients with cracked ice in a shaker or blender. Pour into a chilled rocks glass. Twist an orange peel over the drink and drop it in.

———∞∞∞———

IRISH RASPBERRY

1 oz. Devonshire Irish Cream
½ oz. Chambord

Blend with 1 cup of ice.

———∞∞∞———

IRISH RASPBERRY #2

½ oz. Chambord
1 oz. Carolans Irish Cream
1 cup ice

Blend with ice and serve.

IRISH SHILLELAGH

1½ oz. Irish whiskey
½ oz. sloe gin
½ oz. light rum
1 oz. lemon juice
1 tsp. sugar syrup
2 peach slices, diced

Mix all ingredients with cracked ice in a shaker or blender. Pour into a chilled rocks glass. Garnish with raspberries and a cherry.

———∞∞∞———

ISLAND PLEASURE

1 oz. cream of banana
1/2 oz. Frangelico
2 oz. cream
1 1/2 oz. Angostura Grenadine

Blend all ingredients with crushed ice. Serve in a 12 oz. glass. Garnish with pineapple slice and cherry through a parasol.

———∞∞∞———

ITALIAN ALEXANDER

¾ oz. Di Saronno Amaretto
¾ oz. white creme de cacao
2 oz. half & half
1 scoop vanilla ice cream

Blend until creamy and top with nutmeg.

———∞∞∞———

ITALIAN BANANA

1½ oz. Di Saronno Amaretto
4-5 oz. pina colada mix
½ ripe banana

Blend with ice until milkshake consistency.

ITALIAN COLADA

1½ oz. Puerto Rican White Rum
¼ oz. amaretto
¼ oz. Coco Lopez Cream of
  Coconut
¾ oz. sweet cream
2 oz. pineapple juice

Blend with crushed ice.

JUNGLE JUICE

1½ oz. Cuervo Gold
1½ oz. pineapple juice
1½ oz. cranberry juice
1½ oz. freshly squeezed orange
  juice
splash lemon-lime soda

Blend with ice. Pour in tall
glass with ice.

KAHLUA BANANA

1½ oz. Kahlua
¾ oz. rum
2 oz. pineapple juice
2 oz. cream of coconut
fresh banana
ice

Blend together.

KAHLUA BANANA CREAM FIZZ

⅓ oz. Kahlua
⅓ oz. rum
⅓ oz. creme de banana
top with cream/milk

Blend.

KAHLUA CHI CHI

1 oz. Kahlua
¾ oz. Fris Vodka
2 oz. pineapple juice
1 oz. coconut milk or syrup

Combine all items with 1/2
cup finely crushed ice and
blend. Pour in tall glass.
Garnish with mint sprig.

KAHLUA COLADA

1½ oz. Kahlua
2 oz. cream of coconut
2 oz. pineapple juice

Add ice and blend.

KAHLUA HUMMER

1 oz. Kahlua
1 oz. light rum
2 scoops vanilla or chocolate ice
  cream

Blend with ice.

KAHLUA KOALA FLOAT

½ oz. Kahlua
½ oz. Fris Vodka
½ oz. Carolans Irish Cream
½ oz. coconut cream
1 oz. crushed ice

Blend together.

BLENDED
COCKTAILS

KAHLUA POLAR BEAR

1 oz. Kahlua
¾ oz. Fris Vodka
2 scoops vanilla ice cream

Combine and blend briefly.

———— ∞∞∞ ————

KAHLUA TOP BANANA

1 oz. Kahlua
½ oz. creme de banana
3 oz. milk
1 cup crushed ice

Blend.

———— ∞∞∞ ————

LICORICE WITH A TWIST

1 ½ oz. licorice schnapps
3 oz. coffee ice cream

Combine in blender with ice until smooth.

———— ∞∞∞ ————

LIFESAVER

1 jig Smirnoff Vodka
1 jig DJ Dotson Triple Sec
2 oz. orange juice
2 oz. pineapple juice
½ tsp. Angostura grenadine

Blend and pour over ice.

LIME SORBET LOPEZ

2½ oz. Coco Lopez Cream of Coconut
½ oz. Major Peters' Lime Juice
1 scoops lime sherbet
½ cup ice

Mix in blender until smooth.

———— ∞∞∞ ————

LUCKY IRISH

1½ oz. Irish whiskey
½ oz. sloe gin
½ oz. light rum
1 oz. Angostura Lime Juice
½ oz. Angostura Grenadine
2 peach slices, diced
1 scoop crushed ice
5 to 6 fresh raspberries
1 maraschino cherry

Mix all in blender except fruit. Pour into a chilled old-fashioned glass. Garnish with raspberries & cherry.

———— ∞∞∞ ————

LUCKY LADY

¾ oz. Bacardi Light-Dry Rum
¼ oz. Romana Sambuca
¼ oz. white creme de cacao
¾ oz. cream

Mix in a shaker or blender with ice and strain into a cocktail glass.

MAD MELON-ADE

1½ oz. DeKuyper Mad Melon
  watermelon schnapps
2 oz. lemonade

Combine and serve over ice in
a cocktail glass. Garnish with
a lemon wedge.

⁓

THE MAIDEN MARGARITA

4 oz. Major Peters' Margarita
  Mix
1½ cups small cube ice
2 oz. lemon-lime soda

Blend and serve in a salt-
rimmed glass and garnish
with a wedge of lime. Garnish
with strawberry.

⁓

MAJOR MARGARITA

1½ oz. Cuervo Tequila
½ oz. Major Peters' Lime Juice
4 oz. Major Peters' Margarita
  Mix
1½ cups ice

Blend until slushy. Pour into
salt-rimmed glass. Garnish
with lime slice.

MAJOR PETERS' FROZEN VIRGIN MARY

4 oz. Major Peters' Bloody Mary
  Mix (regular or hot & spicy)
5 oz. orange juice
¼ oz. Major Peters' Lime Juice
1½ cups ice

Blend until smooth and pour
into a 16 oz. glass. Garnish
with lime slice, celery stalk,
and cherry tomato.

⁓

MAJOR STRAWBERRY MARGARITA

1½ oz. Cuervo Tequila
½ oz. Major Peters' Lime Juice
½ cup strawberries (fresh or
  frozen) or 4 oz. Major Peters'
  Strawberry Margarita Mix
1½ cups ice

Blend until slushy. Pour into
salt-rimmed glass.

⁓

MALIBU CARIBBEAN COOLER

2 oz. Malibu
½ ripe banana
½ scoop vanilla ice cream
½ cup crushed ice

Blend until smooth, serve
straight up in stemmed glass-
ware.

BLENDED
COCKTAILS

MALIBU COLADA
1½ oz. Malibu
3 oz. pineapple juice
1 oz. milk or cream
½ cup crushed ice

In a blender, combine ingredients. Serve in a tall glass. Garnish with fresh pineapple.

MALIBU ORANGE COLADA
1½ oz. Malibu
1 oz. triple sec
4 oz. pina colada mix

Blend with ice until smooth.

MALIBU SHAKE
1½ oz. Malibu
1 oz. white creme de menthe
3 oz. pineapple juice
2 oz. cream

Blend with ice until smooth.

MALIBU SLIDE
equal parts:
Baileys Irish Cream
Kahlua
Malibu

Blend with ice.

MALIBU SUNSET
1½ oz. Malibu
2-3 oz. strawberries
1 oz. pineapple juice
2 oz. orange juice
splash of cream

Flash blend with ice, serve in rocks glass.

MALIBU TROPICALE
1 oz. Malibu
½ oz. melon liqueur
¾ oz. creme de banana
2 oz. pineapple juice
2 oz. papaya juice

Blend 30 seconds with crushed iced, garnish with pineapple wedge.

MARGARITA
1 oz. Tequila
1 oz. cointreau or triple sec
1 oz. sweet & sour mix or lime juice

Blend with crushed ice. Serve in a salt-rimmed glass. Garnish with a lime wheel.

MARGARITA MADRES
1¼ oz. Jose Cuervo Gold Tequila
½ oz. cointreau
1½ oz. sweet & sour mix
1½ oz. orange juice
1½ oz. cranberry juice

Blend with crushed ice. Garnish with a lime.

MARGAVERO

3 oz. Agavero Liqueur
1 oz. fresh lime juice
1 dash Stolichnaya Ohranj
coarse salt

Shake with ice or blend and strain into a chilled cocktail glass, the rim of which has been moistened with lime juice and dipped in salt. Garnish with a lime wedge.

———∞———

MEXICAN MIST

1½ oz. Sauza Conmemorativo

Blend with equal parts pineapple juice, orange juice and cranberry juice. Serve over ice in tall glass.

———∞———

MIAMI SPECIAL

1 oz. Bacardi Light-Dry Rum
¼ oz. white creme de menthe
¾ oz. lemon or Major Peters' Lime Juice

Mix in a shaker or blender with ice and strain into a cocktail glass.

———∞———

MIDNIGHT ORCHID

¼ oz. Chambord
1 oz. Absolut Vodka, chilled
2 oz. pineapple juice
½ oz. cranberry juice
½ oz. half & half

Shake. Serve over crushed ice or blend with ice.

MIDNIGHT ORCHID

1½ oz. Finlandia Cranberry Vodka, chilled
¼ oz. Chambord
2 oz. pineapple juice
½ oz. half & half

Shake. Serve over crushed ice or blend with ice.

———∞———

MIDORI COLADA

2 oz. Midori
either
2 oz. cream of coconut and 4 oz. pineapple juice
or
6 oz. colada mix

Blend with crushed ice.

———∞———

MIDORI GREEN IGUANA MARGARITA

½ oz. Midori
1 oz. Tequila
2 oz. sweet & sour mix

Blend and pour into a salt-rimmed glass.

———∞———

MIDORI HOPPER

1 oz. Midori
½ oz creme de cacao
½ oz. cream/milk

Blend ingredients with crushed ice.

MIDORI PINA COLADA

2 oz. Midori
1 oz. rum
either
2 oz. cream of coconut and 4 oz. pineapple juice
or
6 oz. colada mix

Blend with crushed ice.

MIDORI STRAWBERRY COLADA

2 oz. Midori
2 oz. cream of coconut
4 oz. strawberries

Blend with crushed ice and garnish with strawberry.

MILKY WAY

1 oz. cointreau
½ oz. dark creme de cacao
1 oz. cream

Mix with ice in a blender. Pour into balloon glass, top with whipped cream and serve with a cherry.

MIST CREAM

1½ oz. Canadian Mist
1 cup ice in blender
½ cup heavy cream
½ oz. coffee liqueur
dash of grenadine
cherries for garnish

Blend ingredients and garnish with cherries.

MISTRAL

1 oz. Chambord
2 oz. dry white wine
1 Tbsp. frozen strawberries or raspberries

Mix in a blender with 3 tablespoons ice, pour with ice into a champagne glass.

MONT BLANC

1 oz. Chambord
1 oz. Absolut Vodka
1 oz. cream or half & half
1 scoop vanilla ice cream

Mix in a blender for 20 seconds; pour into a wine glass.

MONTEGO MARGARITA

1½ oz. Appleton Estate Rum
½ oz. triple sec
1 oz. lemon or lime juice
1 scoop crushed ice

Blend with ice and serve.

MONTMARTRE

1 oz. Chambord
1 oz. coffee liqueur
1 oz. cream or half & half

Mix in a blender with 1/2 cup crushed ice for 20 seconds; pour into a cocktail glass with ice.

MYERS'S STRAWBERRY DAIQUIRI

1¼ oz. Myers's Dark Rum
½ oz. triple sec
juice of ½ lime
½ cup strawberries
1 tsp. bar sugar

Blend with crushed ice.

NADA COLADA

1 oz. Coco Lopez Cream of
 Coconut
2 oz. pineapple juice
1 cup ice

Mix in blender until smooth.

NEW ORLEANS DAY

2 oz. Coco Lopez Cream of
 Coconut
1 oz. butterscotch topping
1 oz. half & half
1 cup ice

Mix in blender until smooth

NUCLEAR REACTOR

First Mix:
1½ oz. Smirnoff Vodka
½ oz. Bacardi Light Rum
½ oz. Malibu Rum
½ oz. coconut mix
Second Mix:
½ oz. Smirnoff Vodka
½ oz. Bacardi Light Rum
1 oz. Midori Melon
¼ oz. Angostura Lime

Pour 1 oz. Angostura Grenadine
into tall promo or tulip glass.
Blend well. Mix no. 1 and
slowly pour into tilted glass.
Blend Mix no. 2 and add to
tilted glass. Top with 1/2 oz.
Angostura grenadine.

ORANGE ICED TEA

2 oz. Gordon's Orange Vodka
3 oz. iced tea

Start with a collins glass filled
with ice, pour Gordon's
Orange Vodka over ice, top
with your favorite iced tea.
Garnish with orange wedge.
(Joseph Price, Gordon's)

ORANGE MARGARITA

1½ oz. Jose Cuervo Gold Tequila
½ oz. triple sec
3 oz. orange juice
½ oz. sweet & sour mix

Blend. Garnish with strawberries.

BLENDED COCKTAILS

ORANGE SMOOTHIE

2½ oz. Coco Lopez Cream of
  Coconut
3 oz. orange juice
1 scoop vanilla ice cream
1 cup ice
nutmeg

Mix first four ingredients in a blender until smooth. Sprinkle with nutmeg.

ORANGE SORBET LOPEZ

2 oz. Coco Lopez Cream of
  Coconut
1 oz. orange juice
1 scoop orange sherbet
½ cup ice

Mix in blender until smooth.

ORANGE VODKA DELIGHT

2 shots Gordon's Orange Vodka
1 12-oz. can frozen orange juice
2 cups orange-flavored water
1 cup 7-Up (8 oz.)

Pour all ingredients into blender. Fill with ice. Mix until slushy. Pour into frozen long-stemmed bowl glass. Place a slice or orange over rim and serve. (Norma Goodreau, Gordon's)

PADDY COCKTAIL

1½ oz. Irish whiskey
¾ oz. sweet vermouth
9 dashes Angostura Bitters

Mix all ingredients with cracked ice in a shaker or blender. Serve in a chilled glass.

PEACH BANANA DAIQUIRI

1½ oz. Puerto Rican Light Rum
½ medium banana, diced
1 oz. fresh lime juice
¼ cup sliced peaches (fresh, frozen, or canned)

Blend with crushed ice.

PEACH IRISH

1½ oz. Irish whiskey
1 ripe peach (peeled, pitted, and sliced)
½ cup fresh lime juice
1 oz. apricot brandy
1 Tbsp. superfine sugar
dash vanilla extract

Blend with crushed ice.

PEACH MARGARITA

1½ oz. Jose Cuervo Gold Tequila
1 oz. triple sec
1 oz. lime juice
½ cup peaches (canned)

Blend. Garnish with peach slices.

PEACH MELBA

½ oz. Captain Morgan Spiced
  Rum
¾ oz. raspberry liqueur
2 oz. peach cocktail mix
1 oz. heavy cream
2 peach halves
raspberry syrup

Blend with crushed ice. Top
with raspberry syrup.

PEANUT BUTTER CUP

2 oz. Malibu
2 Tbs. creamy peanut butter
2 tbs. chocolate syrup
1 oz. Smirnoff Vodka
2 scoops vanilla ice cream

Blend all ingredients until
smooth and frothy.

PINA COLADA SHAKE

½ cup unsweetened pineapple
  juice
⅓ cup Coco Lopez Cream of
  Coconut
1½ cups vanilla ice cream

Mix in a blender until smooth.
Serve immediately.

PINEAPPLE LOPEZ

2 oz. Coco Lopez Cream of
  Coconut
1½ oz. pineapple juice
½ banana
1 cup ice

Mix in blender until smooth.

PINEAPPLE SORBET LOPEZ

1½ oz. Coco Lopez Cream of
  Coconut
2 oz. pineapple juice
1 scoop pineapple sherbet
1 cup ice

Mix in blender until smooth.

PINK PANTHER #1

1½ oz. Sauza Tequila
½ oz. grenadine
2 oz. cream or half & half

Blend with crushed ice and
strain into a chilled glass.

PINK PANTHER #2

1¼ oz. Bacardi Light Rum
¾ oz. lemon juice
¾ oz. cream
½ oz. Rose's Grenadine

Blend with crushed ice and
strain.

PINK SQUIRREL

1 oz. white creme de cacao
1 oz. creme de noyaux
2 oz. cream/milk

Combine in blender until
smooth. Pour into rocks glass.
Garnish with fresh strawberry.

QUEEN SOPHIA

1 part Licor 43
half part rum
half part coconut cream
1 part evaporated milk or half &
  half

Blend with crushed ice and add cinnamon stick on top.

———— ❧ ————

RASPBERRY SWEET TART

1 jig Chambord
1 jig triple sec
1 jig Angostura Lime Juice
1 scoop ice

Blend until frozen.

———— ❧ ————

RED RACKET

½ cup Ocean Spray Cranberry
  Juice Cocktail, chilled
½ cup Ocean Spray Grapefruit
  Juice, chilled
ice cubes

In a blender, combine cranberry juice cocktail, grapefruit juice and ice cubes. Blend on high speed till frothy. Pour into a tall glass.

———— ❧ ————

REUNION

½ oz. Romana Sambuca
½ oz. vodka
½ oz. strawberry liqueur
6 ripe strawberries
3 oz. orange juice

Blend all ingredients with ice until smooth. Pour into wine or fluted glass.

RHETT BUTLER

1 oz. cointreau
1 oz. Southern Comfort
¾ oz. Rose's Lime Juice

Mix ingredients in a blender and strain into a sour glass. Garnish with an orange peel.

———— ❧ ————

RHUM BARBANCOURT FREEZE

2 oz. Rhum Barbancourt
1 oz. triple sec
1 oz. grapefruit juice
2 oz. orange juice
½ oz. lime juice
⅓ cup ice cubes

Combine ingredients in blender, blend until smooth, about 30 seconds. Pour into glass. Garnish with orange wedge.

———— ❧ ————

THE ROMAN COW

½ oz. Romana Sambuca
1½ oz. Stubbs Australian Rum
½ oz. over-ripe banana
1 oz. lemon or lime juice
½ beaten egg

Blend with ice until frothy. Serve in chilled wine glass, garnish with cherry.

ROOT BEER COLADA

2 oz. Old Fashioned Root Beer
  Schnapps
3 oz. pina colada mix

Combine in blender with ice
until smooth.

※

ROOT BEER FLOAT

2 oz. Old Fashioned Root Beer
  Schnapps
2 oz. milk or cream
4 oz. lemon-lime soda

Combine in blender with ice
until smooth.

※

RUM RUNNER

½ oz. blackberry-flavored brandy
½ oz. creme de banana
1½ oz. light rum
splash grenadine
splash lemon/lime juices

Blend with ice. Serve in rocks
glass. Garnish with pineapple
and cherry.

※

RUM YUM

1 oz. Baileys Irish Cream
1 oz. Malibu Rum
1 oz. cream or milk

Blend with ice and serve.

SAUZA LA BAMBA

¾ oz. Sauza Conmemorativo
¾ oz. Frangelico Liqueur

Blend spirits, banana mix,
orange juice, 7-Up and
crushed ice. Serve in wide-
rimmed glass.

※

SCOTCH SMOOTHIE

1 oz. Coco Lopez Cream of
  Coconut
1¼ oz. scotch
½ oz. Baileys Irish Cream
½ oz. Almond Liqueur
2 scoops vanilla ice cream

Blend with crushed ice.

※

SINGAPORE SLING

1 oz. DeKuyper Cheri-Beri
  Pucker
½ oz. gin, club soda
1 oz. lemon juice
1 cherry
orange slice
lemon twist

Mix Cheri-Beri Pucker, gin
and lemon juice over ice in a
tall glass. Fill with club soda
and garnish with a cherry,
orange slice and lemon twist.

BLENDED
COCKTAILS

※

SLALOM

1 part Absolut Vodka
1 part white creme de cacao
1 part Romana Sambuca
1 tsp. heavy cream

Combine in blender with ice.
Strain into chilled cocktail
glass.

SOUR APPLE MARGARITA

1 oz. DeKuyper Cactus Juice
½ oz. DeKuyper Sour Apple Pucker
1 oz. sour mix
½ oz. lime juice

Combine ingredients. Serve frozen or over ice in a Margarita glass. Garnish with a slice of lime.

———— ⊗⊗⊗ ————

SOVIET COCKTAIL

1½ oz. vodka
½ oz. dry vermouth
½ oz. dry sherry

Shake or blend all ingredients with cracked ice in a shaker or blender and strain into a chilled glass. Twist a lemon peel over the drink and drop it in.

———— ⊗⊗⊗ ————

SPYGLASS

1 oz. Captain Morgan Spiced Rum
2 scoops vanilla ice cream
1 Tbsp. honey
dash milk

Blend until smooth.

STRAWBERRY BANANA LOPEZ

2 oz. Coco Lopez Cream of Coconut
2 oz. strawberries
½ medium banana
1 cup ice

Mix in blender until smooth.

———— ⊗⊗⊗ ————

STRAWBERRY DAIQUIRI ALIZE

2 oz. Alize
½ cup crushed ice
½ cup frozen strawberries
1 Tbsp. freshly squeezed lemon juice
⅛ tsp. superfine sugar

Blend until smooth. Pour into martini glass.

———— ⊗⊗⊗ ————

SUNSHINE FROSTY PUNCH

1¼ oz. vodka
2 scoops vanilla ice cream

Blend until smooth and serve in a 12-oz. brandy snifter.

———— ⊗⊗⊗ ————

TABOO

1½ oz. Finlandia Pineapple Vodka, chilled
½ oz. cranberry juice
½ oz. sour mix
splash triple sec

Blend with crushed ice. Serve in a tall glass. Garnish with a pineapple wedge and a cherry.

TEQUILA GIMLET

1½ oz. tequila
1½ oz. Rose's Lime Juice

Blend tequila and lime juice with crushed ice and pour into a glass. Garnish with a lime wheel or green cherry.

TIJUANA MARGARITA

1 oz. Orchard Orange Schnapps
1½ oz. tequila
1½ oz. sweet & sour mix

Combine in blender until smooth.

TOP TEN

1¼ oz. Captain Morgan Spiced Rum
2 oz. cola
1 oz. Coco Lopez Cream of Coconut
1 oz. heavy cream

Blend with crushed ice.

TROPICAL BREEZE

1 oz. rum
½ oz. creme de banana
1 oz. Coco Lopez Cream of Coconut
2 oz. orange juice

Blend with crushed ice. Garnish with a pineapple slice.

TROPICAL FREEZE LOPEZ

2 oz. Coco Lopez Cream of Coconut
1½ oz. orange juice
1½ oz. pineapple juice
1 cup ice

Mix in blender until smooth.

TROPICAL PASSION

1 oz. Alize
1 oz. Midori
3 oz. pineapple
1 oz. orange juice

Blend. Garnish with pineapple wedge and cherry, speared.

THE TWIST

¾ oz. Absolut Vodka
½ oz. white creme de menthe
2 oz. orange sherbert

Blend. Pour into a champagne glass.

VELVET HAMMER

1 oz. dark creme de cacao
1 oz. triple sec
2 oz. cream/milk

Blend with ice. Serve in a chilled wine glass.

BLENDED COCKTAILS

VODKA STONE SOUR

1½ oz. Gordon's Citrus Vodka
1 tsp. lemon bar mix
2 oz. orange juice

Blend with 1 cup of cracked ice, pour into old-fashioned glass. Garnish with orange slice and cherry. (Jon Campbell, Gordon's)

THE WHITE CAP

1½ oz. Southern Comfort
1½ oz. creme de cacao
1 cup ice cubes
half & half

Pour first 3 ingredients into blender. Add half & half until ice cubes are covered. Blend until foamy.

WHITE VELVET

1½ oz. Romana Sambuca
1 egg white
1 oz. lemon juice

Blend with ice until smooth, strain into chilled cocktail glass.

WILDBERRY ANGEL

2 shots Gordon's Wildberry Vodka
1 shot creme de cassis
1 12-oz. can frozen pink lemonade
2 cups strawberry-flavored water

Pour all into blender. Fill with ice. Mix until slushy. Pour into frozen long-stemmed bowl glass. Place a whole strawberry over rim and serve. (Norma Goodreau, Gordon's)

WYNBREEZER

1 jig dark rum
1 jig triple sec
1 jig Angostura Lime Juice
2 oz. orange juice

Blend. Pour over ice. Fill with 7-Up.

Coffee and Warm Me Up Cocktails

AFTERNOON

1 oz. Kahlua
1 oz. Baileys Irish Cream
½ oz. Frangelico
3 oz. hot coffee and cream

Serve in a hot coffee mug. Top with cream.

———∞∞∞———

AMARETTO CAFE

1½ oz. Disaronno Amaretto
3 oz. hot black coffee

Serve in hot coffee cup. Stir. Top with whipped cream.

———∞∞∞———

ASPEN COFFEE

1 oz. Baileys Irish Cream
1 oz. Grand Marnier
1 oz. Frangelico
2 oz. coffee

Serve in a 5 oz. hot coffee mug.

———∞∞∞———

ATLANTA HOT PEACHED BOURBON

2 oz. Wild Turkey (101 proof)
1 pinch brown sugar
½ oz. peach syrup
3 oz. boiling water

Stir briskly and serve.

AUNT TILLIE'S APPLE TEA

Brew a nice cup of tea and top with 1½ oz. Laird's Applejack. Squeeze in a wedge of lemon.

———∞∞∞———

B&B COFFEE

1¼ oz. B&B Liqueur
4 oz. hot coffee

Top with whipped cream.

———∞∞∞———

BACARDI FIRESIDE

1 tsp. sugar
1 jigger of Bacardi light or dark rum

Add cup of very hot tea and one cinnamon stick. Stir well, top with a slice of lemon.

———∞∞∞———

BACARDI HOT BUTTERED RUM

In a mug put 1 tsp. sugar, ½ tsp. butter, 1 jigger Bacardi light or dark rum, 4 cloves. Fill with boiling water. Stir.

COFFEE AND WARM ME UP COCKTAILS

BACARDI HOT COFFEE

1½ oz. Bacardi Light or Dark
  Reserve Rum to a cup of coffee
Whipped cream optional

———⧢———

BACARDI O COFFEE

2 oz. Bacardi O
3 oz. hot coffee

Serve in cup. Top with Baileys and green creme de menthe.

———⧢———

BAGPIPE

1¼ oz. The Famous Grouse
hot coffee

Top with whipped cream or ice cream.

———⧢———

BAGPIPER

1¼ oz. The Famous Grouse
2 oz. hot coffee

Top with whipped cream or ice cream.

———⧢———

BAILEYS COFFEE

2 parts Baileys Irish Cream
5 parts hot coffee

———⧢———

BARN BURNER

1½ oz. Southern Comfort
small stick cinnamon
slice lemon peel
3 oz. hot cider

Put cinnamon, lemon peel, Southern Comfort in mug; fill with hot cider; stir.

BAVARIAN COFFEE

1 oz. Kahlua
½ oz. peppermint schnapps
hot coffee and whipped cream

———⧢———

BELGIAN COFFEE

1 oz. cointreau
2 oz. Baileys Irish Cream
3 oz. hot coffee

Serve in a hot coffee mug.

———⧢———

BERMUDA COFFEE

1½ oz. Gosling's Black Seal Rum
  of Bermuda
1 oz. Irish cream liqueur
4 oz. hot coffee

Top with fresh whipping cream.

———⧢———

BLACK FOREST COFFEE

1 oz. kirschwasser
3 oz. hot coffee

Serve in a hot mug. Top with whipped cream.

———⧢———

BLACKJACK

1 oz. brandy
1 oz. kirschwasser
3 oz. hot coffee

Serve in a hot coffee mug.

BLUEBERRY TEA
1 oz. Grand Marnier
1 oz. Disaronno Amaretto
3 oz. hot tea

Serve in hot mug. Garnish with an orange slice.

BRANDY BLAZER
3 oz. California Brandy
1 Tbsp. honey
3 oz. hot coffee
lemon peel

Twist the lemon peel over the blazer and drop it into the drink.

BUN WARMER
1 oz. apricot brandy
1 oz. Southern Comfort
3 oz. hot apple cider

Serve in a hot coffee mug.

BURNT RAYBIRD
1 oz. Disaronno Amaretto
½ oz. dark creme de cacao
1 oz. Kahlua
3 oz. hot coffee

Serve in a hot coffee mug

BURNT RAYBIRD
½ oz. Disaronno Amaretto
½ oz. dark creme de cacao
½ oz. Kahlua
3 oz. hot coffee

Serve in a hot coffee mug.

BUSHMILLS HOT IRISH TEA
1½ oz. Bushmills Irish Whiskey
4 oz. hot tea

Add cinnamon stick.

CAFE AMARETTO
1 oz. Disaronno Amaretto
1 oz. Kahlua
3 oz. coffee

Serve in a hot coffee mug.

CAFE CACAO
2 oz. dark creme de cacao
3 oz. coffee

Serve in a hot coffee mug.

CAFE CARIBBEAN
1 oz. Disaronno Amaretto
1 oz. rum
3 oz. coffee
1 tsp. sugar

Serve in a hot coffee mug.

CAFE DISARONNO

Pour 1½ oz. Disaronno Amaretto into a coffee cup. Fill with hot coffee. Garnish with whipped cream and a sprinkling of cinnamon.

CAFE GATES
1 oz. Grand Marnier
1 oz. Tia Maria
½ oz. dark creme de cacao
3 oz. hot coffee

Serve in a hot coffee mug. Stir. Top with whipped cream.

CAFE GROG
2 lumps sugar
1 oz. Gosling's Black Sea Rum
½ oz. brandy
3 oz. hot coffee

Serve in a hot coffee mug with a slice of lemon.

CAFE JOY
½ oz. Frangelico
½ oz. Malibu Rum
1 oz. Baileys Irish Cream
3 oz. hot coffee

Serve in a hot coffee mug.

CAFE L'ARMAGNAC

Stir 1 oz. Armagnac into 4 oz. hot espresso coffee.

CAFÉ MARNIER
1 tsp. powdered sugar
½ oz. Grand Marnier
hot coffee (about 6 oz.)
whipped cream

CAFE MEXICANO
1 oz. Kahlua
½ oz. tequila
3 oz. hot coffee

Serve in a hot coffee mug. Top with whipped cream.

CALYPSO COFFEE
1 oz. Tia Maria
1 oz. dark rum
3 oz. coffee

Serve in a hot coffee mug.

CANADIAN COFFEE
½ oz. Canadian Club
½ oz. Kahlua
½ oz. Hiram Walker Amaretto di Medriana
3 oz. hot coffee

Serve in a hot coffee mug. Top with whipped cream and a maraschino cherry.

CAPPUCCINO DISARONNO

Pour 1½ oz. Disaronno Amaretto into a coffee cup. Fill with fresh cappuccino.

CAPPUCCINO WITH GINGER

Float ½ oz. Canton Delicate Ginger Liqueur on top of the foamy milk of a cup of cappuccino.

CARIBBEAN COFFEE
2 oz. rum
3 oz. coffee

Serve in a hot coffee mug.

CC 'N CIDER
1¼ oz. Canadian Club Classic
3 oz. hot apple cider

Serve in a hot mug. Stir. Dash of grated nutmeg optional.

CELTIC COFFEE
1½ oz. Celtic Crossing Irish
  Liqueur
4 oz. hot coffee
whipped cream

CHAMBORD & COFFEE

Add Chambord to a cup of coffee. Top with whipped cream.

CHIP SHOT
¾ oz. Devonshire Irish Cream
¾ oz. Tuaca
1½ oz. hot coffee

Combine in a glass and stir.

CHRISTIAN COFFEE ROYAL
1½ oz. Christian Brothers Brandy
1 tsp. very fine granulated sugar
3 oz. hot coffee

Serve in a hot coffee mug.

CLUB HOTSY TOTSY
1 oz. Canadian Club
½ oz. Hiram Walker Amaretto
3 oz. hot chocolate

Serve in a hot mug. Stir and top with a half dozen mini-marshmallows.

CO-CO-MO
2 oz. Malibu

Fill with half hot coffee, half hot chocolate.

COFFEE BUSTAMANTE
1 oz. Courvoisier Cognac
½ oz. Kahlua
½ oz. Benedictine
¼ oz. Mozart Liqueur
3 oz. hot coffee

Serve in a hot coffee mug.

COFFEE FLING
2 oz. Drambuie
3 oz. hot coffee
1 tsp. sugar

Serve in a hot coffee mug.

COFFEE AND WARM ME UP COCKTAILS

COMFORT MOCHA

1½ oz. Southern Comfort
1 tsp. instant cocoa or hot chocolate
1 tsp. instant coffee

Add boiling water. Top with whipped cream.

———⟨∞⟩———

COMFORTING COFFEE

1½ oz. Southern Comfort
½ oz. dark creme de cacao
3 oz. coffee

Serve in a hot coffee mug.

———⟨∞⟩———

COSSACK COFFEE

1 oz. Stolichnaya Zinnamon Vodka
1 oz. Stolichnaya Kaffe Vodka
3 oz. coffee
1 tsp. whipped cream

Serve in a hot coffee mug. Top with whipped cream.

———⟨∞⟩———

CREAMED IRISH COFFEE

2 oz. Carolans Irish Cream
3 oz. hot coffee
sugar (to taste)

Serve in a hot coffee mug.

———⟨∞⟩———

CREAMY IRISH COFFEE

1½ oz. Baileys Irish Cream

Fill with hot coffee. Top with whipped cream.

CRUZAN HOT BUTTERED RUM

1 tsp. butter
1 tsp. brown sugar
1½ oz. Cruzan Gold Rum
3 oz. boiling water
dash each:
cinnamon
cloves
nutmeg
lemon slice

Stir. Garnish with lemon slice.

———⟨∞⟩———

DRAMBUIE TEA

Make hot tea in a large mug, add 1 to 1½ oz. of Drambuie. Add milk, cream or lemon peel as desired.

———⟨∞⟩———

DUBLIN COFFEE

1 oz. Kahlua
½ oz. Irish Mist
3 oz. hot coffee
1 tsp. whipped cream

Serve in a hot coffee mug. Top with whipped cream.

———⟨∞⟩———

DUTCH TREAT

1½ oz. Asbach Uralt

Add hot chocolate and whipped cream. Serve in mug with straw.

FINLANDIA COFFEE

2 oz. Finlandia Vodka
¼ oz. cranberry liqueur
3 oz. hot coffee

Serve in a hot coffee mug. Top with whipped cream.

GALLIANO HOT SHOT

1 oz. Galliano
1 oz. hot coffee
dash whipped cream

Combine in a shot glass.

HAZELNUT COFFEE

1 oz. B & B
½ oz. Frangelico Hazelnut
  Liqueur
3 oz. coffee
1 tsp. whipped cream

Serve in a hot coffee mug. Top with whipped cream.

THE HIGHLANDS COFFEE

2 oz. Dewar's Scotch
¼ oz. Drambuie
3 oz. hot coffee
¼ oz. cream

Serve in a hot coffee mug. Top with cream.

HOT BUTTERED COMFORT

1 jigger Southern Comfort
small stick cinnamon
slice lemon peel
pat butter

Float butter. Stir.

HOT CC RIDER

1½ oz. Canadian Club
5 oz. hot cider
dash of cinnamon sugar

Pour Canadian Club in a mug and fill with hot cider. Garnish with a slice of apple and a cinnamon stick.

HOT CHOCOLATE WITH A KICK

6 oz. hot chocolate
1½ oz. Jack Daniel's Old No. 7
½ oz. almond or coffee liqueur

Stir Jack Daniel's and liqueur into mug of hot chocolate. Garnish with a marshmallow.

HOT COFFEE NUDGE

¾ oz. Kahlua
¾ oz. Grand Marnier
¾ oz. brandy
4 oz. coffee

COFFEE AND WARM ME UP COCKTAILS

HOT IRISH NUT

2 oz. Baileys Irish Cream
½ oz. Frangelico
½ oz. amaretto
3 oz. hot coffee

Serve in a hot mug. Top with whipped cream.

HOT MOLTEN JACK

1½ oz. Jack Daniel's Single Barrel
2 sugar cubes
dash bitters
3 oz. boiling water
squeeze of fresh lemon juice

Serve in a hot mug.

HOT OPPLE

Cup hot apple cider
1 oz. OP
cinnamon stick
dash of nutmeg

HOT SCOTCH

1 oz. Chivas Regal
¼ oz. Drambuie
1 oz. lemon juice
½ tsp. sugar

Pour in old fashioned glass and fill with hot water.

HOT TODDY

2 oz. whiskey
1 tsp. sugar
3 oz. boiling water

Serve in hot mug. Garnish with lemon slice and dust with nutmeg or add cinnamon stick.

INSOMNIAC

1 oz. Frangelico
1 oz. Tia Maria
1½ oz. espresso
1½ oz. hot coffee
¼ oz. milk
1 tsp. cream

Serve in hot coffee mug. Top with cream.

IRISH COFFEE (ORIGINAL)

Into a stemmed glass, put 2 tsp. sugar, peferably brown; add ⅓ Irish whiskey and ⅔ really strong black coffee, preferably freshly brewed, not instant. The glass should be filled with this mixture to within half an inch of the brim. Stir well at this point to ensure all of the sugar is dissolved, and then carefully float over the back of a spoon a collar of lightly-whipped cream, so that the cream floats on the top of the coffee and whiskey. Do not stir any more. Serve the drink without a spoon or a straw, as part of the pleasure comes from sipping the hot coffee and whiskey through the cool cream.

IRISH COFFEE (SIMPLE)

2 oz. Tullamore Dew Irish
 Whiskey
3 oz. hot coffee
1 tsp. sugar
1 tsp. whipped cream

Serve in a hot mug. Top with whipped cream.

IRISH CREAM-SICLE

Mix in coffee mug: ½ oz. Bunratty Potcheen, fill ¾ with hot coffee, add scoop vanilla ice cream, sprinkle with nutmeg.

IRISH CUP O' JOE

2 oz. Baileys Irish Cream
¼ oz. chocolate syrup
3 oz. hot coffee

Serve in hot coffee mug.

IRISH KNIT

1 oz. Carolans Irish Cream
1 oz. cointreau
3 oz. hot coffee

Serve in hot coffee mug.

IRISH MIST COFFEE

3 oz. hot coffee
1½ oz. Irish Mist

Serve in a hot coffee mug. Top with whipped cream.

ITALIAN AMARETTO COFFEE

1 oz. Disaronno Amaretto
1 oz. Tuaca
3 oz. coffee

Serve in a hot coffee mug.

ITALIAN COFFEE

1 sugar packet, cube, or bar
 spoon
1½ oz. Galliano

Fill with hot coffee. Top with whipped cream. Straw.

JACK DANIEL'S TENNESSEE MUD

¾ oz. Jack Daniel's
¾ oz. Disaronno Amaretto
3 oz. hot coffee
whipped cream

Serve in a hot coffee mug. Top with whipped cream.

JACK'S WARM FRONT

1 generous tsp. sugar
½ cup boiling water
1 pat butter
2 oz. Jack Daniel's Old No. 7

Spoon sugar into mug. Stir in boiling water to dissolve sugar. Add butter and Jack Daniel's. Stir and sprinkle with nutmeg.

COFFEE AND WARM ME UP COCKTAILS

JAMAICAN COFFEE

1½ oz. Jamaican Rum
¾ oz. Tia Maria

Fill with hot coffee. Top with whipped cream.

KAHLUA & COFFEE

1½ oz. Kahlua
3 oz. hot coffee
½ oz. cream, plain or whipped

Add Kahlua to coffee. Stir in cream or top with whipped cream, if desired.

KAHLUA CAPPUCCINO

1 oz. Kahlua to cup of hot cappuccino

Top with whipped cream.

KAHLUA IRISH COFFEE

1 oz. Kahlua
1 oz. Irish whiskey
3 oz. hot coffee
whipped cream

Add Kahlua and Irish whiskey to coffee and top with whipped cream.

KAHLUA KIOKI COFFEE

1 oz. Kahlua
½ oz. brandy
3 oz. hot coffee
whipped cream

Add Kahlua and brandy to coffee. Top with whipped cream.

KAHLUA PARISIAN COFFEE

½ oz. Kahlua
½ oz. Grand Marnier
1 oz. cognac or brandy
3 oz. hot coffee
whipped cream

Pour first 3 ingredients into a steaming cup of coffee. Top with whipped cream. Garnish with shaved chocolate or orange peel, if desired.

KAHLUA WITCHES BREW

1 oz. Kahlua
½ oz. chocolate mint liqueur
2 oz. hot chocolate
1 oz. whipped cream

Serve in a hot mug.

KEOKE COFFEE

1 oz. Kahlua
½ oz. brandy
½ oz. dark creme de cacao

Fill with hot coffee. Top with whipped cream.

KILBEGGAN & COFFEE

A measure of Kilbeggan Irish
 Whiskey
1 tsp. sugar
1 Tbsp. whipped cream
hot, strong coffee to fill the glass

Pre-warm a stemmed glass. Add whiskey. Add sugar and stir in coffee. Float cream on top. Do not stir after adding cream. Drink coffee through the cream.

LE COFFEE

1½ oz. cointreau
1 tsp. sugar
6 oz. hot coffee

Top with whipped cream and sprinkle with instant coffee, shaved chocolate, or slivers of orange peel.

LEMON MERINGUE

Mix in tall coffee mug:
1 oz. Giori Lemoncillo Cream
¾ oz. Giori Amaretto
½ oz. Amaro Montenegro

Fill with coffee; top with whipped cream.

LUCKY LOVE

Mix in coffee mug:
½ oz. Bunratty Potcheen
½ oz. Giori Amaretto

Fill with hot coffee; top with whipped cream and drizzle with chocolate syrup.

LUDMILA'S CAFE COCOA

1 oz. Stolichnaya Kaffe Vodka
1 oz. Stolichnaya Vanil Vodka
2 oz. hot chocolate
¼ oz. whipped cream

Serve in a hot mug. Top with whipped cream.

MAIN HOT BUTTERED BOURBON TODDY

2 oz. Wild Turkey (101 proof)
1 oz. orange juice
1 tsp. sugar
1 whole clove

Put all ingredients in a mug. Fill with hot water and stir. Add quarter pat of butter to float on top.

MAD MONK

1 oz. Benedictine
1 oz. Kahlua
3 oz. coffee

MALIBU CALYPSO CAFE

1 oz. Malibu
1 oz. Disaronno Amaretto
3 oz. hot coffee

Serve in hot coffee mug.

COFFEE AND WARM ME UP COCKTAILS

MARNIER BODY WARMER

6 oz. hot tea
1 oz. Grand Marnier
½ tsp. sugar

Stir and sweeten to taste. Serve in a hot mug.

MARNISSIMO

2 tsp. sugar
3 oz. hot coffee
1 oz. Grand Marnier

Stir. Top with whipped cream.

MEXICAN COFFEE

1½ oz. tequila
½ oz. Kahlua

Fill with hot black coffee. Top with whipped cream. Straw.

MIDNIGHT IN MALIBU

2 oz. Malibu
fill with hot coffee

Top with whipped cream.

MIDNIGHT MANX

1 oz. Kahlua
1 oz. Baileys Irish Cream
¼ oz. Goldschlager
¼ oz. heavy cream
3 oz. hot coffee

Serve in hot coffee mug. Top with whipped cream.

MIDORI HOT CHOCOLATE

1 oz. Midori
5 oz. hot chocolate

Pour Midori into hot chocolate. Stir.

MIDORI TEA

1½ oz. Midori
5 oz. hot tea
½ oz. cointreau
slice of lemon

Add Midori and cointreau to hot tea. Add lemon to taste.

MILLIONAIRE'S COFFEE

1 oz. Baileys Irish Cream
½ oz. Kahlua
½ oz. Frangelico
3 oz. hot coffee

Serve in hot coffee mug.

MINT KISS

½ oz. peppermint schnapps
1 oz. Baileys
½ oz. creme de cacao
3 oz. coffee

Serve in hot coffee mug.

MISTY-EYED IRISHMAN

¾ oz. Bushmills Irish Whiskey
1 oz. peppermint schnapps
1 pkg. hot chocolate mix
3 oz. hot coffee
¼ oz. whipped cream

Top with whipped cream.

MOCHA-BERRY

2 oz. Chambord
¼ oz. DeKuyper Crème de Cacao
3 oz. hot coffee
¼ oz. whipped cream

Serve in a hot coffee mug. Top with whipped cream.

MONASTERY COFFEE

2 oz. Benedictine
3 oz. coffee

Serve in a hot coffee mug.

MYERS'S COFFEE

Add 1½ oz. Myers's Original Dark Rum and fill with coffee to within 3/4 inch from top of mug. Add sugar or sweetener. Top with whipped cream.

NIKKI COFFEE

2 oz. Baileys Irish Cream
½ oz. butterscotch schnapps
3 oz. hot coffee

Serve in a hot coffee mug.

NUTTY IRISH COFFEE

2 oz. Baileys Irish Cream
½ oz. Frangelico
3 oz. hot coffee
¼ oz. chocolate syrup
¼ oz. whipped cream

Serve in a hot coffee mug. Top with whipped cream.

NUTTY MONK

1 oz. Benedictine
1 oz. Frangelico
3 oz. coffee

Serve in a hot coffee mug.

NUTTY MORGAN

1 oz. Captain Morgan Rum
1 oz. Frangelico
3 oz. coffee

Serve in a hot coffee mug.

THE ORIGINAL JAMAICAN COFFEE

In a glass mug, stir 1 oz. of Tia Maria into hot coffee. Optionally garnish with whipped cream and shaved chocolate.

COFFEE AND WARM ME UP COCKTAILS

PEPPAR TODDY

4 oz. cranberry juice
2 allspice berries
3-inch curl of orange peel
1 tsp. sugar
2 tsp. lemon juice
1 oz. Absolut Peppar Vodka

Heat to boiling and boil two minutes. Pour the hot liquid over vodka in a mug. Add reserved cinnamon stick.

PORTLAND COFFEE

1 oz. Bacardi 151
1 oz. Kahlua
½ oz. triple sec
dash cinnamon
dash nutmeg
½ tsp. sugar
3 oz. hot coffee

Serve in a hot coffee mug.

PSYCHO JOE

1 oz. Kahlua
1 oz. peppermint schnapps
3 oz. hot coffee

Serve in a hot coffee mug.

PURPLE HAZE

5 parts sake
1 part Chambord

Heat.

RICHIE FAMILY

1 oz. Absolut Vodka
½ oz. whiskey
½ oz. Baileys Irish Cream
3 oz. hot coffee
⅛ tsp. brown sugar

Serve in a hot coffee mug.

ROMAN CHOCOLATE

Pour 1½ oz. Romana Sambuca into a large mug with 5 oz. of hot chocolate. Top with whipped cream and chocolate shavings.

ROMAN COFFEE

1½ oz. Galliano
3 oz. hot coffee
¼ oz. whipped cream

Serve in a hot coffee mug and top with whipped cream

ROMANA CAFÉ

Add 1 oz. Romana Sambuca to a 5 oz. cup of hot espresso or regular coffee. Top with sweetened whipped cream.

RÜEDESHEIM COFFEE

Place 3 cubes sugar into a warmed mug. Add 1½ to 2 oz. Asbach Uralt. Stir; fill with hot coffee; cover with layer of whipped cream and sprinkle with vanilla and grated chocolate.

RUMPLE MINTZ PATTY

1 oz. Rumple Minze
½ oz. dark creme de cacao
1 oz. Smirnoff Vodka
3 oz. coffee
¼ oz. whipped cream

Serve in hot coffee mug and top with whipped cream.

RUSSIAN COFFEE

½ oz. Kahlua
½ oz. hazelnut liqueur
1 oz. vodka
3 oz. hot coffee

Serve in hot coffee mug.

SCOTCH COFFEE

1 packet sugar
cube or bar spoon
1½ oz. Drambuie

Fill with hot coffee. Top with whipped cream. Straw.

SKY TOP KIOKI

1 oz. Bacardi Silver
½ oz. brandy
½ oz. Kahlua
dash cinnamon
3 oz. Columbian coffee
¼ oz. whipped cream

Serve in a hot coffee mug. Top with whipped cream.

SMIRNOFF FUZZY COCOA

6 oz. hot water
1 envelope hot cocoa mix
1 oz. Smirnoff Vodka
1 oz. Arrow Peach Schnapps
dash ground cinnamon

Pour hot water in serving cup. (For microwave, pour tap water in cup. Heat in microwave 1½ minutes on high.)

SMIRNOFF PATRIOT PUNCH

5 oz. cranberry juice
1 oz. Smirnoff Vodka
½ oz. Arrow Triple Sec

Heat cranberry juice. Pour in serving cup. (For microwave, pour in cup. Heat in microwave 1½ minutes on high.)

SNOWBALL

½ oz. cinnamon schnapps
1 oz. Kahlua
3 oz. hot coffee

Serve in a hot coffee mug.

SOUTH FORK COFFEE

1½ oz. bourbon
½ oz. dark creme de cacao
3 oz. coffee

Serve in a hot coffee mug.

COFFEE AND WARM ME UP COCKTAILS

SPANISH COFFEE

½ oz. Kahlua
½ oz. Grand Marnier
1 oz. brandy
3 oz. hot coffee
whipped cream

SPIRITED COFFEE LOPEZ

½ oz. Coco Lopez Real Cream of
  Coconut
8 oz. hot coffee
½ oz. Irish whiskey
whipped cream as desired

ST. PATTY'S COFFEE

1 oz. Ashbourne Irish Cream
1 oz. Basilica Coffee Liqueur
1 oz. Gosling's Black Seal Rum

Fill with hot coffee.

STANLEY STEAMER

1 oz. Kahlua
½ oz. Irish Cream
½ oz. cognac
½ oz. cointreau
3 oz. hot coffee
¼ oz. whipped cream

Serve in hot coffee mug. Top
with whipped cream.

SWISS COFFEE

1 ½ oz. peppermint schnapps
3/4 oz. dark creme de cacao
3 oz. hot coffee

Serve in a hot coffee mug. Top
with whipped cream.

TEA WITH LOVE

1½ to 2 oz. Disaronno Amaretto
6 oz. hot tea

Top with chilled whipped
cream.

THERMOSTAT

Pour 1 oz. Romana Sambuca
and ½ oz. hazelnut liqueur
into a cup of hot coffee. Add
nutmeg to taste.

TINKER'S TEA

1½ oz. Baileys Irish Cream
hot tea

TOM & JERRY

Beat until stiff:
1 egg white
2 tsp. sugar
pinch baking soda
½ oz. Rum

Take 1 Tbs. of this batter and
mix it with 2 Tbs. hot milk
and 1½ oz. rum. Put in warm
mug; fill mug with more hot
milk. Float on top ½ oz. five-
star brandy. Dust with nutmeg.

TUACA HOT APPLE PIE

1½ oz. Tuaca Liqueur
5-6 oz. apple cider, warmed

Top with whipped cream and
a sprinkle of cinnamon.

TUACA MEDITERRANEAN COFFEE

¾ oz. Tuaca Liqueur
¾ oz. almond liqueur
¾ oz. Kahlua
5 oz. hot coffee

Top with whipped cream.

———⊗⊗⊗———

TUACACCINO

1 oz. Tuaca Liqueur
2 tsp. instant cocoa
3 oz. hot coffee

Serve in a hot coffee mug. Top with whipped cream.

———⊗⊗⊗———

TUACAJAVA

1½ oz. Tuaca Liqueur
3 oz. hot coffee
whipped cream (optional)

Serve in a hot coffee mug. Top with whipped cream.

———⊗⊗⊗———

TUSCAN WARMER

1 oz. Canadian Club
½ oz. Tuaca
3 oz. hot water

Serve in a hot mug. Add lemon slice studded with cloves.

ULTIMATE IRISH COFFEE

2 oz. Irish Mist
3 oz. coffee

Serve in a hot coffee mug. Top with whipped cream and dash of green creme de menthe.

———⊗⊗⊗———

THE ULTIMATE TEA

1½ oz. Irish Mist
hot tea
a bit of lemon

———⊗⊗⊗———

WARM APPLE SLIDER

1 oz. cognac
1 oz. Alize
3 oz. warm apple juice

Serve in a warm mug.

———⊗⊗⊗———

WINTER WARM-UP

1 oz. Chambord
1 oz. Kahlua
3 oz. hot coffee
¼ oz. whipped cream

Serve in a hot coffee mug. Top with whipped cream.

COFFEE AND WARM ME UP COCKTAILS

Martinis

"007" MARTINI (MR. BABBINGTON'S)

2½ oz. imported vodka
splash Martini & Rossi Extra Dry
  Vermouth
a twist

Shaken, not stirred.

~∞~

1951 MARTINI

2½ oz. Gordons Gin
splash or rinse cointreau
anchovy stuffed olive

~∞~

24-KARROT MARTINI (KETEL ONE VODKA SIGNATURE MARTINI)

This one is pure gold!
2½ oz. Ketel One
2 spicy baby carrots—the best of
  the bunch!

Straight up or over ice, martinis haven't generated this much excitement in years!

~∞~

ABSOLUT CORNET

1½ oz. Absolut Vodka
dash port wine

ABSOLUT VODKA MARTINI

1½ oz. Absolut Vodka
dash Martini & Rossi Extra Dry
  Vermouth

Stir in cocktail glass with ice. Strain and serve up or on the rocks with some ice in cocktail glass. Add lemon twist or olive. OR: Shake and strain and serve up or on the rocks with some ice.

~∞~

AINSWORTH MARTINI

1¼ oz. dry gin
¾ oz. dry vermouth

~∞~

ALASKA MARTINI

7 parts dry gin
1 part yellow Chartreuse
twist of lemon peel

~∞~

ALFONSO SPECIAL

1 oz. dry gin
1 oz. dry vermouth
½ oz. Grand Marnier
¼ oz. sweet vermouth
1 dash bitters

ALL-AMERICAN MARTINI

7 parts Peoria Dry Gin
1 part Modesto Dry Vermouth

Garnish with a California green olive or a twist of Sunkist lemon peel. Serve in a plastic cocktail glass.

ALLIES MARTINI

2 parts dry gin
1 part French vermouth
2 dashes Kummel
green olive (plain or stuffed)

AMBASSADOR MARTINI

7 parts dry gin
1 parts French vermouth
1 tsp. dry white wine
twist of lemon peel

Mix without the wine and pour into a cocktail glass. Gently float the wine from a teaspoon on the surface of the martini.

AMBER DREAM MARTINI

2 parts dry gin
1 part Italian vermouth
1 dash orange bitters
3 dashes yellow Chartreuse

Shake.

ANGEL COCKTAIL (BOWERY BAR, NEW YORK, NY)

1½ oz. Ketel One Vodka (3 Tbsp.)
½ oz. Frangelico (1 Tbsp.)

Shake ingredients with ice and strain into a chilled martini glass.

APRICOT MARTINI

1 part Godiva Liqueur
1 part Absolut Vodka
1 part apricot brandy

Combine with ice; shake well. Serve chilled with cherry.

ARMY COCKTAIL MARTINI

2 oz. dry gin
½ oz. sweet vermouth
orange peel

ARTILLERY MARTINI

1½ oz. dry gin
¾ oz. sweet vermouth
1 dash Angostura Bitters
twist of lemon peel

ATTA BOY MARTINI

2 oz. dry gin
½ oz. dry vermouth
2 dashes grenadine

MARTINIS

ATTY MARTINI
2 oz. dry gin
½ oz. dry vermouth
2 dashes creme de violette
twist of lemon peel

B&B MANHATTAN (STARS, SAN FRANCISCO)
2 oz. B&B Liqueur
¼ oz. Martini & Rossi Sweet
  Vermouth
dash of bitters

Shake and serve over ice or straight up in a chilled martini glass. Garnish with a cherry.

B&B MANHATTAN (HEART AND SOUL)
2½ oz. B&B
⅛ oz. Martini & Rosso Vermouth
dash of Angostura Bitters

Stir and serve up with a cherry.

B&B MARTINI (HEART AND SOUL)
B&B Liqueur
Martini & Rossi Rosso Vermouth
dash of Angostura Bitters
cherry

BACARDI DRY MARTINI
2 oz. Bacardi Rum (light)
½ oz. dry vermouth

BACARDI LIMON MARTINI (HEART AND SOUL)
2½ oz. Bacardi Limon
splash Martini & Rossi Extra Dry
  Vermouth
splash of cranberry juice
lemon twist

BACARDI SWEET MARTINI
2 oz. Bacardi Rum (light)
½ oz. sweet vermouth

BALD HEAD MARTINI
4 parts dry gin
1 part French vermouth
1 part Italian vermouth
1 or 2 dashes Pernod
green olive

Sprinkle the oil from a twist of lemon peel on top.

BALLANTINE'S COCKTAIL
1½ oz. dry gin
¾ oz. French vermouth
1 dash orange bitters
1 dash Pernod

BARON MARTINI

1½ oz. dry gin
½ oz. French vermouth
¼ oz. orange curacao
¼ oz. sweet vermouth

twist of lemon peel

BARRY MARTINI

1½ oz. dry gin
¾ oz. sweet vermouth
1 dash Angostura Bitters
white creme de menthe

Stir into a glass. Float creme de menthe on top. Garnish with a twist of lemon peel.

BELLINI TINI (THE QUIET WOMAN, MARTINI MENU. MAGAZINE: COASTER MAGAZINE)

A smooth blend of Ketel One Vodka and peach schnapps.

BICH'S SPECIAL MARTINI

1½ oz. dry gin
¾ oz. Lillet
1 dash Angostura Bitters
orange peel

BILL LYKEN'S DELIGHT MARTINI

1½ oz. dry gin
½ oz. dry vermouth
¼ oz. sweet vermouth
twist of lemon peel
twist orange peel

BITCH ON WHEELS (STARS, SAN FRANCISO)

2 oz. Bombay Gin
⅛ oz. Martini & Rossi Extra Dry Vermouth
⅛ oz. Pernod
⅛ oz. white creme de menthe

Serve over ice or straight up in a chilled martini glass.

BLACK CURRANT MARTINI

1 oz. Godiva Liqueur
1 oz. Seagram's Gin
¼ oz. creme de cassis
⅙ oz. lemon juice
⅙ oz. lime juice

Combine with ice; shake well. Serve chilled. Garnish with cherry.

BLACK MARTINI

2 oz. Absolut Kurant
¼ oz. Chambord

Serve over ice or straight up in a chilled martini glass.

BLACK TIE MARTINI

2½ oz. Skyy Vodka
⅛ oz. each spritz of Campari &
  Chivas
two onions
black olive

Serve over ice or straight up in a chilled martini glass. Garnish with two onions and black olive.

BLENTON MARTINI

1½ oz. dry gin
¾ oz. dry vermouth
1 dash Angostura Bitters
twist of lemon peel

BLOOD OHRANJ MARTINI

3 parts Stolichnaya Ohranj
  Vodka
1 part Campari
splash club soda

Stirred over ice, served straight up chilled.

THE BLUE KETEL (MORTON'S OF CHICAGO, WASHINGTON DC)

2½ oz. Ketel One Vodka
⅛ oz. Bombay Sapphire
lemon twist

THE BLUE PLATE SPECIAL (HARRY DENTON'S)

3 oz. Bombay Gin
⅛ oz. Martini & Rossi Vermouth

Serve with three olives.

BLUE MOON MARTINI

3 parts classic Finlandia
3 parts Finlandia Pineapple
1 part Blue Liqueur

Garnish: orange zest.

BLUE SKYY MARTINI

2½ oz. Skyy Vodka
¼ oz. blue curacao
twist of lemon

Serve over ice or straight up in a chilled martini glass. Garnish with lemon twist.

BLUES MARTINI (ERIC LINQUEST, DIRECTOR OF OPERATIONS, EMERIL'S. MAGAZINE: MARKET WATCH)

½ oz. Ketel One Vodka
½ oz. Bombay Sapphire Gin
a few drops of blue curacao

BOMBAY MARTINI

1½ oz. Bombay Sapphire Gin
dash extra dry vermouth

Stir in cocktail glass with ice. Strain and serve straight up or on the rocks. Add lemon twist or olive.

BONNIE PRINCE MARTINI

1½ oz. dry gin
½ oz. Lillet
¼ oz. Drambuie

BOOMERANG MARTINI

4 parts dry gin
1 part French vermouth
1 part Italian vermouth
2 dashes maraschino cherry juice
twist of lemon peel

BOSTON BULLET MARTINI

2 oz. dry gin
½ oz. dry vermouth
almond-stuffed green olive

BRADFORD MARTINI

Combine dry gin and dry vermouth in favorite proportions in a cocktail shaker. Shake until frigid and pour.

BRONX COCKTAIL (STARS, SAN FRANCISCO)

⅛ oz. Martini & Rossi Extra Dry
⅛ oz. Rosso Vermouth
2 oz. Bombay Sapphire
splash of orange juice

Serve over ice or straight up in a chilled martini glass.

BRONX MARTINI

1 part dry gin
1 part Italian vermouth
1 part French vermouth
¼ orange

Combine the liquid ingredients, squeezing the orange quarter into a cocktail shaker. Drop in the squeezed orange. Shake with a cracked ice until chilled. Pour through a strainer into a frosted cocktail glass.

BRONX MARTINI (MR. BABBINGTON'S)

London Dry Gin
Martini & Rossi Extra Dry
  Vermouth
Martini & Rossi Rosso Vermouth
orange juice
twist of lemon

BROWN COCKTAIL MARTINI

¾ oz. dry gin
¾ oz. light rum
¾ oz. dry vermouth

BUFF MARTINI

5 parts classic Finlandia
1 part Baileys Irish Cream
1 part Kahlua

Garnish: sprinkle of freshly ground coffee or cinnamon.

CABARET COCKTAIL MARTINI

2 oz. dry gin
¼ oz. dry vermouth
¼ oz. Benedictine
2 dashes Angostura Bitters
cherry

CAJUN MARTINI

2½ oz. Absolut Peppar
⅛ oz. dry vermouth
habernero-stuffed olive

Serve over ice or straight up in a chilled martini glass. Garnish with a habernero-stuffed olive.

CAPITOL "K" MARTINI

2 oz. Ketel One Vodka
⅛ oz. Noilly Prat Vermouth

Stir and garnish with a Tomolive.

CAPRICE MARTINI

1½ oz. dry gin
½ oz. dry vermouth
½ oz. Benedictine
1 dash orange bitters

CASINO COCKTAIL MARTINI

2 oz. Old Tom Gin
2 dashes orange bitters
¼ oz. maraschino liqueur
¼ oz. lemon juice

CHICAGO MARTINI

2 oz. dry gin
½ oz. scotch
green olive

CHOCOLATE MARTINI

1 oz. Absolut Vodka
½ oz. Godiva Chocolate Liqueur

Shaken over ice. Strained into chilled martini glass with lemon twist garnish.

CITRON MARTINI

2½ oz. Absolut Citron Vodka

Serve over ice or in a chilled martini glass with a lemon twist.

CLASSIC DRY MARTINI

2 parts London dry gin
1 part French vermouth
1 dash orange bitters

CLASSIC MANHATTAN (MR. BABBINGTON'S)

2½ oz. Canadian whiskey
⅛ oz. Martini & Rossi Rosso
  Vermouth
1 cherry

Serve chilled, straight up.

CLASSIC MARTINI

2½ oz. Beefeaters Gin
⅛ oz. Noilly Prat Vermouth
dash orange bitters

Serve over ice or straight up in a chilled martini glass with a lemon twist

---

CLASSIC MARTINI (MR. BABBINGTON'S)

2½ oz. London dry gin
⅛ oz. Martini & Rossi Extra Dry
  Vermouth
Olive

THE CLASSIC OLIVE MARTINI (JEFF NACE, OLIVES. MAGAZINE: THE IMPROPER BOSTONIAN)

2½ oz. Ketel One Vodka
1 drop each dry vermouth and
  olive juice "to dirty it up"

Chill until it's "bone-rattling cold," strain into a glass and garnish with three "super-colossal Sicilian olives."

CLUB COCKTAIL MARTINI

1½ oz. dry gin
¾ oz. sweet vermouth
¼ oz. yellow Chartreuse
cherry or green olive

THE CONTINENTAL MARTINI

2½ oz. Stoli
⅛ oz. ghost of dry vermouth
lemon-stuffed olive

Serve over ice or straight up in a chilled martini glass with a lemon-stuffed olive garnish.

COOPERSTOWN MARTINI

4 parts dry gin
1 part French vermouth
1 part Italian vermouth
1 dash orange bitters
1 dash Angostura Bitters
sprig of mint bruised and stirred
  with each cocktail
twist of lemon peel

COPENHAGEN MARTINI

1 oz. dry gin
1 oz. aquavit
½ oz. dry vermouth
green olive

COPPER ILLUSION*

2 oz. gin
¼ oz. Grand Marnier
¼ oz. Campari
orange slice

Serve over ice or straight up in a chilled martini glass. Garnish with an orange slice.
*Sheraton Seattle Hotel & Towers

CORONET MARTINI

2 oz. dry gin
½ oz. sweet vermouth
½ oz. dry vermouth

COSMOPOLITAN MARTINI*

2 oz. vodka
¼ oz. blue curacao
¼ oz. cranberry juice
lemon twist

Serve over ice or straight up in a chilled martini glass. Garnish with a lemon twist.

COSMOPOLITAN MARTINI (KETEL ONE)

2 shots Ketel One Vodka
1 shot cointreau
squeeze ½ lime
splash of cranberry juice

Shake with ice, strain into chilled martini glass and garnish with a twist.

COYOTE MARTINI (COYOTE CAFE IN SANTA FE)

1 liter gin
3 serrano chilies

Add chilies to gin in the bottle and let sit for forty-eight hours or more at room temperature. Put the gin in the freezer until thoroughly chilled. Serve straight from the freezer in chilled shot glasses.

CRANBERRY MARTINI

1 part Godiva Liqueur
1 part Absolut Vodka
1 part cranberry juice

Combine with ice; shake well. Serve chilled. Garnish with lime twist.

CRANBERRY SAUCE MARTINI

1 oz. Stolichnaya Ohranj
¼ oz. cranberry juice

Garnish with cranberries that have been soaked in simple syrup.

———— ∞ ————

CRANTINI (HEART AND SOUL)

2½ oz. Bacardi Limon
splash (1 oz.) of cranberry juice
spritz (2 drops) of Martini & Rossi Dry Vermouth

Shake with ice and serve up with a twist of lemon.

———— ∞ ————

CRANTINI (MR. BABBINGTON'S)

2 oz. Bacardi Limon
⅛ oz. Martini & Rossi Extra Dry Vermouth
⅛ oz. cranberry
garnish: cranberries and lemon twist

Shake and serve over ice or straight up in a chilled martini glass. Garnish with cranberries and a lemon twist.

THE CRANTINI (STARS, SAN FRANCISO)

2½ oz. Bacardi Limon
a touch of Martini & Rossi Extra Dry Vemouth
splash of cranberry

Shake and serve over ice or straight up in a chilled martini glass. Garnish with dried cranberries and a lemon twist

———— ∞ ————

CROCKER MARTINI

1½ oz. dry gin
½ oz. sweet vermouth
½ oz. dry vermouth

———— ∞ ————

DEAN MARTINI

A big, chilled 2½ oz Ketel One, an olive, a Lucky Strike cigarette, and a book of matches.

———— ∞ ————

THE DECADENT MARTINI (MIKE BEAVER, BARTENDER AT THE METROPOLITAN GRILL. MAGAZINE: SEATTLE POST-INTELLIGENCER)

1 oz. Ketel One Vodka
1 oz. Tanqueray Gin
dash of Godiva Chocolate Liqueur

Stir and strain into a chilled martini glass. Garnish with an olive-shaped chocolate truffle (custom made for the Met by Fran's Chocolate's).

DEEP SEA MARTINI

1½ oz. Old Tom Gin
1 oz. dry vermouth
1 dash orange bitters
¼ oz. Pernod
twist of lemon peel

DELMONICO MARTINI

1 oz. dry gin
½ oz. dry vermouth
½ oz. sweet vermouth
½ oz. cognac
1 dash Angostura Bitters
orange peel

DEPTH CHARGE MARTINI

1¼ oz. dry gin
1¼ oz. Lillet
¼ oz. Pernod
orange peel

DERNIER ROUND MARTINI

1½ oz. dry gin
½ oz. dry vermouth
¼ oz. cognac
¼ oz. cointreau
1 dash Angostura Bitters

DEWEY MARTINI

1½ oz. dry gin
1¼ oz. dry vermouth
1 dash orange bitters

DIANA MARTINI

1½ oz. dry gin
¾ oz. dry vermouth
¼ oz. sweet vermouth
¼ oz. Pernod
twist of lemon peel

THE DICKENS MARTINI (HARRY DENTON'S)

2½ oz. Stolichnaya Ohranj
¹⁄₁₆ oz. Martini & Rossi Dry
  Vermouth

No olive or twist.

DICK ST. CLAIRE'S (NOSMO KING IN NEW YORK. MAGAZINE: PAPER GUIDE)

2½ oz. Ketel One Vodka
½ oz. Cherry Herring
freshly squeezed orange and lime
  juices

DILLATINI MARTINI

1½ oz. Absolut Vodka
dash Martini & Rossi Extra Dry
  Vermouth
dilly beam (try and find one)

THE DIRTY MARTINI (BURT & LINDA THORPE)

1½ oz. Ketel One Vodka, chilled
1 jumbo-sized hot spiced garlic
  green olive, chilled
1 capful of the juice from the
  olive jar, chilled

Shake gently, don't stir.

DIXIE MARTINI

2 oz. dry gin
¼ oz. dry vermouth
¼ oz. Pernod

DOUGLAS MARTINI

1¾ oz. dry gin
¾ oz. dry vermouth
orange peel or twist of lemon
  peel

DR. MONAHAN MARTINI

2 oz. dry gin
¼ oz. Pernod
1 dash orange bitters
twist of lemon peel

DRY MARTINI

2 oz. dry gin
½ oz. dry vermouth
green olive or twist of lemon peel

DU BARRY COCKTAIL

1½ oz. dry gin
¾ oz. dry vermouth
¼ oz. Pernod
1 dash Angostura Bitters
orange slice

THE DUTCH KETEL (MORTON'S OF CHICAGO, WASHINGTON DC)

3 oz. Ketel One Vodka
tom-olives

EDDIE BROWN MARTINI

1¾ oz. dry gin
¾ oz. Lillet
2 dashes apricot brandy
twist of lemon peel

EL PRESIDENTE MARTINI

1¾ oz. light rum
¾ oz. dry vermouth
1 dash Angostura Bitters

ELEGANT MARTINI

1¾ oz. dry gin
½ oz. dry vermouth
¼ oz. Grand Marnier

MARTINIS

ELEPHANT'S EAR MARTINI

2 oz. dry gin
¼ oz. dry vermouth
¾ oz. Dubonnet

Serve over ice or straight up in a chilled martini glass.

―⦈⦈⦈―

THE ELEVEN MARTINI (STARS, SAN FRANCISO)

2½ oz. Skyy Vodka
a touch of Martini & Rossi Extra Dry Vermouth

Shake and serve over ice or straight up in a chilled martini glass.

―⦈⦈⦈―

EMERALD CITY MARTINI*

2 oz. vodka
¼ oz. Midori
lime wheel

Serve over ice or straight up in a chilled martini glass. Garnish with a lime wheel.

―⦈⦈⦈―

EMERALD MARTINI (HEART AND SOUL)

2½ oz. Bacardi Limon
⅛ oz. Martini & Rossi Extra Dry Vermouth
Splash(4 drops) of Midori

THE ENCHANTED MARTINI

1 oz. Encantado Mezcal
¼ oz. dry vermouth
1 jalapeno stuffed olive

Shake over ice and strain into a martini glass.

―⦈⦈⦈―

ENOS MARTINI

1¾ oz. dry gin
¾ oz. dry vermouth
¼ oz. Pernod
cherry

―⦈⦈⦈―

ESCOBAR MARTINI

7 parts Tequila
1 part dry vermouth
green olive

―⦈⦈⦈―

FARE-THREE-WELL MARTINI

1¼ oz. dry gin
½ oz. dry vermouth
¼ oz. sweet vermouth
¼ oz. orange curacao

―⦈⦈⦈―

FARMER'S COCKTAIL MARTINI

1½ oz. dry gin
½ oz. sweet vermouth
½ oz. dry vermouth
2 dashes Angostura Bitters

FASCINATOR MARTINI

1¾ oz. dry gin
½ oz. dry vermouth
¼ oz. Pernod
sprig of mint

FERNET BRANCA COCKTAIL

1½ oz. dry gin
½ oz. sweet vermouth
½ oz. Fernet Branca
cherry

FIFTH AVENUE MARTINI

1½ oz. dry gin
½ oz. dry vermouth
½ oz. Fernet Branca

FIFTY FIFTY MARTINI

1¼ oz. dry gin
1¼ oz. dry vermouth
green olive

FIN DE SIECLE COCKTAIL

1½ oz. dry gin
¾ oz. sweet vermouth
¼ oz. Amer Picon
1 dash orange bitters

FINO MARTINI

2 oz. dry gin
½ oz. Fino Sherry
green olive or twist of lemon peel

FLYING DUTCHMAN MARTINI

7 parts dry gin
1 part French vermouth
2 dashes orange curacao

FOGGY DAY MARTINI

1½ oz. dry gin
¼ oz. Pernod
twist of lemon peel

Shake and pour over ice.

FOURTH DEGREE MARTINI

¾ oz. dry gin
¾ oz. dry vermouth
¾ oz. sweet vermouth
¼ oz. Pernod
twist of lemon peel

FRENCH KISS MARTINI

2 oz. Stolichnaya Ohranj Vodka
½ oz. Lillet

Serve over ice or straight up in a chilled martini glass.

FRENCH MARTINI

2 oz. Stolichnaya Ohranj
½ oz. Lillet
a twist

Serve over ice or straight up in a chilled martini glass. Garnish with a twist.

FUZZY NAVAL MARTINI (ED CARLO, BARTENDER, STAGE LEFT. MAGAZINE: HOME NEWS)

2 oz. Ketel One Vodka
½ oz. peach schnapps
½ oz. freshly squeezed orange juice
orange peel for garnish

GENE TUNNEY MARTINI

1¾ oz. dry gin
¾ oz. dry vermouth
1 dash lemon juice
1 dash orange juice
cherry

GENTLEMAN'S MANHATTAN (STARS, SAN FRANCISCO)

⅛ oz. Martini & Rossi Rosso Vermouth
2 ½ oz. Gentleman Jack Whiskey
¹⁄₁₆ oz. bitters
garnish: cherry

Serve over ice or straight up in a chilled martini glass. Garnish with a cherry.

THE GEORGETOWN (THE MARTINI BAR AT CHIANTI RESTAURANT, HOUSTON, TX)

2 oz. Ketel One Vodka
⅛ oz. Grand Marnier
Garnish—orange slice

Serve over ice or straight up in a chilled martini glass.

GIBSON

2 oz. Gordons Gin
⅛ oz. Cinzano Dry Vermouth
1 cured or cocktail onion

GIBSON GIRL MARTINI

1¼ oz. Old Tom Gin
1¼ oz. dry vermouth
twist of lemon peel

GIBSON MARTINI

7 parts dry gin
1 part French vermouth
cocktail onion

GIMLET MARTINI

1½ oz. Absolut Vodka
dash Rose's Lime Juice

Garnish with lime.

GIN AND FRENCH MARTINI

Coat the inside of a glass with dry vermouth. Fill the glass with 2¼ oz. dry gin.

———∞∞∞———

GIN MARTINI

2 oz. dry gin
2 dashes orange bitters
twist of lemon or orange peel

———∞∞∞———

GIN MARTINI (MR. BABBINGTON'S)

2½ oz. Bombay Sapphire Gin
touch (3 drops) of Martini &
  Rossi Extra Dry Vermouth

Shaken and served up.

———∞∞∞———

GIN 'N' IT MARTINI

3 parts dry gin
1 part Italian vermouth
twist of lemon peel

Put large ice cubes in an old-fashioned glass. Pour gin ¾ of the way up the glass. Pour vermouth over the gin to fill the glass. Twist a strip of lemon peel over the drink, splashing oil on the surface. Drop the peel into the glass. Serve with a swizzle stick.

GINKA MARTINI

1¼ oz. dry gin
1¼ oz. vodka
½ oz. dry vermouth
twist of lemon peel or green olive

———∞∞∞———

GLOOM CHASER MARTINI

5 parts dry gin
1 part French vermouth
2 dashes Pernod
2 dashes grenadine

———∞∞∞———

GOLD DIGGER MARTINI

5 parts Finlandia Pineapple
2 parts cointreau

———∞∞∞———

GOLDEN ERMINE MARTINI

1½ oz. dry gin
¾ oz. dry vermouth
¼ oz. sweet vermouth

———∞∞∞———

GOLDEN GIRL MARTINI

1¾ oz. dry gin
¾ oz. dry sherry
1 dash orange bitters
1 dash Angostura Bitters

———∞∞∞———

GOLDEN MARTINI

7 parts golden-colored dry gin
1 part French vermouth
twist of lemon peel

GOLF MARTINI
1¾ oz. dry gin
¾ oz. dry vermouth
2 dashes Angostura Bitters

GORDON MARTINI
5 parts dry gin
1 part Amontillado Sherry
cocktail onion

GREAT SECRET MARTINI
1¾ oz. dry gin
¾ oz. Lillet
1 dash Angostura Bitters
orange peel

GREENBRIER MARTINI
2 parts dry gin
1 part Italian vermouth
sprig of mint bruised and stirred
 with each cocktail
twist of lemon peel

GUARDS MARTINI
1¾ oz. dry gin
¾ oz. sweet vermouth
¼ oz. orange curacao
orange peel or cherry

GUNGA DIN MARTINI
3 parts dry gin
1 part dry vermouth
juice of ¼ orange

Shake. Garnish with a pineapple slice.

GYPSY MARTINI
1¼ oz. dry gin
1¼ oz. sweet vermouth
cherry

H AND H MARTINI
1¾ oz. dry gin
¾ oz. Lillet
¼ oz. orange curacao
orange peel

H.P.W. MARTINI
2 oz. dry gin
¼ oz. French vermouth
¼ oz. Italian vermouth
orange peel

HAKAM MARTINI
1¼ oz. dry gin
1¼ oz. sweet vermouth
¼ oz. orange curacao
1 dash orange bitters
cherry

HALF AND HALF MARTINI
3 parts dry gin
3 parts vodka
1 part French vermouth
twist of lemon peel

HANKY PANKY MARTINI
1¾ oz. dry gin
¾ oz. sweet vermouth
¼ oz. Fernet Branca
orange peel

HAROLD'S MARTINI (FOR THOSE WHO NEVER HAVE MORE THAN ONE)

4 oz. dry gin
½ oz. French vermouth
1 dash orange bitters

Stir and pour into a 6-oz. carafe. Bury the carafe in shaved ice and serve with a frosted cocktail glass and a stuffed green olive.

⸻

HARRY'S MARTINI

1¼ oz. dry gin
¾ oz. sweet vermouth
¼ oz. Pernod
2 sprigs of mint
mint leaf

⸻

HASTY COCKTAIL MARTINI

1¼ oz. dry gin
¾ oz. dry vermouth
¼ oz. grenadine
1 dash Pernod

⸻

HEARST MARTINI

1¼ oz. dry gin
1¼ oz. sweet vermouth
1 dash orange bitters
1 dash Angostura Bitters

HEART & SOUL CLASSIC MARTINI (HEART AND SOUL)

3 oz. Bombay Gin
⅛ oz. spritz of Martini & Rossi dry vermouth

Shaken with ice. Strain and serve up with a jumbo olive.

⸻

THE HENNESSY MARTINI (HARRY DENTON'S)

2½ oz. Hennessy V.S. Cognac
dash(4 drops) of lemon juice
twist

⸻

HILLIARD MARTINI

1¼ oz. dry gin
¾ oz. sweet vermouth
1 dash Peychaud's Bitters

⸻

HILLSBORO MARTINI

1¾ dry gin
¾ oz. dry vermouth
1 dash orange bitters
1 dash Angostura Bitters

⸻

HOFFMAN HOUSE MARTINI

1¾ oz. dry gin
¾ oz. French vermouth
2 dashes orange bitters
green olive

HOMESTEAD MARTINI

1¾ oz. dry gin
¾ oz. sweet vermouth
orange slice

Muddle fruit in glass or mixer.

HONG KONG MARTINI

2 parts dry gin
1 part French vermouth
¼ tsp. sugar syrup
1 tsp. lime juice
1 dash Angostura Bitters

HONOLULU HURRICANE MARTINI

4 parts dry gin
1 part French vermouth
1 part Italian vermouth
1 tsp. pineapple juice

Shake.

HOTEL PLAZA MARTINI

1 oz. dry gin
¾ oz. French vermouth
¾ oz. Italian vermouth

Fill a glass with ice. Garnish with a pineapple spear.

IMPERIAL MARTINI

1¼ oz. dry gin
1¼ oz. dry vermouth
1 dash Angostura Bitters
¼ tsp. maraschino liqueur
cherry or green olive

INCA MARTINI

¾ oz. dry gin
¾ oz. dry sherry
½ oz. French vermouth
½ oz. Italian vermouth
1 dash orgeat syrup
1 dash orange bitters

INDISPENSABLE MARTINI

1½ oz. dry gin
½ oz. French vermouth
½ oz. Italian vermouth
¼ oz. Pernod

INTERNATIONAL MARTINI

4 parts dry gin
1 part French vermouth
1 part Italian vermouth
2 dashes creme de cassis

ITALIAN MARTINI

2 parts Bombay Sapphire Gin
1 part Disaronno Amaretto

Stir on the rocks.

J.O.S. Martini

¾ oz. dry gin
¾ oz. dry vermouth
¾ oz. sweet vermouth
1 dash brandy
1 dash orange bitters
1 dash lemon juice
twist of lemon peel

Jack Sloat Martini

1½ oz. dry gin
½ oz. sweet vermouth
¼ oz. dry vermouth
2 slices pineapple

Shake.

Jackson Martini

1¼ oz. dry gin
1¼ oz. Dubonnet
2 dashes orange bitters

James Bond Martini

3 parts Gordon's Dry Gin
1 part vodka
½ part Kina Lillet

Shake. Add a large thin slice of lemon.

The James Bond Martini (Harry Denton's)

Three parts Bombay Gin
one part Stolichnaya
½ Lillet Blonde with a twist

"Shaken, not stirred."

Jeyplak Martini

1½ oz. dry gin
¾ oz. sweet vermouth
¼ oz. Pernod
twist of lemon peel.

Jimmy Blanc Martini

1¾ oz. dry gin
¾ oz. Lillet
¼ oz. Dubonnet
orange peel

Journalist Martini

1½ oz. dry gin
¼ oz. sweet vermouth
¼ oz. dry vermouth
1 dash Angostura Bitters
1 dash lemon juice
1 dash orange curacao

Jungle Martini

1 oz. dry gin
¾ oz. sweet vermouth
¾ oz. sherry

Juniper Martini

2 oz. dry gin
½ oz. dry vermouth
1 dash grenadine

Kahlua Martini

2 oz. dry gin
½ oz. Kahlua
twist of lemon peel

KANGAROO MARTINI

1¼ oz. vodka
¾ oz. dry vermouth
twist of lemon peel

―――∞∞∞―――

THE KETEL ONE MARTINI, STRAIGHT UP WITH A TWIST (ALEX LEHNEN, LES ZYGOMATES. MAGAZINE: THE IMPORPER BOSTONIAN)

Chill a martini glass with ice and vermouth. Shake Ketel One in a shaker with ice until frost forms on the outside. Dump ice and vermouth from the glass, strain in vodka, and garnish with a twist.

―――∞∞∞―――

KETEL ONE COSMOPOLITAN MARTINI (DIVISION SIXTEEN, BOSTON)

2 oz. Ketel One Vodka, chilled
½ oz. cointrerau
Hint of cranberry

―――∞∞∞―――

KETEL WHISTLE (AJAX LOUNGE. MAGAZINE: SAN JOSE MERCURY)

3 oz. Ketel One Vodka
¼ oz. lime juice
¼ oz. cranberry juice
¼ oz. cointreau

KINA MARTINI

½ oz. dry gin
½ oz. sweet vermouth
½ oz. Kina Lillet
cherry

―――∞∞∞―――

KISS IN THE DARK (STARS, SAN FRANCISCO)

2 oz. Bacardi Limon
⅛ oz. Martini & Rossi Extra Dry
¼ oz. cherry brandy

Serve over ice or straight up in a chilled martini glass.

―――∞∞∞―――

K-TING (NICK AND EDDIE, NEW YORK)

2 oz. Ketel One Vodka
¼ oz. Ting (a grapefruit soda imported from Jamaica)

Serve over ice or straight up in a chilled martini glass.

―――∞∞∞―――

KUP'S INDISPENSABLE MARTINI

1½ oz. dry gin
½ oz. Italian vermouth
½ oz. French vermouth
1 dash bitters
orange peel

―――∞∞∞―――

LADIES' CHOICE MARTINI

1½ oz. dry gin
½ oz. dry vermouth
¼ oz. Kummel

LAMB'S CLUB MARTINI

4 parts dry gin
1 part French vermouth
1 part Italian vermouth
2 dashes Benedictine
twist of lemon peel

LAST ROUND MARTINI

1 oz. dry gin
1 oz. dry vermouth
¼ oz. brandy
¼ oz. Pernod

LEAP YEAR MARTINI

1¼ oz. dry gin
½ oz. orange-flavored gin
½ oz. sweet vermouth
¼ oz. lemon juice

LEMONTINI

cointreau
2 oz. Stolichnaya Limonnaya
  Vodka
½ oz. dry vermouth

Line a cocktail glass with cointreau and pour out excess. Combine Limonnaya Vodka and vermouth over ice in a mixing glass, strain into the cocktail glass.

LIAR'S COCKTAIL MARTINI

1½ oz. dry gin
½ oz. dry vermouth
¼ oz. orange curacao
¼ oz. sweet vermouth

LICIA ALBANESE MARTINI

1½ oz. dry gin
½ oz. Campari
twist of lemon peel

Serve over ice.

LILLET COCKTAIL

1½ oz. Lillet
1 oz. dry gin
twist of lemon peel

LIME LIGHT MARTINI

6 parts classic Finlandia
1 part grapefruit juice
1 part Midori Liqueur

Garnish: thinly sliced lemon and lime twists.

LIMON MARTINI (MR. BABBINGTON'S)

2½ oz. Bacardi Limon
⅛ oz. Martini & Rossi Extra Dry
  Vermouth
⅛ oz. Martini & Rossi Rosso
  Vermouth
dash of bitters
a twist

LIMON TWIST (MR. BABBINGTON'S)

2 oz. Bacardi Limon
½ oz. cointreau
⅛ oz. Martini & Rossi Extra Dry
  Vermouth
wedge of fresh lemon

Serve over ice or straight up in a chilled martini glass. Garnish with fresh lemon wedge.

LONE TREE MARTINI

2 parts dry gin
1 part Italian vermouth
1 dash lemon juice

LOUIS MARTINI

1½ oz. dry gin
½ oz. dry vermouth
¼ oz. Grand Marnier
¼ oz. cointreau

LOYAL MARTINI (BAR D'O, 29 BEDFORD STREET)

2½ oz. Ketel One Vodka (5 Tbsp.)
dash vermouth
20 drops 20-year-old balsamic
  vinegar

Garnish with a black olive (not pitted). Shake vermouth with ice, then strain, leaving ice coated with vermouth. Add vodka and shake. Strain into martini glass and gently stir in vinegar. Garnish with black olive.

LOYAL MARTINI (BAR D'O, COCKTAIL BAR. MAGAZINE: NEW YORK POST)

2/12 oz. Ketel One Vodka
3 drops of very expensive
  Balsamic vinegar

LUCIEN GAUDIN MARTINI

1 oz. dry gin
½ oz. cointreau
½ oz. Campari
½ oz. dry vermouth

MANDARIN MARTINI

1 oz. dry gin
1 oz. dry vermouth
¼ oz. orange curacao
¼ oz. Mandarinette

MANDARIN MARTINI (RHETT DUCHARME, BARTENDER AT THE RACINE. MAGAZINE: CHEERS)

2 oz. Ketel One Vodka
1 oz. Mandarin Napoleon
  Liqueur

Pour ingredients over ice in a mixing glass. Stir and strain into an iced martini glass. Garnish with a cherry.

MARGUERITE MARTINI
2 parts dry gin
1 part dry vermouth
1 dash Angostura Bitters
twist of orange peel
maraschino cherry

MARTINEZ MARTINI
1¼ oz. dry gin
1¼ oz. sweet vermouth
1 dash bitters
1 dash sugar syrup

MARTINI
1¾ oz. dry gin
¾ oz. dry vermouth
green olive

MARTINI BELLINI*
2 oz. Vodka
¼ oz. peach schnapps
twist

Serve over ice or straight up in a chilled martini glass. Garnish with a twist.

MARTINI HOLLAND-STYLE
2 oz. Dutch gin
½ oz. dry vermouth
twist of lemon peel

MARTINI PICANTE*
2½ oz. Absolut Pepper Vodka
jalapeno and olive

Serve over ice or straight up in a chilled martini glass. Garnish with a jalapeno and an olive.

MARTINI SPECIAL (SERVES SIX)
8 jiggers dry gin
3 jiggers Italian vermouth
⅔ jigger orange flower water
1 dash Angostura Bitters

Stir and serve with maraschino cherries.

MAURICE MARTINI
2 parts dry gin
1 part French vermouth
1 part Italian vermouth
juice of ¼ orange
1 dash Angostura Bitters

MAXIM MARTINI
2 parts dry gin
1 part Italian vermouth
2 dashes white creme de cacao

MECCA MARTINI
¾ oz. dry gin
¾ oz. dry vermouth
½ oz. orange juice

Shake.

MEDIUM MARTINI

4 parts dry gin
1 part French vermouth
1 part Italian vermouth
1 dash orange bitters
1 dash Angostura Bitters

MERRY WIDOWER MARTINI

1 part dry gin
1 part dry vermouth
2 dashes Benedictine
1 dash Peychaud's Bitters
2 dashes Pernod
twist of lemon peel

MERRY-GO-ROUND MARTINI

1½ oz. dry gin
½ oz. sweet vermouth
½ oz. dry vermouth
green olive
twist of lemon peel

MICKEY FINN MARTINI

1 oz. dry gin
1 oz. dry vermouth
¼ oz. Pernod
¼ oz. white creme de menthe
sprig of mint

MIDNIGHT EXPRESS MARTINI

2 parts Bombay Sapphire Gin
1 part Caffe Sport Espresso
  Liqueur

Garnish with a few coffee beans.

MIDNIGHT MARTINI

¾ oz. dry gin
¾ oz. sweet vermouth
¾ oz. dry vermouth
¼ oz. Pernod
1 dash orange juice

MIDNIGHT SUN MARTINI

5 parts Finlandia Cranberry
1 part Classic Finlandia
1 part Kahlua

MINNEHAHA MARTINI

1 oz. dry gin
½ oz. dry vermouth
½ oz. sweet vermouth
½ oz. orange juice

Float a teaspoonful of Pernod on the surface.

MINT MARTINI

1 part Godiva Liqueur
1 part Absolut Vodka
splash of white creme de menthe

Combine with ice; shake well. Serve chilled. Garnish with mint leaf.

MINTINI

2 parts Bombay Gin
1 part white creme de menthe

Garnish with mint sprig.

THE MISSION IMPOSSIBLE MARTINI (HARRY DENTON'S)

3 oz. Ketel One Vodka

MO COCKTAIL (MO MCLAUGHLIN, ANCHOVIES. MAGAZINE: THE IMPROPER BOSTONIAN)

2½ oz. Ketel One Vodka
¼ oz. Chambord
5 squeezes of lemon juice

Chill until very cold and serve straight up with a twist.

MODDER COCKTAIL

1½ oz. dry gin
½ oz. dry vermouth
½ oz. Dubonnet
twist of lemon peel

MODERN DRY MARTINI

3 oz. Bombay Sapphire Gin or
  Stolichnaya Cristall
½ oz. dry vermouth

Garnish with lemon twist or olive.

MONTGOMERY MARTINI

2½ oz. Tanqueray Gin
splash Cinzano Dry Vermouth

Serve over ice or straight up in a chilled martini glass with a lemon twist.

MONTPELIER MARTINI

1¼ oz. dry gin
¾ oz. dry vermouth
cocktail onion

MOONSHINE MARTINI

1¾ oz. dry gin
½ oz. dry vermouth
¼ oz. maraschino liqueur
2 dashes Pernod

THE MYSTICAL MARTINI (STARS OF SAN FRANCISCO)

1 oz. Encantado Mezcal
¼ oz. Lillet

Shake over ice and strain into martini glass. Add a long twist of lemon or orange.

NAKED GLACIER MARTINI

7 parts Classic Finlandia
splash peppermint schnapps

Garnish: frost rim of martini glass with superfine sugar.

NAKED MARTINI

3 oz. dry gin
twist of lemon peel or green olive

NAVAL COCKTAIL

1¼ oz. dry gin
1¼ oz. sweet vermouth
cocktail onion
twist of lemon peel

NAVAL COCKTAIL MARTINI

1½ oz. Absolut Vodka
dash Rosso Vermouth
onion
twist

NEGRONI (STARS, SAN FRANCISCO)

2 oz. Bombay Sapphire Gin
⅛ oz. Martini & Rossi Rosso
  Vermouth
⅛ oz. Campari
⅛ Stoli Ohranj

Serve over ice or straight up in
a chilled martini glass.

NEGRONI MARTINI

1 oz. dry gin
1 oz. sweet vermouth
1 oz. Campari

NEW YORKER MARTINI

1½ oz. dry vermouth
½ oz. dry gin
½ oz. dry sherry
1 dash cointreau

NEWBERRY MARTINI

1 oz. dry gin
1 oz. sweet vermouth
½ oz. orange curacao
twist of lemon or orange peel

NINETEEN TWENTY MARTINI

1½ oz. dry gin
½ oz. dry vermouth
½ oz. kirschwasser
1 dash orange bitters
1 dash Groseille syrup

NOME MARTINI

7 parts dry gin
1 part dry sherry
1 dash chartreuse

NUMBER 3 MARTINI

1¾ oz. dry gin
½ oz. dry vermouth
1 dash orange bitters
¼ oz. anisette

NUMBER 6 MARTINI

1¾ oz. dry gin
½ oz. sweet vermouth
¼ oz. orange curacao
twist of lemon peel
orange peel
cherry

NUTTY MARTINI

1 part Godiva Liqueur
1 part Absolut Vodka
splash of Frangelico or amaretto
  liqueur

Combine with ice; shake well.
Serve chilled. Garnish with
three almonds.

OHRANJ MARTINI

1½ oz. Stolichnaya Ohranj Vodka
dash extra dry vermouth
splash triple sec
orange peel

Shake with ice and strain.
Serve up or on the rocks.

OLD ETONIAN MARTINI

1¼ oz. dry gin
1¼ oz. Lillet
2 dashes orange bitters
2 dashes creme de noyaux
orange peel

THE OLD SCHOOL (HARRY DENTON'S)

2½ oz. Bombay Sapphire Gin
⅛ oz. of Martini & Rossi
  Vermouth
onion

OLYMPIC MARTINI

1¾ oz. dry gin
½ oz. sweet vermouth
¼ oz. Pernod

ONE EXCITING NIGHT MARTINI

¾ oz. dry gin
¾ oz. dry vermouth
¾ oz. sweet vermouth
¼ oz. orange juice
twist of lemon peel

Coat the rim of the glass with
sugar before mixing.

ONE OF MINE MARTINI

1 oz. dry gin
½ oz. sweet vermouth
½ oz. dry vermouth
½ oz. orange juice
1 dash bitters

ORANGETINI MARTINI

1½ oz. Absolut Vodka
dash Martini & Rossi Extra Dry
  Vermouth
splash Hiram Walker Triple Sec
orange peel

ORIGINAL MARTINI (MARTINEZ)

1 wineglass sweet vermouth
1 pony Old Tom Gin
2 dashes bitters
1 dash maraschino liqueur

Shake with two small lumps of ice. Add a quarter slice of lemon and serve.

PACIFIC-UNION CLUB MARTINI

5 parts Old Tom Gin
1 part dry vermouth
twist of lemon peel or green olive

PAISLEY MARTINI

2¼ oz. dry gin
¼ oz. dry vermouth
1 dash scotch

PALL MALL MARTINI

¾ oz. dry gin
¾ oz. dry vermouth
¾ oz. sweet vermouth
¼ oz. white creme de menthe
1 dash orange bitters

PARISIAN MARTINI

5 parts dry gin
1 part French vermouth
3 dashes creme de cassis
twist of lemon peel

PEAR MARTINI

2 parts Stolichnaya Vodka
1 part Perle de Brillet Liqueur

Garnish with slice of pear.

PEGGY MARTINI

1½ oz. dry gin
¾ oz. dry vermouth
¼ oz. Pernod
¼ oz. Dubonnet

PEPPAR MARTINI

2½ oz. Absolut Peppar Vodka
splash Cinzano Dry Vermouth
jalapeno-stuffed olive

Serve over ice or straight up in a chilled martini glass. Garnish with a jalapeno-stuffed olive.

PEPPERTINI

1½ oz. Pertsovka
½ oz. dry vermouth
olive

Mix Pertsovka and dry vermouth in cocktail shaker over ice and stir. Strain, leaving out ice and pour into stemmed glass. Add olive for garnish.

PERFECT MARTINI

2 oz. dry gin
¼ oz. French vermouth
¼ oz. Italian vermouth
1 dash bitters
twist of lemon peel

PERFECT ROYAL

¾ oz. dry gin
¾ oz. dry vermouth
¾ oz. sweet vermouth
¼ oz. Pernod
green cherry

———∞∞———

PERFECTION MARTINI

1 3/4 oz. dry gin
1/2 oz. sweet vermouth
1/2 oz. orange juice

———∞∞———

PERNOD MARTINI

2 oz. dry gin
½ oz. dry vermouth
1 dash Pernod

———∞∞———

PHANTOM MARTINI (MORTON'S "MARTINI CLUB." MAGAZINE: NORTH SAN ANTONIO TIMES)

2½ oz. Ketel One Vodka
splash of Johnny Walker Black
  Label
jumbo black olive

———∞∞———

PICCADILLY MARTINI

1½ oz. dry gin
¾ oz. dry vermouth
¼ oz. Pernod
1 dash grenadine

PINK DIAMOND MARTINI

1 part Finlandia Cranberry
2 parts Finlandia Pineapple
3 parts Classic Finlandia
1 part peach schnapps

Garnish: the perfect cherry, or fresh nasturtium or rose petals floated on top.

———∞∞———

PINK GIN MARTINI

Fill an old-fashioned glass with cracked ice. Add 2 dashes bitters and 2½ oz. dry gin.

———∞∞———

PLAZA MARTINI

¾ oz. dry gin
¾ oz. dry vermouth
¾ oz. sweet vermouth.

Shake with ice. Add a slice of pineapple.

———∞∞———

PLYMOUTH COCKTAIL MARTINI

2½ oz. dry gin
2 dashes orange bitters

———∞∞———

POET'S DREAM MARTINI

1 oz. dry gin
¾ oz. dry vermouth
¾ oz. Benedictine
twist of lemon peel

POLO MARTINI

1 oz. dry gin
½ oz. dry vermouth
½ oz. sweet vermouth
½ oz. lime juice

POM POM MARTINI

1½ oz. dry vermouth
¾ oz. dry gin
2 dashes orange bitters

PRINCETON MARTINI

1½ oz. dry gin
1 oz. port
2 dashes orange bitters
twist of lemon peel

THE PROHIBITION MARTINI (HARRY DENTON'S)

bathtub gin or vodka
the right touch of Martini &
 Rossi Vermouth

PSYCHEDELIC MARTINI

6 parts dry gin
1 part French vermouth
1 part Italian vermouth
1/2 part orange juice
1/2 part pineapple juice
1 dash anisette

Shake.

PUNT E MES NEGRONI

¾ oz. dry gin
¾ oz. sweet vermouth
¾ oz. Punt e Mes
twist of lemon peel

PURITAN MARTINI

1¾ oz. dry gin
½ oz. dry vermouth
¼ oz. yellow Chartreuse
1 dash orange bitters

QUEEN ELIZABETH MARTINI

1¾ oz. dry gin
½ oz. dry vermouth
¼ oz. Benedictine

QUEEN MARTINI

2 parts dry gin
1 part Italian vermouth
1 part French vermouth
1 dash orange bitters
1 dash Angostura bitters

RACQUET CLUB MARTINI

1¾ oz. dry gin
¾ oz. dry vermouth
1 dash orange bitters
orange peel

RAIDME MARTINI

1¾ oz. dry gin
½ oz. Pernod
¼ oz. Campari

RAMON MARTINI

1½ oz. dry gin
½ oz. dry vermouth
½ oz. Hercules

RANCH STYLE MARTINI*

2 oz. vodka or gin
½ oz. Patron Tequila
pickled olive

Serve over ice or straight up in a chilled martini glass. Garnish with a pickled olive.

RASPBERRY MARTINI

1 part Godiva Liqueur
1 part Absolut Vodka
splash Chambord or raspberry
 liqueur

Combine with ice; shake well. Serve chilled. Garnish with powdered sugar-dipped glass rim.

RATTLER MARTINI

¾ oz. dry gin
¾ oz. French vermouth
¾ oz. Italian vermouth
½ oz. orange juice

RCA SPECIAL MARTINI

1½ oz. dry gin
½ oz. dry vermouth
2 dashes orange bitters
orange peel

RENDEZVOUS MARTINI

1½ oz. dry gin
½ oz. kirschwasser
¼ oz. Campari
twist of lemon peel

REX MARTINI

1¾ oz. dry gin
¾ oz. sweet vermouth
1 dash orange bitters

RICHMOND MARTINI

1½ oz. Absolut Vodka
dash Lillet
twist of lemon

RICHMOND MARTINI

1¾ oz. dry gin
¾ oz. Lillet
twist of lemon peel

ROLLER DERBY MARTINI

1¾ oz. dry gin
¼ oz. dry vermouth
¼ oz. sweet vermouth
¼ oz. Benedictine

ROLLS ROYA MARTINI

1¼ oz. dry gin
½ oz. sweet vermouth
½ oz. dry vermouth
¼ oz. Benedictine

ROLLS-ROYCE MARTINI

1½ oz. dry gin
½ oz. dry vermouth
½ oz. sweet vermouth
2 dashes Benedictine

———— ∞∞∞ ————

ROMA MARTINI

1½ oz. dry gin
½ oz. sweet vermouth
½ oz. dry vermouth
3 fresh strawberries
 mixed with drink

———— ∞∞∞ ————

ROSA MARTINI

1½ oz. dry gin
½ oz. dry vermouth
½ oz. cherry-flavored brandy

———— ∞∞∞ ————

ROSALIN RUSSELL MARTINI

1½ oz. Absolut Vodka
dash aquavit

———— ∞∞∞ ————

ROSE DU BOY MARTINI

1½ oz. dry gin
½ oz. dry vermouth
¼ oz. cherry-flavored brandy
¼ oz. kirschwasser

———— ∞∞∞ ————

ROSE MARIE MARTINI

1¼ oz. dry gin
½ oz. dry vermouth
¼ oz. Armagnac
¼ oz. cherry-flavored brandy
¼ oz. Campari

ROSELYN MARTINI

1¾ oz. dry gin
½ oz. dry vermouth
¼ oz. grenadine
twist of lemon peel

———— ∞∞∞ ————

ROSINGTON MARTINI

1¾ oz. dry gin
¾ oz. sweet vermouth
orange peel

———— ∞∞∞ ————

ROYAL COCKTAIL

1¾ oz. dry gin
¾ oz. Dubonnet
1 dash orange bitters
1 dash Angostura Bitters

———— ∞∞∞ ————

RUM MARTINI

5 parts light rum
1 part French vermouth
twist of lemon peel

———— ∞∞∞ ————

SAKETINI

2 oz. dry gin
½ oz. sake
twist of lemon peel

———— ∞∞∞ ————

SALOME MARTINI

1 oz. dry gin
¾ oz. dry vermouth
¾ oz. Dubonnet

SAN MARTIN

¾ oz. dry gin
¾ oz. dry vermouth
¾ oz. sweet vermouth
¼ oz. anisette
1 dash bitters

SAPPHIRE MARTINI

Bombay Sapphire Gin
Noilly Prat Vermouth
olive

THE SAPPHIRE (TONY ROMA'S, BARTENDER'S DRINK. MAGAZINE: HAWAII BEVERAGE GUIDE)

2 oz. Ketel One Vodka
½ oz. cointreau
½ oz. sweet & sour
½ oz. triple sec
squeeze of fresh lemon and fresh lime
⅛ oz. blue curacao

Serve over ice or straight up in a chilled martini glass.

SATAN'S WHISKERS MARTINI

½ oz. dry gin
½ oz. dry vermouth
½ oz. sweet vermouth
½ oz. orange juice
¼ oz. Grand Marnier
¼ oz. orange bitters

SAVOY HOTEL SPECIAL

1½ oz. dry gin
½ oz. dry vermouth
1 dash Pernod
2 dashes grenadine
twist of lemon peel

SAVOY MARTINI

1¾ oz. dry gin
½ oz. dry vermouth
¼ oz. Dubonnet
orange peel

SCARLETTINI (GLENN'S RESTAURANT & COOL BAR, NEWBURYPORT, MA)

2 oz. Ketel One Vodka
⅛ oz. Bonny Doon's Raspberry Wine

Serve over ice or straight up in a chilled martini glass.

SCHNOZZLE MARTINI

¾ oz. dry gin
¾ oz. dry vermouth
½ oz. cocktail sherry
¼ oz. Pernod
¼ oz. orange curacao

MARTINIS

SELF-STARTER MARTINI

1½ oz. dry gin
¾ oz. Lillet
¼ oz. apricot-flavored brandy
2 dashes Pernod

SEVENTH REGIMENT

1¾ oz. dry gin
¾ oz. sweet vermouth
2 twists of lemon peel

Stir twists with drink.

SHERRY COCKTAIL

2 oz. dry sherry
½ oz. dry vermouth
2 dashes orange bitters

SILK PANTIES (BOSTON)

2½ oz. Ketel One Vodka
½ oz. peach schnapps

SILVER BULLET

2 parts Bombay Gin or
  Stolichnaya Vodka
1 part dry vermouth

Float of scotch on top. Garnish with lemon twist or olive.

SILVER BULLET MARTINI

2 oz. dry gin
¼ oz. dry vermouth

Stir. Float ¼ oz. scotch on the surface.

SILVER COCKTAIL

1 oz. dry gin
1 oz. dry vermouth
2 dashes orange bitters
¼ tsp. sugar
¼ oz. maraschino liqueur
twist of lemon peel

SKYY COSMOPOLITAN (HEART AND SOUL)

2½ oz. Skyy Vodka
⅛ oz. fresh lime juice
⅛ oz. splash of cointreau
½ oz. splash of cranberry juice

Shake and serve up with a lime squeeze.

SKYY HIGH MARTINI (HEART AND SOUL)

Skyy Vodka
spritz of Martini & Rossi Dry
  Vermouth

Shake with ice. Strain and serve up with a jumbo olive.

SMILER MARTINI

1¼ oz. dry gin
½ oz. dry vermouth
½ oz. sweet vermouth
¼ oz. orange juice
1 dash Angostura Bitters

Shake.

SMOKY MARTINI

7 parts dry gin
1 part scotch
twist of lemon peel

SNYDER MARTINI

1¾ oz. dry gin
½ oz. dry vermouth
¼ oz. orange curacao
orange peel

SO SO MARTINI

¾ oz. dry gin
¾ oz. sweet vermouth
½ oz. apple brandy
½ oz. grenadine

SOCIETY MARTINI

1¾ oz. dry gin
½ oz. dry vermouth
¼ oz. grenadine

SOME MOTHER MARTINI

1¾ oz. dry gin
½ oz. dry vermouth
¼ oz. Pernod
cocktail onion

SOUR KISSES MARTINI

1½ oz. Absolut Vodka
dash Martini & Rossi Extra Dry
 Vermouth

Add egg white. Shake.

SOUR KISSES MARTINI

1¾ oz. dry gin
¾ oz. dry vermouth
1 egg white

Shake.

SOUTHERN GIN COCKTAIL

2¼ oz. dry gin
¼ oz. orange curacao
2 dashes orange bitters

SOVIET SALUTE MARTINI

1 oz. vodka
¾ oz. dry vermouth
¾ oz. dry sherry

SPHINX MARTINI

2 oz. dry gin
¼ oz. sweet vermouth
¼ oz. dry vermouth
lemon wedge

STARLIGHT MARTINI

1¾ oz. dry gin
¾ oz. orange curacao
1 dash Angostura Bitters

Shake.

MARTINIS

STOLI BIKINI MARTINI (BOB BLUMER)

Pour 4 oz. Stoli Ohranj into martini shaker. Add a generous splash (½ oz.) of Framboise. Fill shaker with ice. Shake or stir vigorously. Strain liquid into martini glasses. Garnish with a raspberry.

STOLI CRISTALL BLACK MARBLE MARTINI

2 oz. Stolichnaya Cristall Vodka
black olive marinated in dry vermouth

Shake Stolichnaya Cristall over ice, strain into frosted martini glass, add black olive.

STOLI OH WHAT A NIGHT MARTINI

1½ oz. Stolichnaya Ohranj
splash of Caffe Sport Espresso Liqueur

Shake and strain and serve straight up or on the rocks in a cocktail glass. Garnish with an orange slice.

STOLI POWER MARTINI

1½ oz. Stolichnaya Ohranj Vodka
½ oz. lemon juice
3 oz. orange juice
1 oz. raspberry syrup

Pour ingredients into a mixing glass, add ice and shake well. Strain into a chilled martini glass and garnish with orange peel.

STOLICHNAYA PARADISE MARTINI

2 parts Stolichnaya Ohranj
1 part orange juice

Shake with ice. Pour into martini glass. Garnish with orange slice.

STRAIGHT LAW MARTINI

1¾ oz. dry sherry
¾ oz. dry gin
twist of lemon peel

STRAWBERRY BLONDE MARTINI

7 parts dry gin
1 part Chambraise Strawberry Aperitif
twist of lemon peel

SUBMARINE MARTINI

1½ oz. dry gin
½ oz. Dubonnet
½ oz. dry vermouth
1 dash Boker's Bitters

SUNSHINE MARTINI

1¾ oz. dry gin
¾ oz. sweet vermouth
1 dash bitters
twist of orange peel

SWEET MARTINI

2 parts dry gin
1 part Italian vermouth
1 dash orange bitters
1 dash Angostura Bitters

TAMMANY MARTINI

¾ oz. dry gin
¾ oz. dry vermouth
¾ oz. sweet vermouth
¼ oz. Pernod

TEENY WEENY CHOCOLATE MARTINI (BOSTON)

2½ oz. Ketel One Vodka
½ oz. white creme de cacao
1 chocolate truffle garnish

TEQUINI

2 oz. tequila
½ oz. dry vermouth
green olive or twist of lemon peel

THIRD DEGREE MARTINI

1½ oz. dry gin
¾ oz. dry vermouth
¼ oz. Pernod

TIO PEPE MARTINI

7 parts dry gin
1 part Tio Pepe Sherry
twist of lemon peel

TONIGHT OR NEVER MARTINI

1 oz. dry gin
1 oz. dry vermouth
½ oz. cognac

TOPAZ MARTINI

5 parts Classic Finlandia
1 part creme de cacao (not clear)
1 part Frangelico

Garnish: float three whole roasted coffee beans in glass.

TOPAZ MARTINI (HEART AND SOUL)

2½ oz. Bacardi Limon
⅛ oz. Martini & Rossi Extra Dry Vermouth
⅛ oz. splash of curacao

TRILBY MARTINI

1¼ oz. dry gin
1 oz. sweet vermouth
2 dashes orange bitters

Stir. Float ¼ oz. Creme d'Yvette on the surface.

TRINITY AKA TRIO, PLAZA MARTINI

1½ oz. Absolut Vodka
half rosso and half extra dry
 vermouth
equal parts vermouth and
 Absolut Vodka

TRINITY MARTINI

1 oz. dry gin
¾ oz. dry vermouth
¾ oz. sweet vermouth

TRIO MARTINI

¾ oz. dry gin
¾ oz. dry vermouth
¾ oz. sweet vermouth

TURF MARTINI

1 oz. dry gin
1 oz. dry vermouth
¼ oz. Pernod
2 dashes Angostura Bitters
orange peel

TUXEDO MARTINI

1¼ oz. dry gin
1¼ oz. dry vermouth
¼ oz. maraschino liqueur
¼ tsp. Pernod
2 dashes orange bitters
twist of lemon peel

UNDER THE VOLCANO MARTINI (HARRY DENTON'S)

The Encantado Martini – 2½ oz.
 100% Mescal
⅛ oz. Martini & Rossi Vermouth
one large jalapeño

UNION LEAGUE MARTINI

1¼ oz. Old Tom Gin
¾ oz. port wine
1 dash orange bitters

THE ULTIMATE MARTINI (KETEL ONE VODKA SIGNATURE MARTINI)

Ketel One
Tomolive (no, it's not an olive)

This zesty little pickled green tomato has a lively crunch and a tangy burst of flavor that's sure to please.

UPISSIPPI MARTINI

1½ oz. dry gin
½ oz. sweet vermouth
½ oz. dry vermouth
¼ oz. grenadine

VAMPIRE MARTINI
1 oz. dry gin
1 oz. dry vermouth
½ oz. lime juice

Shake.

VAN MARTINI
1¾ oz. dry gin
½ oz. dry vermouth
¼ oz. Grand Marnier

VANCOUVER MARTINI
1½ oz. dry gin
¾ oz. sweet vermouth
¼ oz. Benedictine
1 dash orange bitters

Shake.

VELOCITY MARTINI
1½ oz. Absolut Vodka
dash Martini & Rossi Extra Dry
 Vermouth

Add orange slice and shake.

VELOCITY MARTINI
1½ oz. sweet vermouth
¾ oz. dry gin
orange slice

Shake.

VENDOME MARTINI
1 oz. dry gin
1 oz. Dubonnet
½ oz. dry vermouth
twist of lemon peel

VERMOUTH RINSE MARTINI

Coat the inside of a glass with dry vermouth. Shake off the excess. Fill the glass with chilled dry gin. Add a twist of lemon peel or a green olive.

VERMOUTH TRIPLE SEC MARTINI
1 oz. dry vermouth
1 oz. dry gin
½ oz. triple sec
2 dashes orange bitters
twist of lemon peel

VERY DRY MARTINI
5 parts dry gin
1 part French vermouth
twist of lemon peel

VESPER MARTINI
1 oz. Gordons Gin
1 oz. Gordons Vodka
½ oz. Blonde Lillet
garnish: lemon twist

Serve over ice or straight up in a chilled martini glass. Garnish with a lemon twist.

VICTOR MARTINI
1½ oz. dry vermouth
½ oz. dry gin
½ oz. brandy

VIOLETTA MARTINI

5 parts Classic Finlandia
1 part cranberry juice cocktail
splash blue curacao liqueur

VIP MARTINI

Fill a stemmed cocktail glass
with chilled dry gin. Waft a
fine spray of dry vermouth
gently on the surface from an
atomizer. Add a twist of
lemon peel or a green olive.

VODKA GIBSON

2 oz. vodka
½ oz. dry vermouth
cocktail onion

VODKA MARTINI

2 oz. vodka
½ oz. dry vermouth
twist of lemon peel or green olive

VODKA MARTINI (MR. BABBINGTON'S)

Stolichnaya Vodka
touch of Martini & Rossi Extra
 Dry Vermouth

Shake and serve up.

WALLICK MARTINI

1¼ oz. dry gin
1¼ oz. dry vermouth
¼ oz. orange curacao

WALTER MARTINI

5 parts dry gin
½ part dry vermouth
½ part dry sherry
2 drops lemon juice

WARDEN MARTINI

1½ oz. dry gin
½ oz. dry vermouth
½ oz. Pernod

WEMBLEY MARTINI

1½ oz. dry gin
¾ oz. dry vermouth
¼ oz. apple brandy
1 dash apricot-flavored brandy

WHITE CHOCOLATE MARTINI

2½ oz. vodka
½ oz. white creme de cacao

Serve over ice or straight up in
a chocolate-rimmed martini
glass.

WHITE CHOCOLATE MARTINI (DIVISION SIXTEEN, BOSTON)

Ketel One Vodka
white creme de cacao

WHITE PELICAN MARTINI

1¾ oz. dry gin
½ oz. dry vermouth
¼ oz. sweet vermouth

— ∞∞ —

WHITE STALLION MARTINI

2½ oz. Stolichnaya Vodka
⅛ oz. dry vermouth
pearl onion

Serve over ice or straight up in a chilled martini glass. Garnish with a pearl onion.

— ∞∞ —

"WILD" MANHATTAN (MR. BABBINGTON'S)

2 oz. Wild Turkey
⅛ oz. Martini & Rossi Rosso
  Vermouth
cherry

Serve over ice or straight up in a chilled martini glass. Garnish with cherry.

— ∞∞ —

WILD ROSE MARTINI

1½ oz. dry gin
½ oz. dry vermouth
½ oz. sweet vermouth
1 dash orange bitters
1 dash Angostura Bitters

— ∞∞ —

WILSON SPECIAL

2 oz. dry gin
¼ oz. dry vermouth
2 orange slices

Shake.

YACHTING CLUB

1¾ oz. Hollands Gin
¾ oz. dry vermouth
2 dashes Peychaud's Bitters
1 dash Pernod

Sweeten with sugar to taste.

— ∞∞ —

YALE MARTINI

1¾ oz. dry gin
½ oz. dry vermouth
2 dashes orange bitters
¼ oz. maraschino liqueur

Sweeten with sugar to taste.

— ∞∞ —

YELLOW DAISY MARTINI

1½ oz. dry gin
¼ oz. dry vermouth
¼ oz. Grand Marnier
¼ oz. Pernod
cherry

— ∞∞ —

YOLANDA MARTINI

¾ oz. dry gin
¾ oz. brandy
½ oz. dweet vermouth
¼ oz. grenadine
¼ oz. Pernod

— ∞∞ —

YORK MARTINI

7 parts dry gin
1 part French vermouth
1 drop of scotch
twist of lemon peel

YVETTE MARTINI (YVETTE WINTERGARDEN, CHICAGO)

2 oz. Ketel One Vodka
¼ oz. Grand Marnier
orange twist

Serve over ice or straight up in a chilled martini glass. Garnish with orange twist.

———∞∞∞———

ZAZA MARTINI

1¾ oz. Old Tom Gin
¾ oz. Dubonnet
1 dash orange bitters

———∞∞∞———

ZORBATINI

1½ oz. Stolichnaya Vodka
¼ oz. Metaxa Ouzo

Garnish with a green olive.

ALIZÉ GOLDEN APPLE MARTINI

3 oz. Alizé Gold Passion
½ oz. apple liqueur

Shake vigorously. Garnish with a lime wedge.

THE APPLE TARTINI

1½ oz. Wyborowa
1 oz. sour apple schnapps
1 oz. sour mix

Shake well over ice and pour into martini glass. Garnish with sugared cinnamon and Granny Smith apple wedge.

APPLETINI

1 oz. 99 Apples
3 oz. Effen Vodka
splash of orange-flavored liqueur

Shake with ice and strain into chilled, cinnamon & sugar rimmed martini glass.

ATTITUDE ADJUSTER

1 oz. Jose Cuervo Especial
½ oz. triple sec
2 oz. cranberry juice
1 oz. orange juice

Mix ingredients in a cocktail shaker with ice. Strain and pour into chilled martini glass.

BACARDI BIG APPLE CARAMEL APPLE MARTINI

2 parts Bacardi Big Apple
½ part butterscotch schnapps

Shake first two ingredients with ice and strain. Top with Sprite, if desired.

BACARDI BIG APPLE CINNATINI

1½ parts Bacardi Big Apple
½ part cinnamon schnapps
½ part coffee liqueur
1½ part half & half

Shake ingredients with ice and strain. Garnish with cinnamon stick.

FLAVORTINIS

BACARDI BIG APPLE MARTINI

1½ parts Bacardi Big Apple
½ part sweet & sour

Shake ingredients with ice and strain. Garnish with apple slice.

———— ✸ ————

BACARDI BIG APPLE MOJITO MARTINI

3 parts Bacardi Big Apple
2 parts lemon-lime soda
1 part sweet & sour mix

Shake all ingredients with ice and strain.

———— ✸ ————

BACARDI BIG APPLE TART MARTINI

1½ parts Bacardi Big Apple
½ part triple sec
2 parts cranberry juice

Shake and strain into chilled martini glass.

———— ✸ ————

BADA-BLING

1 oz. Pallini Limoncello
1 oz. Hpnotiq
1 oz. Courvoisier

Serve in a martini glass.

———— ✸ ————

BAHAMA BANANA

1¼ oz. Mount Gay Vanilla Rum
½ oz. white crème de cacao
½ oz. banana Liqueur
½ oz. half & half

Shake and strain.

THE BLUE GROTTO

2 oz. super premium gin
1 oz. Hpnotiq

Shake with ice, strain. Garnish with star fruit slice.

———— ✸ ————

BLUE MANGO-TINI

1¼ oz. Mount Gay Mango Rum
1 oz. sweet & sour schnapps
1 oz. pineapple juice
½ oz. simple syrup

Shake and strain.

———— ✸ ————

BLUE ORCHARD COSMOPOLITAN

2 parts Vox Green Apple
  Flavored Vodka
1 part DeKuyper Pucker Island
  Blue Schnapps
1 part cranberry juice
1 part DeKuyper Triple Sec
splash fresh lime juice

Shake and strain. Garnish with a pineapple ring, a pineapple square, or a slice of apple or pear.

———— ✸ ————

THE BLUE RAZZBERRY MARTINI

1½ oz. Bacardi Razz
½ oz. blue curaçao
½ oz. Rose's Lime Juice
½ oz. cranberry juice

Shake all ingredients with ice. Strain.

CANDY APPLE MARTINI

1 oz. 99 Apples
2½ oz. Effen Vodka
½ oz. grenadine

Shake with ice and strain into chilled, sugar-rimmed martini glass. Garnish with a maraschino cherry.

―――⋙⋘―――

CARAMEL APPLE MARTINI

1 oz. 99 Apples
2 oz. Effen Vodka
½ oz. coffee-flavored liqueur
¼ oz. butterscotch schnapps

Shake with ice and strain into chilled, sugar-rimmed martini glass.

―――⋙⋘―――

CINNAMON TWIST

1 part Starbucks Coffee Liqueur
½ part DeKuyper Buttershots Schnapps
½ part Irish Cream
2 parts cream
splash Goldschlager Liqueur

Shake and strain into a cinnamon-sugar rimmed martini glass.

―――⋙⋘―――

CITRON FLIRTINI

2 oz. Absolut Citron
½ oz. cointreau
⅛ oz. dry vermouth

Serve over ice or straight up in a chilled martini glass.

CITRUS BELLINI

2 oz. Skyy Citrus
1 oz. peach schnapps
splash lime juice

Shake ingredients with ice and strain.

―――⋙⋘―――

CLOVER-HONEY-MOON

1½ oz. Celtic Crossing
1½ oz. Boru Citrus Vodka
3 lemon wedges
1 tablespoon of clover honey

In a mixing glass, muddle the 3 lemon wedges with the honey. Add the Celtic and Boru, shake with ice and strain. Garnish with half a lemon slice.

―――⋙⋘―――

COCO NUTTY MARTINI

3 parts Bacardi Cóco
1 part Disaronno Originale Liqueur
2 parts pineapple juice
splash orange juice

Shake all ingredients with ice and strain.

―――⋙⋘―――

CÓCOTINI

3 parts Bacardi Cóco
1 part triple sec

Shake well with ice. Strain into chilled martini glass rimmed with coconut shavings. Garnish with lime wheel.

CRAZZMOPOLITAN

1½ oz. Boru Crazzberry Vodka
1 oz. cranberry juice
½ oz. fresh lime juice
½ oz. cointreau

Place all ingredients in a shaker with ice. Shake vigorously. Strain. Garnish with a luscious raspberry.

―∞∞―

CRUZAN CARIBBEAN MARTINI

¾ oz. Cruzan Banana Rum
¾ oz. Cruzan Coconut Rum
¾ oz. Cruzan Pineapple Rum

Combine ingredients into a mixing glass with ice. Shake till chilled and strain.

―∞∞―

DADDY WARBUCKS

1½ oz. Ultimat Vodka
4 oz. Godiva Chocolate Liqueur
¼ oz. Hennessy Richard

Serve in crystal Riedel Sommelier martini glass garnished with two handmade truffles.

―∞∞―

DAM BLONDIE MARTINI

1½ oz. Damrak Gin
1½ oz. cointreau
squeezed orange chunk

Serve up. Garnish with an orange slice.

DOUBLE SHOT DUTCH MOCHA

1 oz. Van Gogh Espresso Vodka
1 oz. Van Gogh Dutch Chocolate Vodka
1 oz. Chocolate Cream Liqueur

Garnish with a small whipped cream drop.

―∞∞―

FRENCH MARTINI

2 parts Vox Vodka
2½ parts pineapple juice
½ part Chambord Black Raspberry Liqueur

Shake ingredients with ice and strain.

―∞∞―

GINGERLY VOX

1½ parts Vox Vodka
1 part ginger liqueur
1 thin banana leaf
sliced fresh ginger

Mix in a shaker half-filled with ice. Pour into a chilled martini glass. Garnish: edge the glass with a piece of fresh ginger. Roll a banana leaf and place it into glass.

―∞∞―

GORGEOUS GISELLE'S BLUEBIRD

1½ oz. Hpnotiq
1½ oz. Super Premium Coconut Rum
splash lime juice

Shake with ice and strain into martini glass rimmed with coconut.

GREEN APPLETINI TWIST

1½ oz. Smirnoff Green Apple Twist
splash sour mix

Shake and strain. Garnish with a green apple twist.

~~~

HEATED ICE MARTINI

2 oz. Polar Ice Vodka
½ oz. bourbon

Shake with a splash of maple syrup and serve well chilled.

~~~

HPNOCRAZZ

1 oz. Boru Crazzberry Vodka
1 oz. Hpnotiq
1 oz. passion fruit juice or pineapple juice
splash of blue curaçao

Shake the first 3 ingredients in a shaker with ice, strain. After the drink is poured, drop the splash of blue curaçao right in the center of the glass. It will form a blue layer at the bottom of the martini glass.

~~~

HPNOTIQ AVANTINI

1½ oz. Hpnotiq
1 oz. super-premium vodka
splash of freshly squeezed watermelon juice
splash of guava juice

Shake well, strain. Garnish with a floating star fruit. Signature drink for Ava at the Mirage Casino, Las Vegas, NV

HPNOTIQ LOVE POTION NUMBER 9

1 oz. Hpnotiq
1 oz. watermelon liqueur
1 oz. super-premium vodka

Shake well, strain into a martini glass. Garnish with a heart-shaped stir stick. Signature drink for both Ghostbar & Rain at the Palms Casino, Las Vegas, NV

~~~

HPNOTIQ SUB ZERO MARTINI

1 oz. Hpnotiq
1 oz. orange rum
1 oz. coconut rum
splash pineapple juice

Shake well, strain. Garnish with mini-sugar cubes stir stick. Signature drink for Mist Bar and Lounge at the Treasure Island Casino, Las Vegas, NV

~~~

HPNOTIQ-O

2 oz. Hpnotiq
1 oz. fresh-squeezed orange juice
Shake with ice, strain

Garnish with an orange wheel floating on top.

~~~

HYPNOTIQ BLUE GOOSE MARTINI

2 oz. Hpnotiq
1 oz. Grey Goose Vodka
splash pineapple juice

Shake with ice, strain. Garnish with a lemon twist.

HYPNOTIQ COSMO

2 oz. Hpnotiq
1 oz. super premium citrus
 vodka
splash white cranberry juice

Shake with ice, strain. Garnish
with lemon or lime twist.

IGUANA MARTINI

2 oz. Absolut Citron
¼ oz. Midori
¼ oz. triple sec
lemon pinwheel

Serve over ice or straight up in
a chilled martini glass. Garnish
with lemon pinwheel.

IRISH PASSION MARTINI

1 oz. Celtic Crossing
1½ oz. Alizé Red Passion
1 oz. Boru Vodka

Shake all ingredients thoroughly with ice and strain.
Garnish with a lemon peel.

IRISH STRAWBERRY

1¼ oz. Tequila Rose
¾ oz. McCormick's Irish Cream
1 oz. butterscotch schnapps

Shake and serve over ice.

JIM BEAM BLACK & ORANGE MARTINI

4 parts Jim Beam Black Bourbon
1½ parts DeKuyper Amaretto
 Liqueur
2 drops bitters
splash fresh-squeezed orange
 juice
2 lime wedges

In a martini shell, combine
bourbon, amaretto, bitters and
orange juice. Muddle with lime
wedges. Serve up with orange
wheel.

JIM BEAM BLACK COFFEE & CREAMTINI

1½ parts Jim Beam Black
 Bourbon
¼ parts Starbucks Coffee Liqueur
¼ parts Irish Cream

Shake hard. Serve in martini
glass with a dash of cinnamon.

KEKE V

½ oz. KeKe Beach
½ oz. Polar Ice Vodka

Shaken and strained.

LIMÓN APPLETINI

4 parts Bacardi Limón
2 parts apple schnapps
1 part sweet & sour

Shake. Garnish with lemon
twist.

LIMÓN MOJITO MARTINI

3 parts Bacardi Limón
2 parts lemon-lime soda
1 part sweet & sour

Shake with ice and strain. Lemon wheel and mint leaves for garnish.

—⊶⊷—

MAGNIFICENT MELON

1½ parts Vox Vodka
¼ oz. DeKuyper Melon Liqueur
splash pineapple juice
pineapple leaves
¼ oz. watermelon
¼ oz. honeydew
¼ oz. cantaloupe

Serve over ice or straight up in a chilled martini glass. Garnish: overlap three long pineapple leaves and place into glass. Spear large watermelon, honeydew and cantaloupe balls and place over the leaves.

—⊶⊷—

MANGO BANANA

1¼ oz. Mount Gay Mango Rum
½ oz. white crème de cacao
½ oz. banana liqueur
½ oz. half & half

Combine in mixing tin with ice. Shake and strain. Garnish with a banana slice.

MINT CHOCOTINI

¾ oz. Sgt. Peppermint
¾ oz. coffee liqueur
¾ oz. white crème de cacao
½ oz. half & half

Add ice, shake vigorously. Strain.

—⊶⊷—

MOCHA BUZZ

1 oz. Van Gogh Espresso Vodka
1 oz. chocolate cream liqueur
1 shot of espresso coffee
1 oz. half & half

Garnish with small whipped cream drop.

—⊶⊷—

O CHOCOLATE MARTINI COCKTAIL

2 parts Bacardi O
1 part crème de cacao

Shake ingredients with ice. Strain into martini glass with chocolate rim. Garnish with orange twist.

—⊶⊷—

O-MARTINI

4 parts Bacardi O
½ part Martini & Rossi Extra Dry Vermouth

Shake with ice and strain.

—⊶⊷—

PALLINI MARTINI

1 part Pallini Limoncello
1 part Boru Vodka

Shaken on ice, served straight up.

PINK PASSION

1½ shot Crema Di Limone
1¼ shot Bacardi Rum
½ shot grenadine

Mix in blender with ice, serve in martini glass topped with a raspberry and mint leaves. Consistency should be that of a Piña Colada. (Julie, Beacon Hill Club, Summit, NJ)

PINK SIN MARTINI

¾ part cinnamon schnapps
1 part white crème de cacao
1½ parts Vox Vodka
1 part cranberry juice

Shake all ingredients with cubed ice and strain.

POLAR BREEZE MARTINI

1½ oz. Polar Ice Vodka
1 splash blue curaçao
lychee juice
1 splash tart lemonade
lemon wheel

Mix, chill and serve with the lemon wheel as a garnish.

RASMOPOLITAN

1¼ parts Vox Raspberry
½ part cointreau
1 part cranberry juice
squeeze fresh lime juice

Mix in a shaker half-filled with ice. Strain. Garnish with fresh raspberries or a lime peel.

RASPBERRY TRUFFLE MARTINI

1½ parts Vox Raspberry Flavored Vodka
½ part DeKuyper White Creme de Cacao
¾ part cream
½ part Chambord Liqueur

Mix in a shaker half-filled with ice. Pour into a cocoa-rimmed martini glass. Garnish with raspberries or a maraschino cherry.

RED APPLE TWIST

1½ oz. Smirnoff Green Apple Twist
1 oz. sour mix
splash grenadine

RED, WHITE AND HPNOTIQ BLUE MARTINI

2 oz. Hpnotiq
1 oz. super premium citrus vodka
splash lemon-lime soda
splash grenadine

Shake with ice and strain. Garnish with chopped coconut.

THE ROTHMANN'S MARTINI

2 oz. Absolut Mandrin
½ oz. cointreau
½ oz. pineapple
⅛ oz. lime juice

Serve over ice or straight up in a chilled martini glass.

ROYAL MARTINI

1 oz. Crown Royal
½ oz. peach schnapps
1 oz. cranberry juice

Shake ingredients with ice, strain and garnish with an orchid or lemon twist.

SILK ROSE

1 oz. Tequila Rose
½ oz. butterscotch schnapps
½ banana schnapps
½ oz. milk
¼ oz. half & half

Mix in a shaker with ice and strain.

SKYY APPLETINI

2 oz. Skyy Vodka
1 oz. sour apple liqueur

Shake ingredients with ice and strain. Garnish with an apple slice.

THE SPARKLER

2 oz. Wyborowa
½ oz. lime juice
1 tsp. simple syrup

Fill with champagne or sparkling wine. Pour into champagne glass.

STRAWBERRY MARTINI

2½ oz. Tequila Rose
1 oz. Polar Ice Vodka

Shake and pour into martini glass.

SUNBURNED MARTINI

1 oz. Jose Cuervo Clasico
½ oz. Grand Marnier
2 oz. orange juice
1 oz. cranberry juice
ice

Mix ingredients in a cocktail shaker filled with ice. Serve.

THE SUNDRENCH

2 oz. Wyborowa
½ oz. peach schnapps
½ oz. Midori
dash grenadine

Fill with pineapple juice.

SWEET & SOUR APPLETINI

Equal parts:
DeKuyper Sour Apple Pucker
Vox Vodka
splash sweet and sour mix

Chill. Serve in a martini glass.

THREE BERRY SHORTCAKE

1 oz. Boru Crazzberry
1 oz. Licor 43
3 oz. cranberry juice
1 oz. heavy cream

Combine all ingredients in a cocktail shaker over ice. Shake well and strain into a chilled martini glass with a sugar rim. Garnish with a strawberry.

TIRAMISU

1 oz. coffee-flavored liqueur
½ oz. rum
1 shot of espresso

Shake with ice, strain. Pour into glass of choice, martini or other stemmed glass preferred. Garnish with whipped cream. (Veritable Quandary, Portland, OR)

VAN GOGH'S ESPRESSOTINI

2 oz. Van Gogh Espresso Vodka
½ oz. Kahlua
½ oz. half & half

VANÍLA MARTINI

1½ oz. Bacardi Vaníla
1 oz. lemon juice
simple syrup to taste

Shake all ingredients with ice and strain into martini glass.

VODKA AMERICANO

1 part Starbucks Coffee Liqueur
1½ parts Absolut Vanilia Vodka

Shake and strain into a martini glass. Garnish with three coffee beans.

VOX APPLETINI

2 parts Vox Vodka
1 part DeKuyper Pucker Sour Apple Schnapps
splash sweet & sour
2 apples

Mix in a shaker half-filled with ice. Pour into a chilled martini glass.

VOX FRUITS OF THE FOREST

2 oz. Vox Vodka
¼ oz. simple syrup
⅛ oz. lime juice
1 oz. each fresh berries: strawberry, raspberry, blackberry
1 bunch of edible flowers: pansies, roses

Muddle the berries in a mixing glass with a muddler. Add dash of simple syrup and Vox Vodka and shake. Double strain into a pre-chilled martini glass. Garnish: rim the glass with simple syrup and dip into a plate of finely chopped flowers to match the cocktail's color.

VOX POMEGRANATE

1½ parts Vox Vodka
1 pomegranate
2 oz. fresh pomegranate juice
dash simple syrup
1 white orchid

Muddle 10 pomegranate seeds in a mixing glass. Add pomegranate juice, Vox Vodka, and a dash of simple syrup. Shake and strain. Garnish: float a white orchid on cocktail.

WASHINGTON APPLE TWIST

¾ oz. Smirnoff Green Apple Twist
¾ oz. Crown Royal
2 oz. cranberry juice

Shake with ice and strain over crushed ice in a tumbler glass. Garnish with a red apple slice.

WATERMELON MARTINI

2 cups cubed watermelon flesh
2 parts Vox Vodka
¼ part sugar syrup
½ part watermelon liqueur

Muddle watermelon in base of shaker, add other ingredients. Shake with ice and strain.

THE "WHITE" COSMOPOLITAN

2 oz. Absolut Citron
¼ oz. cointreau
2 oz. white cranberry juice
⅛ oz. lime

Serve over ice or straight up in a chilled martini glass.

WILD BERRI TINI

3 parts Island Breeze Wild Berry

Shake with ice and strain.

ABSOLUT HURRICANE WARNING

1½ oz. Absolut Vodka
2 oz. pineapple and cherry juice

Garnish with maraschino cherry. (Hurricane Restaurant, Passagrille, FL)

ALIZÉ PASSIONATE MARTINI

2 oz. Alizé
½ oz. Absolut Vodka
½ oz. cranberry juice

Shake and strain.

ALIZÉ RED PASSION MARTINI

2½ oz. Alizé Red Passion
1 oz. super premium vodka

Fill martini shaker ¾ with ice. Shake and serve. Garnish with thin slice of lime.

ALIZÉ TROPICAL MARTINI

2 oz. Alizé
½ oz. Malibu

Fill shaker with ice, add above ingredients, cover and shake. Garnish with maraschino cherry.

THE ALL-AMERICAN MARTINI

1½ oz. Glacier Vodka
dash vermouth

Garnish with two olives skewered by an American flag toothpick.

APPLE MARTINI

1½ oz. Glacier Vodka
½ part Schoenauer Apfel
 Schnapps
dash cinnamon

Garnish with a slice of apple.

APPLE SAUCE MARTINI

chilled Finlandia Vodka
¼ oz. apple brandy

APPLETINI

1½ oz. Ketel One Vodka
2 oz. Sour Apple Pucker

Serve in chilled martini glass. Garnish with slice of apple. (Bobby McGee's, San Bernadino, CA)

BACARDI LIMÓN MARTINI

2 oz. Bacardi Limón
¾ oz. Martini & Rossi Extra Dry
 Vermouth
splash cranberry juice

Shake and strain. Garnish with lemon twist.

———∞∞∞———

BACARDI SPICE CARIBBEAN MARTINI

2½ oz. Bacardi Spice Rum
½ oz. creme de banana

Shake and strain. Serve up. Garnish with pineapple wedge.

———∞∞∞———

BAFFERTS BULL

1 oz. Bafferts Gin
5 oz. Red Bull

———∞∞∞———

BAFFERTS GIN

3 oz. Bafferts Gin

Shaken over ice—enough said. Serve ever so slowly in a martini glass.

———∞∞∞———

BANANA SPLIT MARTINI

1 oz. chilled Finlandia Arctic
 Cranberry Vodka
¼ oz. banana liqueur
¼ oz. Chambord

BELLINI MARTINI

2 oz. Stolichnaya Vodka
½ oz. fresh white peach puree
zest of lemon

Serve over ice or straight up in a chilled martini glass. Garnish with zest of lemon.
(Martini's, New York, NY)

———∞∞∞———

BERI-BERI NICE

1 part Stoli Strasberi Vodka
1 part Stoli Razberi Vodka
splash Chambord

Garnish with fresh raspberry. (Peggy Howell, Cotati Yacht Club & Saloon, Cotati, CA)

———∞∞∞———

BERRY BERRY MARTINI

2 oz. Beefeater Gin
½ oz. cranberry juice cocktail

Shake and strain. Garnish with a fresh berry.

———∞∞∞———

BLACKBERRY MARTINI

2 oz. Stoli Vanil Vodka
¼ oz. Chambord

Serve over ice or straight up in a chilled martini glass.
(Tunnel Bar Raphael, Providence, RI)

BLONDE MARTINI

2 oz. Bombay Sapphire

Enlivened with Lillet Blonde. Serve over ice or straight up in a chilled martini glass. (Brasserie Jo Martini's, Chicago, IL)

BLUE DOLPHIN MARTINI

2 oz. chilled finlandia vodka
¼ oz. blue curacao
¼ oz. Grand Marnier
1 oz. grapefruit juice
2 drops Rose's Lime Juice

BLUE LAGOON MARTINI

1¼ oz. Bacardi Limón
½ oz. blue curacao
¼ oz. dry vermouth

Garnish with strawberry or olives. Alex Refojo, Club Mystique, Miami, FL

BLUE MOON MARTINI

½ oz. Marie Brizard Blue Curacao Liqueur
2 oz. vodka

Coat a chilled martini glass with vermouth, add ingredients. Garnish with orange slice.

BLUE SHARK MARTINI

1½ oz. vodka
1½ oz. tequila
½ oz. blue curacao

Shake and strain into martini glass or over ice.

BLUE VELVET MARTINI

A few ice cubes
1 oz. Beefeater Dry Gin
1 oz. Bols Blue Curacao

Stir and pour into a chilled cocktail glass. Garnish with an orange zest.

CAMPARTINI

2 oz. Campari
2 oz. Stoli Ohranj Vodka
dash Rose's Lime Juice
splash orange juice

Shaken not stirred, serve with orange slice.

CELTIC MARTINI

Equal parts of Celtic Crossing and lemon vodka. Garnish with a lemon twist.

CELTIC CONTINENTAL

2 oz. Celtic Crossing
dash Chambord
splash peach schnapps

Serve over ice or straight up in a chilled martini glass.

CHICAGO LAKE BREEZE MARTINI

1½ oz. Stoli Persik Vodka
splash 7-Up
splash cranberry juice

Garnish with a lemon twist.

CHOCO-RASPBERRY MARTINI

3 oz. Stoli Vanil Vodka
3 oz. Stoli Razberi Vodka
1 oz. creme de cacao

Shake and strain.

CITRON MARTINI

1¼ oz. Absolut Citron Vodka
dash extra dry vermouth

Pour Citron and vermouth over ice. Shake or stir well. Garnish with twist or olive.

THE CLASSIC COSMO

2 oz. Absolut Citron Vodka
splash cointreau and cranberry juice
lime wedge garnish

(Columbus Inn, Wilmington, DE)

CLASSIC HENDRICK'S MARTINI

1½ oz. Hendrick's Gin
¾ oz. dry vermouth

Stir vermouth and Hendrick's Gin over ice cubes in a mixing glass. Strain into a chilled martini glass. Serve with cucumber slice.

COINTINI

2 oz. Stoli Ohranj Vodka
⅛ oz. cointreau

(Brasserie Jo Martini's, Chicago, IL)

COSMOPOLITAN WAY BACK WHEN!

2 oz. cointreau
1 oz. cranberry
⅛ oz. lime juice

Serve over ice or straight up in a chilled martini glass. Garnish with an olive and orange twist.

COSMOPOLITAN MARTINI

2 oz. Vodka
1 oz. cointreau
squeeze ½ lime
splash cranberry juice

Shake and strain. Garnish with a lemon twist.

DEEP SEA MARTINI

1½ oz. gin
1 oz. dry vermouth
1 dash orange bitters
¼ oz. Pernod

Garnish with lemon peel.

───── ⸎ ─────

DEPTH CHARGE MARTINI

1¼ oz. gin
1¼ oz. Lillet
¼ oz. Pernod
orange peel

───── ⸎ ─────

ELECTRIC PEACH MARTINI

1 oz. Finlandia Vodka, chilled
¼ oz. peach schnapps
½ oz. cranberry juice cocktail
¼ oz. orange juice

───── ⸎ ─────

THE EROICA*

2 oz. OP
splash Grand Marnier
1 oz. lime juice

Mix in a shaker. Float a lime slice.
*Drink inspired by The Eroica Trio.

───── ⸎ ─────

FERNET BRANCA COCKTAIL MARTINI

1½ oz. dry gin
¼ oz. sweet vermouth
½ oz. Fernet Branca

Garnish with a maraschino cherry.

FINLANDIA GOLD DIGGER MARTINI

5 parts Classic Finlandia Vodka
1 part pineapple juice
2 parts cointreau

───── ⸎ ─────

FUZZY MARTINI II

2 oz. Stoli Vanil Vodka
1 oz. Stoli Persik Vodka
1 splash peach schnapps

Garnish with thin peach slice.

───── ⸎ ─────

GOLD DIGGER MARTINI

1 oz. Finlandia Vodka
½ oz. cointreau
½ oz. pineapple juice

Stir with ice; serve straight up or over ice.

───── ⸎ ─────

GOLDEN GIRL MARTINI

1¼ oz. Beefeater Gin
¾ oz. dry sherry
1 dash orange bitters
1 dash Angostura Bitters

───── ⸎ ─────

GRANITINI

2 oz. orange vodka
½ oz. cherry liqueur
splashes of fresh lime and lemon
  juice

Serve over ice or straight up in a chilled brown sugar rimmed martini glass.

Green Opple (Apple Martini)

2 oz. OP
splash apple juice
splash Calvados

Mix in a shaker. Float a green apple slice.

Green Hornet Martini

1 oz. chilled Finlandia Vodka
¼ oz. Midori
½ oz. sweet & sour mix

Hawaiian Cocktail Martini

2 oz. gin
½ oz. triple sec
½ oz. unsweetened pineapple juice

Shake and strain.

Iceberg Martini

2 oz. Beefeater Gin
splash white creme de menthe

Stir with ice and strain. Garnish with mint.

Kahlua Dawn Martini

2 oz. dry gin
1 oz. Kahlua Liqueur
½ oz. lemon juice

Shake and strain. Serve with maraschino cherry.

Kentucky Martini

1½ oz. Maker's Mark Bourbon
½ oz. amaretto
2 oz. Orange Slice soda

Stir with ice; strain.

Kiev Coffee Delight Martini

2 oz. Stoli Kafya Vodka
splashes: Stoli Zinamon and Stoli Vanil Vodka.

Serve over ice or straight up in a chilled martini glass.

Lemon Chiffon Martini

2 oz. Chilled Finlandia Vodka
¼ oz. triple sec
1 oz. sweet & sour mix

Serve over ice or straight up in a chilled martini glass. Squeeze and drop in fresh lemon wedge.

Lillet Cocktail Martini

1½ oz. Lillet
1 oz. dry gin
twist of lemon peel

THE LILY PAD

2 oz. Absolut Mandrin
¼ oz. banana liqueur
¼ oz. Midori
¼ oz. sour mix

Serve over ice or straight up in a chilled martini glass. (Columbus Inn, Wilmington, DE)

MAD MARTINI

Coat a chilled martini glass with vermouth, then simply add ½ oz. of your favorite Marie Brizard Fruit Bursters Liqueur flavor to 2 oz. of gin or vodka. Garnish with fruit.

MALACCA MARTINI

2½ oz. Tanqueray Malacca Gin
splash dry vermouth to taste

Garnish with olive or lemon twist.

MALIBU RAIN MARTINI

2 oz. chilled Finlandia Vodka
1½ oz. pineapple juice
½ oz. Malibu
splash orange juice

THE MALIBU TEASE

2 oz. Finlandia Cranberry Vodka
splash cranberry juice
splash pineapple juice

Pour ingredients over ice, shake vigorously and strain into chilled martini glass. (Columbus Inn, Wilmington, DE)

MINT MARTINI

1 part Godiva Liqueur
1 part Absolut Vodka
splash white creme de menthe

Shake and serve straight up. Garnish with a mint leaf.

OP PASSION

2 oz. OP
splash of Grand Marnier
splash passion fruit juice

Mix in a shaker. Garnish with lime twist.

OPAL

2 oz. OP
½ oz. white creme de menthe

Shake. Serve straight up or on the rocks.

ORANGE BOWL

1 oz. Tanqueray Gin
1 oz. orange vodka
¹⁄₁₆ oz. vermouth
¹⁄₁₆ oz. Grand Marnier
garnish: orange slice

Serve over ice or straight up in a chilled martini glass. Garnish with orange slice. (Shulas No Name Lounge, Tampa, FL)

ORCHARD BEACH MARTINI

2 oz. Vincent Van Gogh Wild Appel Vodka
1 oz. cranberry juice

Serve over ice or straight up in a chilled martini glass.

PAISLEY

2 oz. Bombay Sapphire Gin
½ oz. single malt scotch whiskey
½ oz. dry vermouth

Garnish with a twist.

PEPPERMINT MARTINI

2 oz. vodka
½ oz. Rumple Minze

Shake.

PINK MARTINI TWIST

2 oz. Absolut Kurant Vodka
½ oz. Chambord

Serve over ice or straight up in a chilled martini glass. (Portland's Best, Portland, OR)

PINK ROSE

2 oz. Skyy Vodka
½ oz. DeKuyper Peachtree Schnapps
½ oz. cranberry juice

Serve over ice or straight up in a chilled martini glass. (Hamiltons, Miami, FL)

PURPLE HAZE

Coat a chilled martini glass with vermouth, pour ½ oz. of Marie Brizard Parfait Amour Liqueur to 2 oz. of vodka or gin. Garnish with fruit.

QUEEN ELIZABETH MARTINI

1½ oz. Bombay Gin
dash Martini & Rossi Extra Dry Vermouth
splash Benedictine

Stir in cocktail glass. Strain and serve up or on the rocks. Add lemon twist or olives.

RED OPPLE (APPLE MARTINI)

2 oz. OP
splash apple juice
splash Chambord

Mix in a shaker. Float a red apple slice.

RED PASSION MARTINI

1½ oz. Alizé
½ oz. Campari

Stir well and serve up. Garnish with orange peel.

RISING SUN MARTINI

2 oz. Skyy Vodka
⅛ oz. Grand Marnier

Serve up in an oversized chilled stem. Shaken, not stirred. Garnish with an orange twist.

ROYAL DEVIL

2 oz. Stoli Razberi Vodka
¼ oz. Chambord
¼ oz. Black Haus Liqueur

Serve over ice or straight up in a chilled martini glass.

SAPPHIRE MARTINI

Bombay Sapphire Gin
Cinzano Vermouth

Garnish with an olive.

SCOTTISH ROSE

1½ oz. Hendrick's Gin
½ oz. cassis
⅛ oz. Schweppes Tonic Water

Stir Hendrick's Gin and cassis in a mixing glass over ice cubes. Strain into a chilled martini glass. Add a dash of tonic. Garnish with a cucumber slice.

SHARKBITE MARTINI

2 oz. Leyden Dry Gin
⅛ oz. Sprite
1/16 oz. lemon

Serve over ice or straight up in a chilled martini glass.
(Red Lobster, Memphis, TN)

SMOOTH OPERATOR

2 oz. OP
½ oz. Irish Cream
½ oz. coffee liqueur
½ oz. white creme de menthe

Shake. Serve on the rocks or in a martini glass.

SOPRANO

2 oz. OP
¼ oz. dry vermouth
float Sambuca on top

Serve on the rocks.

SOPRANO ROYAL

2 oz. OP
¼ oz. Campari

Shake with ice. Serve up or on the rocks.

SOUR KISSES MARTINI

1½ oz. Bombay Gin
dash Martini & Rossi Extra Dry Vermouth

Add egg white. Strain and serve straight up or on the rocks. Add lemon twist or olive.

STARLIGHT MARTINI

1¾ oz. Beefeater Gin
¾ oz. orange curacao
1 dash Angostura Bitters

Shake.

STARRY NIGHT MARTINI

1 part Vincent Van Gogh Vodka
2 parts lemonade
splash curacao

STOLI BELLINI MARTINI

2 oz. champagne
½ oz. Stoli Persik Vodka
⅛ oz. peach schnapps

Serve over ice or straight up in a chilled martini glass.

STRAWBERRY BLONDE MARTINI

2 oz. Beefeater Gin
1 oz. Chambraise Strawberry Aperitif
twist of lemon peel

STRING OF PEARLS

2½ oz. Leyden Gin
4 cocktail onions

(Bill Chiusano, Bloomfield, NJ)

SUN KISSED LEMONADE

2 oz. Absolut Citron Vodka
¼ oz. triple sec
½ oz. sour mix and sugar

Serve over ice or straight up in a chilled martini glass.
(Columbus Inn, Wilmington, DE)

SUNFLOWER MARTINI

2 oz. Van Gogh Gin
¼ oz. cointreau
½ oz. pineapple juice
1/16 oz. grenadine

SUNRISE MARTINI

2 oz. Smirnoff Vodka
1 oz. Cuervo 1800 Tequila
splash Grand Marnier
splash grenadine

Garnish with orange slice.

SUNSET

2½ oz. Stoli Ohranj Vodka
¹⁄₁₆ oz. bitters

Serve over ice or straight up in
a chilled martini glass. Garnish
with an orange slice.

SWEDISH COSMOPOLITAN

2 oz. OP
splash Grand Marnier
splash lime juice
splash cranberry juice

Shake and serve. Float a lime
slice.

TAKE OFF MARTINI

Tanqueray Gin
splash cointreau
orange peel

(The Windsock Bar & Grill,
San Diego, CA)

TANQUERAY "PERFECT TEN" MARTINI

2 oz. Tanqueray No. Ten
1 oz. Grand Marnier
½ oz. sour mix

TANQUERAY NO. TEN MARTINI

2¼ oz. Tanqueray No. Ten
1¾ oz. lime juice

Shake and serve. Add squeeze
of one lime wedge.

TEMPLE TINI

2½ oz. Absolut Kurant Vodka
⅛ oz. Chambord
maraschino cherry

Serve over ice or straight up in
a chilled martini glass. Garnish
with maraschino cherry.

THIGH OPENER

2 oz. OP
¼ oz. lime juice
¼ oz. triple sec

Shake. Serve on the rocks.

TWO LIPS MARTINI

2 oz. Leyden Gin
¼ oz. Chambord

Serve over ice or straight up in
a chilled martini glass.
(Bill Chiusano, Bloomfield,
NJ)

ULTIMATE MARTINI

1 oz. Stoli Vodka
½ oz. Campari
¼ oz. sweet vermouth

VANILLA RAIN

1 part Rain Vodka, chilled
1 part Dr. Vanillacuddy, chilled

Strain into martini glass.

VIOLETTA

2½ oz. Absolut Vodka
½ oz. blue curacao
splash cranberry juice

Garnish with a twist.

WILD APPELTINI

3 oz. Vincent Van Gogh Wild
  Appel Vodka

Shake it cold and pour into
martini glass. Garnish with
green apple slice.

ZORBATINI MARTINI

1½ oz. Stolichnaya Vodka
¼ oz. Metaxa Ouzo

Stir gently with ice and strain.
Garnish with a green olive.

SUMMERTINIS

Springtinis

ABSOLUT MESS

1¼ oz. Absolut Mandrin
¼ oz. Absolut Citron
¼ oz. Absolut Kurant
¼ oz. triple sec
1 oz. lime juice
1 oz. cranberry juice

ABSOLUT TROPICAL MARTINI

1 part Absolut Mandrin
1 part DeKuyper Tropical
   Pineapple

AIR GUITAR

2 oz. Stoli Vanil Vodka
½ oz. Hiram Walker White Crème
   de Menthe

Garnish with lemon twist.

ALOHA

1 oz. Stolichnaya Vodka
½ oz. Hiram Walker apricot
   brandy
2 oz. pineapple juice

Garnish with pineapple wedge.

BACARDI LIMÓN COSMOPOLITAN

2 oz. Bacardi Limón Rum
1 oz. triple sec
½ oz. lime juice
cranberry juice

Garnish with lemon twist.

BACARDI MARTINI COCKTAIL

1½ oz. Bacardi Carta Blanca Rum
dash Martini & Rossi Extra Dry
   Vermouth

Add olive.

BACARDI TU TU CHERRY

1 oz. Bacardi Gold Rum
¼ oz. cherry liqueur
2 oz. orange juice
3 oz. cranberry juice

BANANA APPLE

1 oz. Stolichnaya Vodka
1 oz. Hiram Walker Sour Apple
   Schnapps
1 oz. crème de banana

Garnish with apple wedge.

BANANA MARTINI

2½ oz. Skyy Vodka
splash creme de banana
splash extra-dry vermouth

Garnish with a caramelized banana slice.

———— ✺ ————

BELVEDERE STARTINI

1½ oz. Belvedere Vodka
¼ oz. Grand Marnier
⅛ oz. Chambord
1½ oz. lemonade

Garnish with slice of starfruit.

———— ✺ ————

BERI-BERI

equal parts:
Stoli Strasberi
Stoli Razberi
Chambord

———— ✺ ————

THE BIKINI MARTINI

2 oz. Bombay Sapphire Gin
¼ oz. freshly squeezed lime juice
¼ oz. blue curacao
¼ oz. peach schnapps
sugar syrup

———— ✺ ————

BLACK & WHITE MARTINI

Pour 2 oz. Cruzan Vanilla Rum into a mixing glass, add ice. Strain into martini glass rimmed with powdered gourmet chocolate. Garnish with strawberry.

BLOODY MARY ON A STICK

1½ oz. Teton Glacier
1 cherry tomato, think vermouth

Garnish with cherry tomato.

———— ✺ ————

BLOOMING ROSE

2 oz. Tequila Rose
1 oz. raspberry liqueur
3 oz. milk or heavy cream

Serve in martini glass, drizzle in chocolate sauce and swirl. Optional: substitute 3 scoops of ice cream for milk or serve over ice.

———— ✺ ————

BLUE BORU

2 oz. Boru Orange
½ oz. Malibu Rum
⅛ oz. blue curacao
1 oz. pineapple juice

———— ✺ ————

BLUE DOLPHIN

2 oz. Stolichnaya Vodka
1 oz. grapefruit juice
½ oz. Hiram Walker Blue
  Curacao
garnish with lemon peel

———— ✺ ————

BLUE MARTINI

equal parts:
Pucker Island Blue
Absolut Citron

Garnish with a lemon twist.

SPRINGTINIS

THE BLUE RIBAND

1½ oz. Bombay Sapphire Gin
¼ oz. triple sec
¼ oz. blue curacao

BLUE VELVET

1 part Pucker Island Blue
1 part Absolut
1 part DeKuyper Triple Sec
splash lime
splash cranberry

Garnish with lime wedge.

BOMBAY CLOUD

2 oz. Bombay Sapphire Gin
¼ oz. apricot brandy
1 oz. orange juice
grenadine syrup

BORU 007

2 oz. Boru Orange
1 oz. orange juice
7-Up

BRAZEN MARTINI

2 oz. Smirnoff Vodka
⅓ oz. Parfait Amour (Violet Liqueur)
orange slice

BREAKFAST MARTINI

2 oz. Bombay Sapphire Gin
⅛ oz. Martini Extra Dry Vermouth
½ oz. freshly squeezed lemon juice
⅛ tsp. light orange marmalade
orange peel garnish

CAPPUCCINO MARTINI

2 oz. Absolut Vodka
½ oz. Godiva Chocolate
½ oz. cappuccino liqueur

CARAMEL APPLE MARTINI

½ oz. Kahlua
½ oz. butterscotch schnapps
½ oz. 99 Apples Liqueur
1 oz. vodka

CARIBBEAN COSMO

equal parts (1 oz.) Cruzan Orange and Estate Light Rums
equal parts cranberry and fresh orange juice
squeeze of lime

Garnish with an orange slice.

CELTIC CITRUS MARTINI

Equal parts:
Celtic Crossing
Boru Citrus Vodka

CHAMBORD MARTINI

½ oz. Chambord
1 oz. Vodka
2 oz. pineapple juice

CHICAGO MARTINI

2½ oz. Absolut Vodka

Serve in a glass rinsed with cointreau.

CHOCOLATE

2 oz. Stolichnaya Vodka
1 oz. Hiram Walker Coffee
  Brandy
1½ oz. Hiram Walker Brown
  Crème de Cacao

Garnish with whipped cream
and drizzle of Coffee Brandy.

CHOCOLATE COVERED APPLE

1 oz. Godiva Chocolate
1 oz. Smirnoff Vanilla
½ oz. Apple Pucker

CHOCOLATE SWIRL

2 oz. Stolichnaya Vanil Vodka
1½ oz. Hiram Walker Crème de
  Cacao

Coat rim of glass with chocolate shavings. Swirl glass with
chocolate syrup.

CIROC ASIAN SCENE

1½ oz. Ciroc Snap Frost Vodka
1 oz. dry sake
splash Chambord

CIROC FROSTY GRAPE MARTINI

2 oz. Ciroc Snap Frost Vodka
½ oz. Grand Marnier
½ oz. red grape juice
splash blue curacao

CIROC N ROLL

2½ oz. Ciroc Snap Frost Vodka
1 oz. orange juice
1½ oz. energy drink
lemon twist garnish

CIROC RIVIERA

2 oz. Ciroc Snap Frost Vodka
½ oz. triple sec
½ oz. cranberry juice
½ oz. lime juice

CITRON FLIRTINI

1 oz. Absolut Citron
¼ oz. cointreau
a hint of dry vermouth

CITRUS BELLINI

2 oz. Skyy Citrus
1 oz. peach schnapps
splash lime juice

CITRUS DROP MARTINI

2 oz. Skyy Citrus
1 oz. triple sec
squeeze fresh lime

Garnish with a lemon.

CLARIDGE CLASSIC

2 oz. Bombay Sapphire Gin
⅛ oz. Martini Extra Dry
  Vermouth
brine from cocktail olives
cocktail olives garnish

COUNTRY ROSE

1 oz. Tequila Rose
½ oz. Southern Comfort
½ oz. strawberry schnapps
½ oz. amaretto
3 oz. milk

COWBOY MARTINI

2 oz. Bombay Sapphire Gin
⅛ oz. sugar syrup
fresh mint leaves
orange bitters

CREAMSICLE MARTINI

1 oz. Absolut Mandrin
½ oz. cointreau
½ oz. Licor 43
shaken with cream

CRUZAN CARIBBEAN MARTINI

Equal parts (¾ oz.) Cruzan
  Banana, Coconut and Pineapple
  Rums

Serve over ice.

CUERVO TEQUINI

3 parts Jose Cuervo Especial
½ part dry vermouth
dash Angostura Bitters

Garnish with lemon twist.

CUERVOPOLITAN

2 parts Jose Cuervo Especial
1 part orange liqueur
½ part cranberry juice
juice of ½ lime
dash orange bitters, orange
  wedge

Shake and strain into martini
glass. Squeeze in juice from
orange wedge.

DESERT MARTINI

1½ oz. Absolut Vodka
½ oz. cointreau
1 oz. orange juice
splash grenadine

DEWAR'S SIDECAR

1½ oz. Dewar's White Label
  Blended Scotch Whiskey
½ oz. cointreau
1 oz. sour mix

Optional garnish: cherry or
orange peel.

ELECTRIC MARTINI

2 oz. Absolut Vodka
½ oz. blue curacao
lime wedge garnish

ELROY'S MARTINI

2 oz. Skyy Vodka
splash orange juice
dash lime juice

EXPLOSION MILLENNIUM

2 oz. Bacardi 151 Rum
1 oz. amaretto

FOR A GOOD TIME

1 oz. Absolut Mandrin Vodka
½ oz. Appel Berentzen
½ oz. Grand Marnier
1 oz. cranberry
¼ oz. lime juice

FRÏS VODKA APPLE MARTINI

1 oz. Frïs Vodka
1 oz. apple schnapps

Garnish with a Granny Smith apple slice.

FRÏS VODKA LIME COSMOPOLITAN

2 oz. Frïs Vodka Lime
dash triple sec
dash lime juice
dash cranberry juice

Garnish with a lime peel.

FRÏS VODKA LIME MARTINI

2 oz. Frïs Vodka
Lime

FROZEN MARTINI

1½ oz. Beefeater
¾ oz. dry vermouth
crushed ice

Garnish with fresh berries.

FUZZY MARTINI

1 part DeKuyper Peachtree
  Schnapps
2 parts Absolut Mandrin Vodka
splash orange juice

Garnish with orange slice.

GIN BERRY BLOSSOM

1½ oz. Fruja Raspberry
1½ oz. Beefeater Gin
½ oz. grapefruit juice

Top with club soda.

GLAMOROUS MARTINI

2 oz. Skyy Vodka
¼ oz. orange juice
¼ oz. grapefruit juice
splash orange liqueur

Garnish with an orange slice.

GREEN EYED LADY

2 oz. Van Gogh Wild Appel
  Vodka
1 part Applefest Sour Apple
  Liqueur
1 part Midori Melon
1 squeeze fresh lemon
1 squeeze fresh lime

Garnish with a green apple curl.

SPRINGTINI

HAVANA WHITE

1½ oz. Three Olives Raspberry
 Vodka
1 oz. white crème de cacao

Serve in martini glass rimmed
with powdered chocolate.

HAWAII THREE-O

1½ oz. Three Olives Vanilla Vodka
¾ oz. coconut rum
splash pineapple juice

Garnish with slice of pineapple.

HEATED ICE MARTINI

2 oz. Polar Ice Vodka
½ oz. bourbon

Shake with a splash of maple
syrup. Serve well chilled.

IGUANA MARTINI

1 oz. Absolut Citron
½ oz. Midori
½ oz. triple sec

lemon pinwheel garnish

JACKIE-O MARTINI

1½ oz. Skyy Vodka
splash apricot brandy
dash grenadine
⅓ oz. pineapple juice

Garnish with a pineapple
wedge.

JAPANESE SEDUCTION

2 oz. Beefeater
1 oz. Midori
½ oz. peach schnapps

KEKE V

½ oz. Keke Beach
½ oz. Polar Ice Vodka

KEY LIME MARTINI

1½ oz. Cruzan Vanilla Rum
½ oz. fresh lime juice
½ oz. pineapple juice
dash Midori

Garnish with lime.

KEY WEST MARTINI

1 oz. Absolut Mandrin
½ oz. coconut rum
½ oz. Midori
½ oz. peach schnapps
½ oz. cranberry juice

KISS FROM A ROSE

1¼ oz. Tequila Rose
¾ oz. strawberry liqueur

Garnish with strawberry.

LENINADE

2 oz. Absolut Citron
splash grenadine
½ oz. lemon juice
¹⁄₁₆ oz. sugar
fresh mint leaves

Limón Cosmo

2 oz. Bacardi Limón Rum
1 oz. triple sec
½ oz. lime juice
2 oz. cranberry juice

Liquorice Martini

1 oz. Kahlua
1 oz. anisette
1 oz. half & half

Love Cocktail

2 oz. Beefeater
2 dashes raspberry syrup
2 dashes lemon juice
1 egg white

Garnish with fresh raspberry and lemon peel.

Mad Martini

1 part DeKuyper Mad Melon
  Watermelon
2 parts vodka
splash lime juice

Garnish with a lemon twist.

Mandrini

3 parts Absolut Mandrin
1 part triple sec
splash orange juice

Mango Tango Martini

1 oz. Fruja Mango
1 oz. Fruja Tangerine
1 oz. Stoli Ohranj Vodka
1 oz. orange juice

Mangotini

2 oz. Fruja Mango
2 oz. Stoli Vodka

Martini Bopper

3 oz. Three Olives Cherry Vodka
splash grenadine

Garnish with cherry.

Melontini

1 part DeKuyper Pucker
  watermelon schnapps
1 part Vox Vodka
splash lemon-lime soda

Garnish with watermelon slice.

A Midsummer Night's Dream

1½ oz. Jose Cuervo Especial
2½ oz. pineapple juice
½ oz. lemonade
1/2 oz. grenadine

Minta

2 oz. vodka
fresh crushed mint
1 tsp. sugar

Monkey Gland

2 oz. Bombay Sapphire Gin
1 oz. orange juice
¼ oz. absinthe/anis
shot grenadine

SPRINGTINIS

THE NIGHTMARE

1½ oz. Beefeater
½ oz. Madeira
½ oz. cherry-flavored brandy
1 tsp. orange juice

Garnish with lime peel.

NUTTY TEQUINI

3 parts Jose Cuervo Especial
1 Tbsp. hazelnut liqueur
½ tsp. sugar syrup

ORANGE TEQUINI

3 parts Jose Cuervo Especial
dash Angostura Bitters
dash orange juice
dash orange liqueur

Garnish with orange slice.

PEARL'S WITCHY WART JUICE

1 oz. Pearl Vodka
1 oz. coconut rum
1 oz. Irish Cream
½ oz. hazelnut liqueur

Garnish with sprinkle of nutmeg.

PIÑA COLADA MARTINI

equal parts (1 oz.) Cruzan
 Coconut and Pineapple Rums
splash pineapple juice
ice

Garnish with pineapple wedge.

PINK LADY

3 oz. Beefeater
5 dashes grenadine
¼ oz. egg white
maraschino cherry

Garnish with cherry.

POLAR ICE APPLE MARTINI

1 oz. Polar Ice Vodka
1 oz. sour apple schnapps
splash apple juice

RED MARTINI

2 oz. Absolut Vodka
¼ oz. Campari
lemon twist garnish

ROCKAPOLITAN

equal parts (1 oz.) Cruzan Citrus
 Rum, "Junkanu" and Cruzan
 Orange Rum
splash of lime juice
splash cranberry juice

ROSE DE MENTHE

¾ oz. Tequila Rose
¼ oz. white crème de menthe

ROTHMANN'S MARTINI

2 oz. Absolut Mandrin
¼ oz. cointreau
½ oz. pineapple juice
splash lime juice

SAPPHIRE ROSE

2 oz. Bombay Sapphire Gin
fresh grapefruit juice
sugar syrup
maraschino liqueur

SAVE THE PLANET

1 oz. Smirnoff Vodka
1 oz. melon liqueur
½ oz. blue curacao
1-2 dashes green chartreuse

SIBERIAN SUNRISE

1½ oz. Stolichnaya Vodka
4 oz. grapefruit juice
½ oz. Hiram Walker Triple Sec

SILK ROSE

1 oz. Tequila Rose
½ oz. milk
½ oz. butterscotch schnapps
½ oz. banana schnapps
¼ oz. half & half

SNICKERTINI MARTINI

1½ oz. Van Gogh Dutch
  Chocolate Vodka
¾ oz. Frangelico Liqueur
¾ oz. Amsterdam Chocolate
  Liqueur

Garnish with an orange rind
and chocolate shavings.

SOUR APPLE MARTINI

1 oz. Midori Melon
½ oz. Apple Pucker
1 oz. vodka

STOLI BUTTERFLY

1 oz. Stoli Vanil
1 oz. Stoli Razberi
1 oz. Hiram Walker Creme de
  Banana
splash soda

Garnish with cherry.

STRAWBERRY MARTINI

2½ oz. Tequila Rose
1 oz. Polar Ice Vodka

SWEET & SOUR APPLETINI

equal parts:
DeKuyper Sour Apple Pucker
Vox Vodka
splash sweet & sour mix

TANGERINI

2 oz. Fruja Tangerine
2 oz. Stoli Vodka

TANQUERAY GREEN APPLE MARTINI

Fill cocktail shaker with 1½ oz. Tanquery and 1½ oz. sour apple schnapps. Add equal splashes ginger ale and sweet & sour. Garnish with thinly sliced green apple.

THIN MINT
½ oz. KeKe Beach
½ oz. white crème de cacao
½ oz. peppermint schnapps

TROPICO 2000 COCKTAIL
2 oz. Bacardi 151 Rum
4 oz. Tropico
1 drop Martini & Rossi Sweet
  Vermouth

TUACATINI
1 oz. Tuaca Liqueur
1½ oz. Finlandia Vodka

Shake with ice, garnish with lemon twist.

VESPER MARTINI
3 oz. Stoli Vodka
½ oz. Blond Lillet

Garnish with lemon peel.

VODKA LIME AND CRANBERRY
1½ oz. Finlandia Lime Vodka
3 oz. cranberry juice

Garnish with a fresh squeeze of lime.

WATERMELONTINI
1 part DeKuyper Watermelon
  Pucker
1 part Vox Vodka

Garnish with watermelon slice.

WHISPER MARTINI
1½ oz. Teton Glacier
1 or 2 drops dry vermouth

Garnish to taste.

THE "WHITE" COSMOPOLITAN
1½ oz. Absolut Citron
¼ oz. cointreau
1 oz. white cranberry juice
squeeze of lime

YACHTING MARTINI
1½ oz. Skyy Vodka
splash peach schnapps
splash melon liqueur

Garnish with a fresh peach wedge.

A Cillo Mia

2 oz. Giori Lemoncillo Cream
½ oz. Tia Maria

After Eight

½ oz. Baileys Irish Cream
½ oz. coffee brandy
½ oz. green creme de menthe

After Five

1 oz. Carolans Irish Cream
  Liqueur
1 oz. peppermint schnapps
½ oz. Kahlua

Amarula French Toast

½ oz. Appleton Rum (preferably
  amber or dark)
1½ oz. Amarula Fruit Cream
  Liqueur
1½ oz. milk

Garnishes: ground cinnamon,
cinnamon stick.

Avalanche

1½ oz. Carolans Irish Cream
  Liqueur
splash cold milk
1 scoop vanilla ice cream

Blend.

Baileys B-52

Layer in shot glass equal parts:
Baileys Irish Cream, Kahlua,
orange liqueur.

Baileys Chocolate Covered Cherry

½ oz. Baileys Irish Cream
½ oz. Grenadine
½ oz. Kahlua

Layer grenadine, Kahlua, then
Baileys.

Baileys Coconut Frappe

2 parts Baileys Irish Cream
1 part Malibu Rum
2 parts milk

Baileys Cream Dream

2 oz. Baileys Irish Cream
2 oz. half & half
4 oz. ice cubes

Baileys Dublin Double

1 part Baileys Irish Cream
1 part Disaronno Amaretto

Serve in a shot glass.

BAILEYS EGGNOG

1 oz. Baileys Irish Cream
½ oz. Irish whiskey
1 medium egg
2 cups milk
nutmeg

BAILEYS O'

equal parts: Baileys Irish Cream,
  Stolichnaya Ohranj

BANANA SPLIT

2 oz. Vermeer
dash creme de banana or small
  ripe banana
½ scoop vanilla ice cream

Blend. Top with fresh whipped
cream and a maraschino cherry.

BEAM ME UP SCOTTY

equal parts: Carolans Irish
  Cream Liqueur, Kahlua, Hiram
  Walker Creme de Banana

BOURBON CREME

¾ oz. Amarula Cream Liqueur
¾ oz. Woodford Reserve Bourbon
¾ oz. Tuaca
¾ oz. dark creme de cacao

Sprinkle nutmeg, garnish
with cherry.

BRANDY BUTTER CREAM

¾ oz. Christian Brothers Amber
  Cream Liqueur
¼ oz. butterscotch schnapps
¾ oz. coffee liqueur
⅛ oz. cream or milk

Shake. Strain over ice and top
with cream or milk.

BROWN SUGAR

Chilled Vermeer straight up

Serve as a chilled shot.

CAFE COCORANGE

1 oz. Vermeer
¾ oz. coffee liqueur
splash Grand Marnier
3 oz. hot coffee

CAFE VERMEER

1 part Vermeer
3 parts fresh hot coffee

Top with whipped cream and
shaved chocolate.

CARAMEL CREME BRULEE

2 Tbs. Just Desserts Creme
  Brulee Liqueur
1 cup coffee
2 Tbs. caramel syrup

CARIBBEAN MUDSLIDE

1 oz. Christian Brothers Amber Cream Liqueur
1 oz. coffee liqueur
1 oz. coconut rum

CAROLANS' CONCERTO COFFEE

equal parts Carolans Irish Cream and Tia Maria

Stir.

CHEER OF VERMEER

1½ oz. Vermeer
½ oz. melon liqueur
½ oz. peppermint schnapps

CHERRILLO

1½ oz. Giori Lemoncillo Cream
½ oz. Chambord

CHOCOLATE ELEPHANT

1 oz. Vanilla Flavored Vodka
½ oz. Godiva Chocolate Liqueur
½ oz. Amarula Cream Liqueur

Garnish with a cherry.

CHOCOLATE ORANGE TRUFFLE

2 parts Vermeer
1 part Grand Marnier

Shake. Garnish with orange peel.

CILLO AMORE

1½ oz. Giori Lemoncillo Cream
½ oz. amaretto

Shake with ice.

CILLO FELLOW

1¼ oz. Giori Lemoncillo Cream
3 oz. orange juice

Stir. Serve in tall glass with ice.

CINNAMON TOAST

½ oz. Cinnamon Flavored Spirit
1½ oz. Amarula Cream Liqueur

Shake. Splash Coke on top of mixture; garnish with sprinkled cinnamon, and a cinnamon stick.

COCO COLADA

2 oz. Vermeer
1 oz. coconut rum
2 oz. whole milk

Pour into a tall glass over crushed ice. Garnish with orange or pineapple slice and maraschino cherry.

COFFEE SHAKE

1 oz. O'Mara's Irish Cream
2 scoops vanilla ice cream
1 Tbs. instant coffee

Blend.

CREAM

COMFORT & CREAM

½ oz. Southern Comfort
½ oz. Irish Cream

Mix in ½ shaker of ice.

———— ⨯ ————

CREAM FIZZ

Pour O'Mara's Irish Cream over ice in a tall glass. Add lemon lime soda and garnish with a lemon wedge.

———— ⨯ ————

CREME BRULEE FRAPPUCCINO

½ cup Just Desserts Creme Brulee Liqueur
3 scoops vanilla ice cream
¼ cup milk

Blend.

———— ⨯ ————

CREME BRULEE LATTE

1 Tbs. crème brûlée liqueur
1 cup coffee
steamed milk

———— ⨯ ————

DEVIL MINT

2 parts Vermeer
1 part white creme de menthe

———— ⨯ ————

DIRTY ITALIAN

1½ oz. Giori Lemoncillo Cream
½ oz. Giori Amaretto

Shake.

DIRTY NELLY

1 oz. Carolans Irish Cream Liqueur
1 oz. Tullamore Dew

Shake.

———— ⨯ ————

DUBLIN HANDSHAKE

½ oz. Baileys Irish Cream
½ oz. Irish whiskey
¾ oz. sloe gin

Shake.

———— ⨯ ————

DUCK FART

1 oz. Carolans Irish Cream Liqueur
1 oz. Kahlua
¼ oz. Canadian Club

Layer, first Kahlua, then Carolans Irish Cream. Top with Canadian Club.

———— ⨯ ————

DUTCH DREAMSICLE

2 parts Vermeer
1 part Skyy Citrus
½ oz. amaretto

Shake. Garnish with orange twist.

———— ⨯ ————

DUTCH VELVET

2 oz. Vermeer
½ oz. Skyy Vodka
½ oz. dark creme de cacao

Shake.

EASY EGGNOG

1 cup Southern Comfort
1 qt. dairy eggnog
ground nutmeg

Chill ingredients. Combine and blend in punch bowl. Dust with nutmeg.

EGG CREAM

1 oz. Giori Lemoncillo Cream
1 oz. vodka

Shake.

ESPRESSO BLANCO MARTINI

1 part illy Espresso Liqueur
3 parts Glacier Vodka
1 part cream

Shake.

FATMANCILLO

1 oz. Giori Lemoncillo Cream
½ oz. hazlenut liqueur
½ oz. triple sec

Blend. Garnish with maraschino cherry.

FIFTH AVENU

½ oz. Baileys Irish Cream
½ oz. apricot brandy
½ oz. white creme de cacao

Shake.

FLAMINGO FLIP

2 oz. Giori Lemoncillo Cream
½ oz. grenadine

Shake.

FRENCH CREAM

1½ oz. Baileys Irish Cream
½ oz. Chambord
2 oz. half & half
4 oz. ice cubes

Blend for 30 seconds.

FRUIT BURST

1½ oz. Giori Lemoncillo Cream
½ oz. orange juice
½ oz. cranberry juice
½ oz. pineapple juice

Shake with ice. Serve over rocks or straight up.

HOLLY BERRY

2 parts Vermeer
½ part blackberry liqueur
½ part raspberry liqueur

Shake. Garnish with mini candy cane.

HORNY DEVIL

2 parts Vermeer
1 part orange liqueur

HOT CHOCOLATE CREME BRULEE

2 Tbsp. Just Desserts Creme
  Brulee Liqueur
1 cup hot chocolate
¼ cup whipped cream

ILLY & CREAM

1 part illy Espresso Liqueur
1 part milk or cream

Serve over ice.

IRIE ELEPHANT

1 oz. Appleton Estate VX Jamaica
  Rum
1 oz. Amarula Cream Liqueur
splash butterscotch schnapps
3 oz. orange juice

ITALIAN DREAM

1½ oz. Baileys Irish Cream
½ oz. Disaronno Amaretto
2 oz. half & half
4 oz. ice cubes

Blend for 30 seconds.

ITALIAN TOASTED ALMOND

1 part illy Espresso Liqueur
1 part Glacier Vodka
1 part amaretto
1 part cream

Shake.

JAVA O'MARA'S

1 oz. O'Mara's Irish Cream
hot coffee

Stir in O'Mara's and top with
whipped cream and cinnamon.

JUNIOR MINTINI

2 oz. Vermeer
dash creme de menthe
dash cream

Shake. Garnish with fresh mint.

LEMEACH

1 oz. Giori Lemoncillo Cream
1 oz. peach schnapps

Shake.

LEMON HEAVEN

1½ oz. Giori Lemoncillo Cream
½ oz. coffee liqueur

Shake.

LEMON NOG

1½ oz. Giori Lemoncillo Cream
½ oz. rum

Shake. Top with nutmeg.

LUCK OF THE IRISH

2 parts Carolans Irish Cream
  Liqueur
2 parts Tullamore Dew Irish
  Whiskey
1 part Irish Mist

Shake.

MALIBU SLIDE
equal parts:
Baileys Irish Cream
Kahlua
Malibu

Blend.

MINT KISS
2 parts Baileys Irish Cream
5 parts coffee
1 part Rumple Minze
  Peppermint Schnapps

Top with fresh whipped cream.

MOCHA ALMOND CREAM
1 oz. Christian Brothers Amber
  Cream Liqueur
1 oz. amaretto
1 oz. coffee liqueur
1 oz. cream

Mix.

MUDSLIDE
1 oz. Baileys Irish Cream
1 oz. Kahlua
1 oz. Smirnoff Vodka

Mix and pour. Serve straight
up or on the rocks.

NEW MEER EVE COCKTAIL
1½ oz. Vermeer
½ oz. cognac
½ oz. white creme de menthe

Shake.

NUTTY IRISHMAN
1 part Carolans Irish Cream
  Liqueur
1 part Frangelico

Shake well and pour over ice.

OATMEAL COOKIE
equal parts:
Baileys Irish Cream
Goldschlager
butterscotch schnapps

PINK ELEPHANT
½ oz. Amarula Cream Liqueur
½ oz. Tuaca
½ oz. Woodford Reserve Bourbon
½ oz. Chambord
½ oz. Frangelico

Shake.

RUM YUM
1 oz. Baileys Irish Cream
1 oz. Malibu Rum
1 oz. cream or milk

Blend.

SCOTCH IRISH
1 part Baileys Irish Cream
1 part J&B Scotch

Shake or stir.

SIMPLY O'MARA'S
O-Mara's Irish Cream served on
  the rocks.

CREAM

SNOWBALL

1 oz. Amarula Cream Liqueur
½ oz. white creme de cacao
½ oz. Korbel Brandy
1 scoop vanilla ice cream

SNOWFLAKE

1 oz. Vermeer
½ oz. Frangelico
1 oz. Skyy Vodka
3 oz. cream or milk

Shake.

SOUTHERN ALEXANDER

1½ oz. Southern Comfort
1½ oz. creme de cacao
1 cup ice

Blend.

TARZAN O'REILLY

1 oz. Carolans Irish Cream
  Liqueur
1 oz. Fris Vodka
1 oz. Hiram Walker Creme de
  Banana

Stir.

TEMPTRESS

2 parts Vermeer
1 part Tequila Rose

TOOTSIE ROLL

½ oz. Baileys Irish Cream
1 oz. root beer schnapps

Topped with dash of Baileys
Irish Cream.

TUACA CREAMSICLE

1 oz. Tuaca Liqueur
1 oz. vanilla-flavored vodka
1 oz. orange juice
1 oz. cream

Shake.

TUACA ON HEAVEN'S DOOR

½ oz. Tuaca Liqueur
½ oz. vanilla flavored vodka
½ oz. hazelnut liqueur
½ oz. Irish Cream liqueur

Shake. Garnish with peppermint patty.

TWISTED NUTS

1½ oz. Giori Lemoncillo Cream
½ oz. Frangelico

Shake.

ULTIMATE IRISH COFFEE

2 oz. Carolans Irish Cream
  Liqueur
hot coffee

VERMEER AMORE

1 oz. Vermeer
1 oz. amaretto

Shake. Garnish with a stemmed cherry.

———⊗⊗⊗———

VERMEER BANANA SPLIT

2 oz. Vermeer
small ripe banana or dash creme
  de banana
½ scoop vanilla ice cream

Blend. Top with whipped cream and a stemmed cherry.

———⊗⊗⊗———

VERMEER CHOCOLATE MARTINI

2 parts Vermeer
1 part Skyy Vodka

Shake.

———⊗⊗⊗———

VERMEER FROZEN MUDSLIDE

1 part Vermeer
1 part Skyy Vodka
1 part milk
ice

Blend.

———⊗⊗⊗———

VERMEER MEEERACULOUS

1½ oz. Vermeer
½ oz. Molinari Sambuca

Shake.

VERMEER PAINTERS PALETTE

½ oz. grenadine
½ oz. Vermeer
½ oz. triple sec

Layer.

———⊗⊗⊗———

VERMEER SNOWFLAKE

1 oz. Vermeer
½ oz. Frangelico
1 oz. Skyy Vodka
3 oz. cream or milk

Serve over ice.

———⊗⊗⊗———

VERMEER THIN MINT

2 oz. Vermeer
1 oz. Kahlua
dash creme de menthe

Shake well over ice and strain into a frosted martini glass. Garnish with fresh mint leaf.

———⊗⊗⊗———

VERMEER TRONIE

1½ oz. Vermeer
½ oz. gin
½ oz. triple sec

Shake with ice. Pour in a stemmed glass.

VERMEER VALENTINE

2 parts Vermeer
1 part Skyy Vodka
½ part Chambord

Shake over ice and pour into a martini glass.

VERMEER VENUS

2 parts Vermeer
1 part Skyy Vodka
½ part vanilla schnapps
Shake over ice and pour into a
  martini glass.

VERMEER VER MOO

2 oz. Vermeer
2 scoops vanilla ice cream

Blend until smooth. Serve in a champagne glass.

WHITE RUSSIAN

Pour 1½ parts Kahlua
1 part Stoli Vodka over ice

Top with 1½ parts cream.

WILD ROVER

1 part Carolans Irish Cream
  Liqueur
1 part Irish Mist

Serve on the rocks.

BEER

At Anheuser-Busch, Inc., the phrase "Somebody Still Cares About Quality" accurately depicts the philosophy of the world's largest and most successful brewing operation.

With thirty-four domestic brands and five imports, Anheuser-Busch, Inc. offers consumers the most diverse, high-quality family of beers in the brewing industry.

Since its establishment as a small South St. Louis brewery in 1860, the company has maintained key commitments to product quality, tradition, and leadership. Through the years, the beer brands of Anheuser-Busch have become part of the American scene, quality products consumed responsibly by an overwhelming majority of American beer consumers.

History of Beer

The origins of beer are older than recorded history, extending into the mythology of ancient civilizations. Beer, the oldest alcoholic beverage, was discovered independently by most ancient cultures—the Babylonians, Assyrians, Egyptians, Hebrews, Africans, Chinese, Incas, Teutons, Saxons, and the various wandering tribes that were found in Eurasia.

In recorded history, Babylonian clay tablets more than six thousand years old depict the brewing of beer and give detailed recipes. An extract from an ancient Chinese manuscript states that beer, or "kiu" as it was called, was known to the Chinese in the twenty-third century B.C.

With the rise of commerce and the growth of cities during the Middle Ages, brewing became more than a household activity. Municipal brew houses were established, which eventually led to the formation of the brewing guilds. Commercial brewing on a significantly larger scale began around the twelfth century in Germany.

Although Native Americans had developed a form of beer, Europeans brought their own version with them to the New World. Beer enjoys the distinction of having come over on the Mayflower and, in fact, seems to have played a part in the Pilgrims' decision to land at Plymouth Rock instead of farther south, as intended. A journal kept by one of the passengers—and now in the Library of Congress—states, in an entry from 1620, that the Mayflower landed at Plymouth because "we could not now take time for further search, our victuals being much spent, especially our beer..."

The first commercial brewery in America was founded in New Amsterdam (New York) in 1623. Many patriots owned their own breweries, among them Samuel Adams and William Penn. George Washington even had his own brew house on the grounds of Mount Vernon, and his handwritten recipe for beer—dated 1757 and taken from his diary—is still preserved.

Brewing at Anheuser-Busch

In 1876, Adolphus Busch created a beer that would become known for its uncompromising quality. The original Budweiser label guaranteed a beer brewed by a unique process, using only the highest quality ingredients.

Today Budweiser's label gives the same assurance of quality. On the label for all to see are the words: "This is the famous Budweiser beer. We know of no brand produced by any other brewer which costs so much to brew and age. Our exclusive beech wood aging produces a taste, a smoothness and a drinkability you will find in no other beer at any price." Today, more than a century later, the quality is still there, still uncompromised.

The secret of fine, traditional brewing is really no secret at all—take the choicest, most costly ingredients, skillfully brew them, allowing plenty of time for nature to work its wonders, age the beer slowly and naturally, and take intense pride and care in every step along the way. That's the way Anheuser-Busch has always brewed beer.

Ingredients

Beer is a food product made from barley malt, hops, grain adjuncts, yeast, and water. The alcohol in beer results from the fermentation by yeast of an extract from barley, malt, and other cereal grains. In addition to alcohol, beer commonly contains carbohydrates, proteins, amino acids, vitamins (such as riboflavin and niacin), and minerals (such as calcium and potassium) derived from the original food materials.

All Anheuser-Busch beers vary in the type and mix of ingredients and in certain refinements in the brewing process to achieve their distinctive and unique characteristics. But all are like in one respect—every Anheuser-Busch beer is completely natural without any artificial ingredients, additives, or preservatives.

Superior ingredients are basic in the brewing of truly great beers. Anheuser-Busch uses only the finest, choicest, most costly ingredients available, selected through the most exacting requirements and specifications in the brewing industry. Again, nothing secret or mysterious, just the same basic ingredients that have been known for centuries as the way to make fine beers—barley malt, hops, rice or corn, yeast, and water.

Malt is the soul of all great beers and Anheuser-Busch uses more malt per barrel than any other major brewer in the country. The malt it uses begins with the choicest golden barley selected from the finest fields in America—from the sweeping plains of Minnesota and the Dakotas and from the Western states of Idaho, Washington, Wyoming, Colorado, Oregon, Montana, and California.

There are two basic types of malting barleys. One produces two rows of kernels on each stalk, the other, six rows. The flavor of the two varieties differs, with two-row barley malt being a choicer ingredient because it produces a smoother-tasting beer. Anheuser-Busch beers contain a varying percentage of two-row barley malt. Michelob contains the highest percentage.

In a carefully controlled malting procedure, the barley is cleaned, steeped, germinated and kilned. Malt is a natural source of carbohydrates, enzymes, and flavor compounds. Most of the enzymes are developed during the malting process. During brewing, the complex malt carbohydrates are broken apart by the enzymes. As a result, simple sugars are formed. These sugars are used by the yeast as an energy source during fermentation.

Hops, the cone-shaped clusters of blossoms from the vine-like hop plant, are the spice of beer, adding their own special aroma, flavor, and character. Anheuser-Busch uses only the choicest imported and domestic hops, hand-selected by company agents from the world's finest fields in Europe and Washington, Oregon, and Idaho.

Rice adds lightness and crispness to Budweiser and Michelob brands, while some of our other brands are made with corn to produce a milder flavor.

The brewer's yeast used in all Anheuser-Busch beers has been perfected and protected over decades, and all of the company's breweries are supplied from one carefully maintained pure-culture system.

Pure water is also a key ingredient in brewing great beer. Water is checked just as rigidly as other ingredients and, when necessary, the water is treated to ensure conformity to Anheuser-Busch's exacting standards.

Brewing Process

Next comes the brewing process. Here, too, there is no secret—visitors have always been welcome to tour Anheuser-Busch breweries and witness the painstaking and exacting care it takes to produce its beers. As an example, following are the steps in the Budweiser brewing process.

Brewing at Anheuser-Busch is a long, natural process taking up to thirty days or longer. It may appear old-fashioned to brew beer principally the way they have been brewing it for more than a hundred years, but Anheuser-Busch has never found a better way to brew than by combining the finest ingredients with slow, precise steps which give nature the time it needs to create great beer. There are modern shortcuts such as forcing fermentation by mechanical agitation, using enzyme preparations for chillproofing or artificially injecting carbon dioxide into the beer for carbonation—but they don't create great beers.

Modern Technology and Quality Assurance

While it chooses not to use chemical advances to cut corners in brewing, Anheuser-Busch has always been innovative in the use of science to promote quality. The company pioneered in the application of pasteurization in the brewing industry and developed the use of refrigeration railcars and a nationwide system of rail delivery.

Today, the Anheuser-Busch traditional brewing process is strictly maintained using modern technology in a rigorous program of quality assurance. Scientists and technicians use every skill available to ensure that each bottle, can or keg of beer is the very finest that can be produced, and to ensure that each Anheuser-Busch beer has its own great taste glass after glass, year after year.

Quality assurance at Anheuser-Busch begins with the testing of ingredients before brewing ever begins. Perfection is sought through close scrutiny extending down to the smallest detail of the packaging operation, including bottle crowns and can lids.

No scientific test, however, can replace tasting as the final judgment of quality. Numerous flavor panels meet daily at company headquarters and at each brewery to judge the aroma, appearance, and taste of packaged, filtered, and unfiltered beer. In addition, samples are flown into St. Louis from each brewery for taste evaluation.

Control of quality does not cease at the brewery. Anheuser-Busch's wholesalers play a key role in seeing that the quality that begins with the ingredients and continues through the brewing and packaging processes is preserved until it reaches the consumers. Anheuser-Busch wholesalers, at their expense, provide controlled environment warehouse systems that maintain beer freshness during storage.

In the marketplace, quality standards and beer freshness are maintained through Anheuser-Busch's unique "Born On" Freshness Dating program. Initiated in September of 1996, the program tells consumers the exact day, month, and year the beer was packaged so they know how fresh it is. All Anheuser-Busch domestic brands feature "Born On" dates, with an alpha-numeric code that is easy for consumers to read and understand. The

"Born On" date is accompanied by a "Brewery Fresh Taste Guaranteed" seal and a "Freshest Taste Within 110 Days" tag.

The final result of all these efforts is a family of naturally-brewed beers that the company believes is the freshest in the industry. And millions of consumers agree.

Anheuser-Busch remains firmly committed to quality, which it believes is, and has always been, the fundamental, irreplaceable ingredient in its successful performance.

Anheuser-Busch further believes that the consuming public will increasingly come to recognize and appreciate the natural quality and value that it has been brewing into its beers for more than a century.

Budweiser Mobile Beer School

The Budweiser Mobile Beer School is a classroom on wheels that enables Anheuser-Busch to bring its brewmasters anywhere in the United States to teach people who serve and sell beer—such as bartenders, bar managers, and wholesaler personnel—as well as beer drinkers, about the art, science, and tradition of brewing beer. There are currently four Budweiser Mobile Beer Schools traveling the country.

The Budweiser Mobile Beer School program includes a brief look at the history of beer around the world, a description of the all-natural ingredients Anheuser-Busch uses to brew its beers and an overview of the principles of brewing, allowing participants to see the step-by-step process by which barley malt, brewer's rice, hops, yeast, and water are crafted into fresh Budweiser. Brewmasters then introduce guests to the wide variety of beer styles that are popular today and discuss the benefits of drinking brewery-fresh beer.

The Budweiser Mobile Beer School is an extension of the Budweiser Beer School, a program also taught by Anheuser-Busch brewmasters that began in early 1995. Budweiser Beer School is taught primarily at Anheuser-Busch brewery sites, along with a few off-site locations, and in 1996 more than twenty-seven hundred attendees completed the program. With the addition of the mobile exhibits, Anheuser-Busch has been able to make the popular Beer School program available to the public.

History of Anheuser-Busch

It was 1852 and a tiny brewery on St. Louis' south side operated by George Schneider opened for business. From 1857 to 1860, ownership of that brewery changed hands—three times. But it wasn't until 1860 that a great tradition of beer would begin.

His name was Eberhard Anheuser, a successful manufacturer turned brewery owner. And, in 1860, an expanded brewery reopened its doors under the name of E. Anheuser & Co.

The following year, Eberhard's daughter, Lily, married a young St. Louis brewery supplier named Adolphus Busch. Enticed by his father-in-law's offer, Adolphus joined the brewery in 1864 as a salesman. In 1865, E. Anheuser & Co. produced eight thousand barrels of beer, featuring St. Louis Lager, the company's original flagship beer.

By 1873, Adolphus was a full partner in the brewery, serving as the company's secretary. And in 1876, with his close friend, Carl Conrad, Adolphus created a new beer—Budweiser Lager—which became the brewery's new flagship beer, and 120 years later, still owns that title.

Upon the death of Eberhard in 1880, Adolphus became president and production of beer was up to 141,163 barrels, largely representative of an increase in the popularity of Budweiser Lager.

Michelob was introduced in 1896, and by 1901, production of Anheuser-Busch beer broke the million-barrel mark.

Adolphus Busch died in 1913 and August A. Busch Sr. was named president—entering an era in which Anheuser-Busch was to face a variety of social and political changes: The First World War...Prohibition...and the Great Depression.

Intent on the survival of the company and protecting the jobs of its many hundreds of loyal employees during Prohibition, August focused the company's expertise and energies in new directions—including the production of corn products, baker's yeast, ice cream, soft drinks, commercial refrigeration units, and truck bodies.

During this period, the company also introduced Bevo, a non-alcohol malt-based beverage, as well as a number of carbonated soft drinks, including chocolate-flavored Carcho; coffee-flavored Kaffo; Buschtee, flavored with imported tea leaves; Grape Bouquet grape drink; and Busch Ginger Ale. Each enjoyed various levels of success, but all were eventually discontinued when Prohibition ended and Anheuser-Busch could return to its core business—beer.

Baker's yeast proved to be another story—a long-term success story. This product, first manufactured in St. Louis in 1927, made great gains under the watchful eye of Adolphus Busch III, who became the company's president in 1934. Anheuser-Busch eventually became the nation's leading producer of compressed baker's yeast, a position it held until its Busch Industrial products subsidiary was sold in 1988.

August A. Busch Jr. succeeded his brother as president in 1946 and served as the company's chief executive officer until 1975. He continued to serve as chairman of the board until 1977, when he was named honorary chairman. During his tenure, eight branch breweries were constructed; annual sales increased from three million barrels in 1946 to more than thirty-four million in 1974; Busch beer was introduced; and corporate diversification was extended to include family entertainment, real estate, can manufacturing, transportation, and major league baseball. August Busch Jr. died in 1989.

August A. Busch III became president in 1974 and was named chief executive office in 1975, becoming the fourth generation of his family to serve the company in that capacity. In 1977, he was elected chairman of the board.

Under his leadership, the company has: opened two breweries; introduced more than twenty new beer brands; launched the Anheuser-Busch Specialty Brewing Group; acquired a 25 percent stake in the Redhook Brewery of Seattle, Washington; acquired a minority equity interest in Widmer Brothers Brewing Co. of Portland, Oregon; opened new family entertainment attractions through its Busch Entertainment Corp. subsidiary; launched the largest brewers expansion projects in company history; increased vertical integration capabilities with the addition of new can manufacturing and malt production facilities; and diversified into container recovery, metalized label printing, international marketing, and creative services.

Beer Brands

Anheuser-Busch has developed products to meet a wide range of consumer tastes and price preferences. And, although each brand is produced according to a time-honored Old World brewing method, using only the finest natural ingredients, all Anheuser-Busch beers have their own unique characteristics.

Budweiser, the company's flagship brand, reigns as the top-selling beer brand in the world. Budweiser was introduced in 1876 when company founder Adolphus Busch set out to create the nation's first truly national beer brand—a beer that would be universally popular and transcend regional tastes.

Today, Budweiser leads the premium beer category. In fact, it outsells all other domestic premium beers combined. With broad appeal among virtually all demographic consumer groups, the brand truly lives up to its reputation as the "King of Beers."

Bud Light is the company's premium entry in the light beer category and continues to be the industry's fastest-growing light beer. Introduced in 1982, Bud Light became the best-selling light beer in America in 1994...and the number two brand overall, trailing only Budweiser.

Introduced in 1993 as Ice Draft from Budweiser, Bud Ice is ice-brewed to create a taste that is rich, smooth, and remarkably easy to drink. Bud Ice Light, introduced in 1994, incorporates advanced, state-of-the-art brewing methods to deliver a smooth taste at only ninety-six calories per serving.

Anheuser-Busch launched Bud Dry in 1989. An American Dry Lager, Bud Dry is not as sweet as Budweiser and has little aftertaste.

In 1896, Anheuser-Busch developed another beer brand, Michelob. Considered a "beer for connoisseurs," Michelob was served only on draught in the finest retail establishments.

Michelob became available in bottles—with the distinctive hourglass shape and red ribbon—in 1961 and in cans in 1966.

In recent years, Michelob and the Michelob Family of beers have experienced a sales and awareness resurgence never before seen in American brewing—all the result of a combination of integrated marketing campaigns, renewed wholesaler confidence in the brands, strong retailer support, and renewed value for the Michelob name in the consumer's eye.

In 1978, Michelob Light was introduced as the industry's first super premium light beer, for consumers who prefer a full-bodied, rich-tasting beer with reduced calories. Michelob Light's growing popularity in recent years—its sales volume was up 6 percent in 1996—has sparked the Michelob Family's strong performance.

Three years later, in 1981, Michelob Classic Dark was introduced, offering consumers Michelob's smooth taste in a rich, dark beer. A two-time Great American beer festival gold medal winner in the dark lager category, Michelob Classic Dark is brewed using black malt, which gives the brand its deep color and a pleasant, malty character.

Michelob Dry was introduced nationally in 1988 as America's first super premium dry beer. It derives its distinct, clean taste from the use of the exclusive DryBrew method of brewing. The longer brewing process produced a less sweet beer with no aftertaste.

Michelob Golden Draft was introduced in 1991 as Anheuser-Busch's first entry into the clear bottle, packaged draft market. Its smooth, full taste is packaged in unique bottles and cans that feature exclusive faceted edges.

Michelob Golden Draft Light, also introduced in 1991, offers the same brewing and packaging features as Michelob Golden Draft, but with significantly fewer calories.

Busch, a popular priced beer, has achieved strong growth in many key markets. Introduced in 1955, the brand is now available in forty-eight states and the District of Columbia, and it ranks as one of the nation's ten largest selling beers.

In 1989, Anheuser-Busch introduced Busch Light, the low calorie partner of the successful Busch brand.

Popular priced Busch Ice, introduced in 1995, combines the smooth refreshing taste of Busch beer with Anheuser-Busch's exclusive ice-brewing process to produce a very drinkable beer.

Natural Light, the sub-premium priced beer unveiled in 1977, offers an excellent price/value for light beer drinkers seeking a quality product at an attractive price.

Introduced in 1995, sub-premium priced Natural Ice was developed in response to continued consumer interest in ice-brewed beers.

Michelob Malt was introduced in 1995 and is Anheuser-Busch's premium brand in the malt liquor category. It offers a smooth, full-bodied taste to consumers looking for a step up from their normal malt liquor brand.

Hurricane Malt Liquor, with a slightly sweet, robust taste, was introduced in 1996.

King Cobra was the first Anheuser-Busch entry into the malt liquor category. First available in 1984, the brand is now sold in more than 300 markets across the United States, offering a smooth, high quality malt liquor taste.

O'Doul's non-alcohol brew was introduced in 1989. It contains less than 0.5 percent alcohol by volume—about the same amount of alcohol found in some soft drinks and fruit juices. O'Doul's is marketed to consumers who want the great taste of an Anheuser-Busch beer, but without the alcohol.

Busch NA, Anheuser-Busch's first sub-premium priced non-alcohol brew, was introduced in 1994 to help meet the demands of the growing non-alcohol segment. It contains less than 0.5 percent alcohol by volume.

ANHEUSER-BUSCH SPECIALTY BREWING GROUP

In the 1990s, "The Specialty Brewing Group of Anheuser-Busch" was launched. The group was created by selecting some of the most independent-minded, creative brewmasters and beer enthusiasts within Anheuser-Busch and the industry. The result is a team of autonomous, self-driven beer lovers committed to nothing short of excellence.

The family of beers that has been born out of the Specialty Brewing Group has already garnered tremendous support from the beer drinking community. Although some of the beers are currently available only in selected markets, some, such as the Michelob Specialty Ales & Lagers, the American Originals, and Red Wolf are available nationwide. Each of the beers constitutes an important part of the Anheuser-Busch family.

Michelob Specialty Ales & Lagers

When Adolphus Busch first brewed Michelob in 1896, he had just one goal in mind—to create a specialty beer, the finest in the world. Today, Anheuser-Busch continues the spirit and quality brewing heritage inspired by Michelob for over a century with the next generation of specialty beers—the Michelob Specialty Ales & Lagers.

Anheuser-Busch's top-selling specialty beer, Michelob Amber Bock is an American-style bock beer that debuted in 1995. It is brewed with the finest dark roasted malts to produce a rich, malty flavor, amber color, and full body, while its unique blend of hops and a touch of brewer's rice give Amber Bock its characteristic smooth, clean finish.

Michelob Golden Pilsner is a classic European-style pilsner. Full-bodied and deep golden in color, Golden Pilsner has a rich malty flavor and a spicy aroma. It was introduced in early 1997.

An unfiltered American wheat ale, Michelob Hefeweizen (pronounced hay-fuh-vise-un) was introduced in Oregon in late 1995, and after expanding throughout the Northwest in 1996, Hefeweizen was released nationally in 1997. It is brewed with 50 percent wheat malt to produce a beer with a smooth, refreshing taste and cloudy golden color.

Michelob Honey Lager is brewed with natural wild-flower honey to enhance the naturally sweet, creamy flavor of the beer. Also introduced in early 1997, Honey Lager is a very drinkable specialty beer, with a balanced taste and a uniquely soft, slightly sweet finish.

Michelob Pale Ale is a full-bodied golden pale ale. In addition to being brewed with the finest, all-natural barley, malt, and hops, Pale Ale is dry-hopped, adding a pronounced hop character to its malty aroma.

Michelob Porter, available in several select Northwestern markets, is brewed with a distinct blend of chocolate, black, caramel, and pale malts and roasted barley, producing a hearty, full-bodied and robust dark ale.

American Originals

The three beers in the American Originals family were originally introduced by Adolphus Busch at the turn of the century. Close to the style, taste, and look of the original beers, today's American Originals were created from a variety of handwritten notes and sales literature from the late 1800s, found in the Anheuser-Busch archives. They are available nationally on draught and in bottles in select markets.

Originally brewed in 1895, American Hop Ale was Anheuser-Busch's first mail-order beer. Customers could order cases of the brand and have it shipped directly to their homes. Today's American Hop Ale is a full-bodied amber ale, brewed with only American Fuggles and Cluster hops.

First brewed in 1885, Faust is an all-malt lager that is aged in lager tanks with beech wood chips for twenty-five days. Its deep golden color complements its complex malt, hoppy flavor.

Black & Tan porter was particularly popular on draught in saloons when it was first brewed in 1899. This full-bodied, porter-style ale has extra malt to soften the flavor. Its taste is slightly fruity, with chocolate notes, and a roasted and hearty flavor.

First introduced on the East Coast in October 1994, Red Wolf Lager met with immediate consumer support, and became available nationally in January of the next year. Red Wolf is a very drinkable, smooth, and subtly sweet red lager made from 100 percent all-natural ingredients, including choice hops, select grains, water, yeast and specially roasted barley malt.

Currently available only in Texas, Ziegenbock is rich and dark in color with a rich, smooth, full-bodied taste. The beer was first introduced in selected cities in Texas in March 1995, and became available statewide in June 1995.

Pacific Ridge Pale Ale is an intensely hopped, full-bodied pale ale, brewed in Northern California exclusively for beer drinkers in Northern California. This regional beer, released in November of 1996, was created by the brewmasters at Anheuser-Busch's brewery in Fairfield, California.

Special Winter Brew, Anheuser-Busch's first seasonal beer, is a hearty, flavorful lager, reminiscent of traditional German-style holiday beers. Adolphus Busch first created a Christmas beer in the 1890s and in 1995, Anheuser-Busch brought back that tradition.

IMPORTS

In addition to the wide variety of recently introduced domestic brews from the Specialty Brewing Group, several other beers in the family are imported into the United States by Anheuser-Busch.

Brewed under license from Denmark's Carlsberg A/S by Labatt Brewing Company in Canada, Elephant Red is distributed in the U.S. by Anheuser-Busch, Inc. Its dark red color is complemented by a drinkable, yet very full-bodied taste.

Brewed in Denmark by Carlsberg A/S since 1959, Elephant Malt Liquor has been available stateside since Anheuser-Busch began importing it in 1985. Very much in the European style, this malt liquor has a very strong, bold, and distinctive taste.

The full-bodied character and smooth and pleasing flavor of Carlsberg has been available in Europe since Carlsberg began brewing it in 1847. Americans have been enjoying the classic lager since it was first imported by Anheuser-Busch in 1985.

Nearly a century and a half after Carlsberg Beer was first brewed in Europe, its lighter-calorie version was introduced to consumers. Carlsberg Light was made available to Europeans in 1985 and was first imported into the United States the next year. Using the same fine ingredients as its namesake, Carlsberg Light offers the flavor of Europe without all of the calories.

Rio Cristal is brewed in Brazil by Companhia Antarctica Paulista and imported by Anheuser-Busch. Originally test-marketed in Norfolk, Virginia, and Key West, Florida, Rio Cristal is now available in Miami, Fort Lauderdale, and West Palm Beach as well. A smooth, refreshing golden lager, Rio Cristal captures the mystery and allure of Rio de Janeiro and its famous Carnaval celebration.

Anheuser-Busch—dedication, quality and tradition—trademarks that have dictated the growth of the company and positioned it as the largest and most successful brewer in the world.

Beer Clean Glasses

Anheuser-Busch, the world's largest brewer, assures excellence in its draught beer from the brewery to the wholesaler. Likewise, Anheuser-Busch wholesalers take the necessary steps to make certain that the product is delivered to retail establishments in first-class condition. However, it's up to the bartender to draw the best possible glass of draught beer for the consumer.

The first step is to serve the draught beer in a clean glass...a Beer Clean Glass. A glass may look clean, but is it near clean or beer clean?

Following are a few tips for obtaining a "Beer Clean Glass," the eye-appealing glass filled with one of Anheuser-Busch's great beers with a clear, golden color, and a good tight collar of foam.

A three or four-sink setup is ideal for getting glasses beer clean; a three-tank setup is most common. The first tank is for washing followed by two rinsing compartments.

A beer glass should be washed each time it is used—unless the customer requests that his glass be refilled. Proper cleaning and drying can be accomplished in four simple steps.

1. Used glasses should be emptied and rinsed with clear water to remove any foam or remaining beer which will cause dilution of the cleaning solution.

2. Each glass should be brushed in water containing a solution of odor-free and non-fat cleaning compound that will thoroughly clean the surface of the glass, and rinse away easily in clear water.

3. The glass must then be rinsed twice in fresh, clean, cool water—with the proper sanitizer in the last tank. Proper and complete rinsing is most important for a "beer clean" glass.

4. Dry glasses upside down on a deeply corrugated surface or stainless steel glass rack. Never towel dry glasses. Store air-dried glasses away from sources of unpleasant odors, grease, or smoke that are emitted from kitchens, restrooms, or ashtrays.

And, another secret to serving a perfect glass of beer...rinse the "beer clean" glass with cold, fresh water just before filling with Anheuser-Busch draught beer.

Dispensing Draught Beer

Obtaining a "beer clean" glass is just one step involved in the proper dispensing of perfect "brewery fresh" draught beer. Equally important are proper refrigeration, cleanliness of dispensing equipment, and proper pressures.

Since draught beer is perishable, it must not be exposed to warm temperatures. The retailer must preserve it by providing equipment that will maintain the temperature of the beer in the barrel 38–42 degrees Fahrenheit. These temperatures should be maintained throughout the dispensing equipment so the beer in the glass as it is served to the consumer will also be 38–42 degrees Fahrenheit. This range of temperature seems to satisfy the majority of tastes and is too small a variation to affect its flavor or quality.

Cleanliness is a most vital consideration. The beer faucets, tubing, hose, coils, taps, and vents, including direct draw systems, must be thoroughly cleaned regularly. Glasses should be "beer clean," and no effort should be spared to keep the bar clean and bright.

Finally, proper pressure in the barrel is very important. To maintain the brewery fresh taste in the beer, its natural or normal carbonation must be preserved. The dispensing equipment through which the beer flows must have a pressure that corresponds to the normal carbonation of the beer at the temperature of the beer in the barrel. The size and length of the coil in the dispensing equipment will determine the pressure to be used.

With the dispensing equipment properly set up, you are ready to serve fresh draught beer.

The right head of foam is important to giving a glass of beer that essential eye appeal. The size of the head is controlled by the angle at which the glass is held at the beginning of the draw. If the glass is held straight, so that the beer drops into the bottom, a deep head will result. If the glass is tilted sharply so that the beer flows down the side, the head of foam will be minimized.

For most beer glasses—and to please most customers—the head should be allowed to rise just above the top of the glass without spilling over, then settle down to a three-fourths of an inch or one inch head of frothy white foam.

Remember, there are two key steps for serving a truly perfect glass of draught beer: Use a "beer clean" glass, and before filling, rinse the glass in cold, running water.

POUSSE CAFE

Pousse-Cafe, French for "after coffee," was and is the quintessential test of a bartender's ability as a mixologist. Pousse-Cafes are French in origin and are layered specialty drinks. Bartenders in New Orleans first popularized Pousse-Cafes in the late 1840s and the drinks became a fad in bars and restaurants throughout the United States in the early 1900s.

A bartender is really put to the "test" when making a Pousse-Cafe. One needs a steady hand and the knowledge of specific gravities of cordials, syrups, and brandies. From three to twelve different types of the above-mentioned are poured over the back of a spoon into a cordial glass. The spoon breaks the fall of the liquids, enabling them to layer more easily. By adding the ingredients in order of their specific gravities, they remain separate and the result is a colorful rainbow effect. Pousse-Cafes can be prepared ahead of time for use at a party or to end a special dinner. They will keep for at least an hour in the refrigerator before the layers start to blend. If brandy is your last ingredient, the "show" would go on further by flaming it when served or even squeezing an orange peel on the lit brandy to heighten the effect.

Bartender Magazine's Ultimate Bartender's Guide is happy to present a listing of the Hiram Walker cordial line and their specific gravities. So grab your spoons and cordial glasses and "Pousse-Cafe the night away!!"

The Hiram Walker cordials, liqueurs, and products shown below can be used in Pousse-Cafes. Be sure to pour slowly over the back of a spoon. For best results allow at least five units between each liqueur starting with the type having the highest number.

POUSSE-CAFE SPECIFIC GRAVITY INDEX*

NO.	PROOF	PRODUCT	SPECIFIC GRAVITY	COLOR
1	40	Creme de Cassis	1.1833	Light Brown
2	25	Grenadine Liqueur	1.1720	Red
3	54	Creme de Cacao	1.1561	Brown
4	48	Hazelnut Schnapps	1.1532	Tawny
5	40	Praline	1.1514	Brown
6	54	Creme de Cacao, White	1.1434	Clear
7	56	Creme de Noyaux	1.1342	Red
8	48	Licorice Schnapps	1.1300	Clear
9	54	Chocolate Cherry	1.1247	Brown
10	56	Creme de Banana	1.1233	Yellow
11	54	Chocolate Mint	1.1230	Brown
12	48	Blue Curacao	1.1215	Blue
13	54	Swiss Chocolate Almond	1.1181	Brown
14	60	Creme de Menthe, White	1.1088	Clear
15	60	Creme de Menthe, Green	1.1088	Green
16	60	Orange Curacao	1.1086	Tawny
17	60	Anisette, White and Red	1.0987	Clear/Red
18	48	Creme de Strawberry	1.0968	Red
19	48	Wild Strawberry Schnapps	1.0966	Clear
20	48	Red Hot Schnapps	1.0927	Red
21	60	Triple Sec	1.0922	Clear
22	60	Rock & Rye	1.0887	Yellow
23	40	Cranberry Cordial	1.0872	Red
24	50	Amaretto	1.0842	Tawny
25	48	Old Fashioned Root Beer Schnapps	1.0828	Tawny
26	84	Sambuca	1.0813	Clear
27	40	Country Melon Schnapps	1.0796	Pink

28	70	Coffee Flavored Brandy	1.0794	Brown
29	48	Red Raspberry Schnapps	1.0752	Clear
30	48	Snappy Apricot Schnapps	1.0733	Tawny
31	48	Cinnamon Schnapps	1.0732	Red
32	48	Spearmint Schnapps	1.0727	Clear
33	60	Shamrock Schnapps	1.0617	Green
34	60	Peppermint Schnapps	1.0615	Clear
35	48	Jubilee Peach Schnapps	1.0595	Clear
36	70	Raspberry Flavored Brandy	1.0566	Red
37	70	Apricot Flavored Brandy	1.0548	Tawny
38	70	Peach Flavored Brandy	1.0547	Tawny
39	70	Cherry Flavored Brandy	1.0542	Red
40	70	Blackberry Flavored Brandy	1.0536	Purple
41	90	Peach Schnapps	1.0534	Clear
42	90	Root Beer Schnapps	1.0441	Brown
43	50	Amaretto and Cognac	1.0394	Tawny
44	90	Cinnamon Spice Schnapps	1.0358	Red
45	60	Sloe Gin	1.0241	Red
46	70	Ginger Flavored Brandy	0.9979	Light Brown
47	90	Kirschwasser	0.9410	Clear

*If you use other brands, the specific gravity will vary from one manufacturer to another.

Some Simple Recipes

ANGEL'S KISS
1 oz. dark creme de cacao
1 oz. cream

It's an Angel's Tit when you garnish with a cherry on a toothpick centered across the top.

FIFTH AVENUE
equal parts:
dark creme de cacao—brown
apricot brandy—gold
cream—white

FOURTH OF JULY
⅓ shot grenadine
⅓ shot vodka
⅓ shot blue curacao

GRAVURE
equal parts:
grenadine—red
brown creme de cacao—brown
triple sec—clear

IRISH FLAG
⅓ shot green creme de menthe
⅓ shot Irish Cream
⅓ shot Grand Marnier

SAVOY HOTEL
½ oz. white creme de cacao
½ oz. Benedictine
½ oz. brandy

TRAFFIC LIGHT
⅓ oz. green creme de menthe
⅓ oz. creme de banana
⅓ oz. sloe gin

YELLOW MORNING
1 part creme de banana
1 part cherry herring
1 part cognac

FACTS ON LIQUOR AND PROOF

The Meaning of Proof

Proof spirit, underproof, and overproof are terms difficult to explain in easy language since they are arbitrary standards set up by governments for collection of revenue.

Proof spirit is defined by law to be spirit which at 51 degrees. weighs $\frac{12}{13}$ of an equal measure of distilled water. At 51 degrees. it has a specific gravity of .92308. It is a mixture of about 57 percent pure alcohol and 43 percent water.

An underproof mixture of alcohol and water contains less than 100 percent of the mixture called proof spirit. So in 100 gallons of 20 underproof whiskey there is 80 gallons at proof strength and 20 extra gallons of water.

Overproof whiskey contains more alcohol and less water than proof spirit.

This proof chart shows these differences.

BRITIAN & CANADA		AMERICAN		ALCOHOL BY % VOL.
75.25		200	Proof	100.0%
	Overproof			
50	Overproof	172	Proof	86.0%
30	Overproof	149		74.5%
	Proof	114.2	Proof	57.1%
12.5	Underproof	100	Proof	50.0%
30	Underproof	80	Proof	40.0%
50	Underproof	57	Proof	28.5%
100	Underproof	0	Proof	0.0%

CHARTS &
MEASURES

Measurements

	METRIC	STANDARD
1 dash	0.9 ml.	⅟₃₂ ounce
1 teaspoon	3.7 ml.	⅛ ounce
1 Tablespoon	11.1 ml.	⅜ ounce
1 Pony	29.5 ml.	1 ounce
1 Jigger	44.5 ml.	1½ ounces
1 Wineglass	119.0 ml.	4 ounces
1 Split	177.0 ml.	6 ounces
1 Miniature (nip)	59.2 ml.	2 ounces
1 Half Pint	257.0 ml.	8 ounces
1 Tenth	378.88 ml.	12.8 ounces
1 Pint	472.0 ml.	16.0 ounces
1 Fifth	755.2 ml.	25.6 ounces
1 Quart	944.0 ml.	32.0 ounces
1 Imperial Quart	1.137 Liter	38.4 ounces
1 Half Gallon	1.894 Liter	64.0 ounces
1 Gallon	3.789 Liter	128.0 ounces

Dry Wine and Champagne

Split (¼ bottle)	177.0 ml.	6 ounces
"Pint" (½ bottle)	375.2 ml.	12 ounces
"Quart" (1 bottle)	739.0 ml.	25 ounces
Magnum (2 bottles)	1.534 Liter	52 ounces

Jeroboam (4 bottles)	3.078 Liter	104 ounces
Tappit-hen	3.788 Liter	128 ounces
Rehoboam (6 bottles)	4.434 Liter	
Methuselah (8 bottles)	5.912 Liter	
Salmanazar (12 bottles)	8.868 Liter	
Balthazar (16 bottles)	11.829 Liter	
Nebuchadnezzar (20 bottles)	14.780 Liter	
Demijohn (4.9 gallons)	18.66 Liter	

Distilled Spirits *

EQUIVALENT BOTTLE SIZE FLUID OZ.	BOTTLES/ CASE	LITERS/ CASE	GALLONS/ CASE	CORRESPONDS TO	
1.75 Liters	59.2	6	10.50	2.773806	1/2 Gallon
1.00 Liter	33.8	12	12.00	3.170064	1 Quart
750 ml.	25.4	12	9.00	2.377548	4/5 Quart
500 ml.	16.9	24	12.00	3.170064	1 Pint
200 ml.	6.8	48	9.60	2.536051	1/2 Pint
50 ml.	1.7	120	6.00	1.585032	1, 1.6, 2 oz

Wine *

EQUIVALENT BOTTLE SIZE FLUID OZ.	BOTTLES/ CASE	LITERS/ CASE	GALLONS/ CASE	CORRESPONDS TO	
4 Liters	135				1 Gallon
3 Liters	101	4	12.00	3.17004	⅘ Gallon
1.5 Liters	50.7	6	9.00	2.37753	⅖ Gallon
1 Liter	33.8	12	12.00	3.17004	1 Quart

750 ml.	25.4	12	9.00	2.37763	⅕ Quart
375 ml.	12.7	24	9.00	2.37753	⅒ Pint
187 ml.	6.3	48	8.976	2.37119	⅖ Pint
100 ml.	3.4	60	6.00	1.58502	2, 3, 4 oz.

*DEPARTMENT OF THE TREASURY
BUREAU OF ALCOHOL, TOBACCO AND FIREARMS

CALORIES & CARBOHYDRATES

	CALORIES	CARBOHYDRATES
Ale	72	
Beer (12 oz. bottle or can)	144	11.7
Light Beer	110	6.9
Bourbon		
80 proof, distilled	65	trace
86 proof, distilled	70	trace
90 proof, distilled	74	trace
94 proof, distilled	77	trace
100 proof, distilled	83	trace
Brandy		
80 proof, distilled	65	trace
86 proof, distilled	70	trace
90 proof, distilled	74	trace
94 proof, distilled	77	trace
100 proof, distilled	83	trace
Champagne		
Brut (4 fl. oz.)	92	2.1
Extra Dry	97	2.1
Pink	98	3.7
Coffee Liqueur		
53 proof	117	16.3
63 proof	107	11.2
Creme de Menthe, 72 proof	125	14.0
Gin		
80 proof (1 oz.)	65	0.0
86 proof (1 oz.)	70	0.0
90 proof (1 oz.)	74	0.0
94 proof (1 oz.)	77	0.0
100 proof (1 oz.)	83	0.0
Rum		
80 proof (1 oz.)	65	0.0
86 proof (1 oz.)	70	0.0

90 proof (1 oz.)	74	0.0
94 proof (1 oz.)	77	0.0
100 proof (1 oz.)	83	0.0
Scotch		
80 proof, distilled	65	trace
86 proof, distilled	70	trace
90 proof, distilled	74	trace
94 proof, distilled	77	trace
100 proof, distilled	83	trace
Tequila		
80 proof, distilled	64	0.0
86 proof, distilled	69	0.0
90 proof, distilled	73	0.0
94 proof, distilled	76	0.0
100 proof, distilled	82	0.0
Vodka		
80 proof (1 oz.)	65	0.0
86 proof (1 oz.)	70	0.0
90 proof (1 oz.)	74	0.0
94 proof (1 oz.)	77	0.0
100 proof (1 oz.)	83	0.0
Whiskey		
80 proof (1 oz.)	65	0.0
86 proof (1 oz.)	70	0.0
90 proof (1 oz.)	74	0.0
94 proof (1 oz.)	77	0.0
100 proof (1 oz.)	83	0.0
Wine		
Aperitif (1 oz.)	41	2.3
Port (1 oz.)	41	2.3
Sherry (1 oz.)	41	2.3
White or red table (1 oz.)	29	1.2
NON-ALCOHOLIC		
Club soda (1 oz.)	0	0.0

Cola (1 oz.)	12	3.1
Cream soda (1 oz.)	13	3.4
Fruit-flavored soda (1 oz.)	13	3.7
Ginger ale (1 oz.)	9	2.4
Root beer (1 oz.)	13	3.2
Tonic water (1 oz.)	9	2.4

HOME BAR
RECOMMENDATIONS
& TIPS

Location

Choosing the proper locations is essential. Select an open area that is easily accessible. A kitchen counter or a sturdy table near the kitchen counter is well suited. It should be convenient to the refrigerator and sink. The kitchen also becomes a gathering point for many partiers. Cleaning up water and spills is a lot easier on your kitchen floor than on your carpet.

If your kitchen is too small, choose a location near your kitchen on a sturdy table, and if you're worried about your carpet, spread a small rug beneath.

Bar Tools

The following should be displayed on your bar top (or table):

1. Ice Bucket. Try to find one with a vacuum seal, large enough to hold at least three trays of ice.
2. Wine/Bottle Opener. A good wine opener or waiter type church key or bottle opener that can open cans as well as snap off bottle tops.
3. Bar Spoon. One long spoon for stirring drinks or pitchers of drinks.
4. Cocktail Shaker and Mixing Glass. Mixing glass for use in stirring drinks. Shaker fits over glass to shake drinks.
5. Ice Scoop/Tongs. Use to pick up ice cubes from an ice bucket and place in glass. A must for every home bar. Never use your hands. If necessary, a large-mouth spoon can be used.
6. Blender. Blending margaritas, pina coladas, and daiquiris. Can also be used for crushing ice and making three or more drinks at once.

7. Napkins/Coasters. To place drink on or hold drink.

8. Stirrers/Straws. For mixing and sipping drinks.

9. Pitcher of water. A large pitcher for water only.

10. One Box of superfine sugar.

11. Three Large Bowls. One for cut fruit, two for garnish (olives, onions, etc.)

12. Knife and Cutting Board. Use to cut more fruit.

13. Jigger/Measuring Glass. All drinks should be made with a measuring glass or jigger. Drinks on the rocks or mixed drinks should not contain more than 1 1/2 oz. of alcohol. Doubles should not be served.

14. Muddler. To muddle your fruit.

15. Pourer.

16. Strainer.

STOCKING THE BAR FOR HOME

The traditional bartender's formula for setting up a simple home bar is:

– Something white (vodka, gin, rum or tequila)

– Something brown (scotch, Canadian whiskey or bourbon)

– Something sweet (a liqueur)

– Wine and/or vermouth if you want an aperitif or plan on making martinis.

In stocking your home bar for the first time, don't attempt to buy all types of exotic liquors and liqueurs. Your inventory should be based on items you and your friends will use most. Keep in mind that people will bring their favorite brands as gifts.

Folks might be drinking less, but they're drinking the best. Buy the best. It's only pennies more and saves a lot of excuses and embarrassment. Treat yourself and your guests to the best!

BASIC BAR STOCK AND PARTY TABLE

PRODUCT	BASIC STOCK (QUANTITIES IN LITERS)	NUMBER OF GUESTS				
		10/30	30/40	40/60	60/100	
White Wine						
Domestic	750 ml.	2	4	4	6	8
Imported	750 ml.	1	2	2	2	3
Red Wine						
Domestic	750 ml.	2	1	2	3	3
Imported	750 ml.	1	1	1	2	2
Blush Wine		1	1	2	2	2
Champagne						
Domestic	750 ml.	1	2	3	4	4
or						
Imported	750 ml.	1	2	2	2	2
Vermouth						
Extra Dry	750 ml.	1	1	1	2	2
Rosso (Sweet)	750 ml.	1	1	1	1	1
Liquors						
Vodka (choice of imported/domestic		1	2	3	3	4
Rum		1	1	2	2	2
Gin (choice of imported/domestic		1	1	2	2	3
Scotch		1	1	2	2	3
Whiskey (choice of American/Canadian)		1	1	1	2	2
Bourbon		1	1	1	1	1
Irish Whiskey		1	1	1	1	2
Tequila		1	2	2	2	3
Brandy/Cognac		1	1	2	2	3
Beer (12 oz. bottles)		6	48	72	72	96
Others						
Aperitifs: (choice of 1)						
Campari	750 ml.	1	1	2	2	

Dubonnet

Red*	750 ml.	1	1	1	2
Blonde	750 ml.	1	1	1	2
Lillet	750 ml.	1	1	1	2

Cordials/Specials
(choice of 3)

Grand Marnier*	750 ml.	1	1	1	1
Creme de Menthe					
White	750 ml.	1	1	1	1
Green	750 ml	1	1	1	1
Peach Schnapps	750 ml.	1	1	1	1
Kahlua*	750 ml.	1	1	1	1
Creme de Cacao					
White	750 ml.	1	1	1	1
Dark	750 ml.	1	1	1	1
Irish Cream*	750 ml.	1	2	3	3
Romana Sambuca	750 ml.	1	2	3	3
Amaretto	750 ml.	1	2	2	2

* Recommended

Total Cost (approximate): $250-300

Number of Guests	10/30	30/40	40/60	60/100
Cost:	$300-400	$400-550	$550-700	$700-800

1. This chart is based on 1-3/4 oz. per drink; this is a basic.
2. Product will vary based on age (usually the younger the crowd, 21-35, the more beer and mixed drinks); so increase by one-half the amount of vodka, rum, tequila, and beer.
3. Geographical location is also important in selecting and determining cost of your liquor stock for your guests. Consult your local bartender or liquor clerk to find the most popular products in your area.
4. The time of the year or season should also be considered—in fall/winter serve less beer; in spring serve more beer, vodka, gin and tequila.

Other Supplies

PRODUCT	BASIC STOCK (QUANTITIES IN LITERS)	NUMBER OF GUESTS 10/30	30/40	40/60	60/100
Soda (2 Liters):					
Club/Seltzer		1	3	3	4	5
Ginger Ale		1	2	2	2	3
Cola		1	3	3	3	4
Diet Cola		1	3	3	3	4
7-Up		1	2	3	3	4
Tonic		1	2	2	3	3
Juice (Quart):					
Tomato		1	2	2	3	3
Grapefruit		1	2	2	3	3
Orange		1	2	2	3	3
Cranberry		1	2	2	3	
Miscellaneous:					
Ice (trays)		2	10	15	20	30
Napkins (dozen)		1	4	4	6	8
Stirrers (1,000/box)		1	1	1	1	1
Major Peters' Grenadine		1	1	1	1	2
Superfine Sugar (box)		1	1	1	1	1

Other Miscellaneous:

1 Quart Milk

2 Large Bottle Mineral Water

2 Bottles Major Peters' Lime Juice

1 Bottle Angostura Bitters

1 Bottle Worcestershire Sauce

1 Bottle McIlhenny Tabasco sauce

1 Small Jar Horseradish for Bloody Marys

1 Can Coco Lopez Cream of Coconut

101 WEBSITES

ABSENTE - www.absente.com

ABSOLUT VODKA - www.absolutvodka.com

AGAVERO EL ORIGINAL LICOR TEQUILA - www.agavero.com

ALIZE - www.kobrandwine.com

AMSTEL - www.amstel.nl

ANHEUSER-BUSCH - www.anheuser-busch.com

APPLETON RUM - www.appletonrum.com

AUTOFRY - www.autofry.com - Ventless, hoodless, fully-enclosed, automatic deep-frying system. Designed for bartender use. It's as easy as 1-2-3.

BACARDI RUM - www.bacardi.com - Also see:

BACARDI CÓCO, Original Coconut Rum - www.barcardicoco.com

BACARDI O - www.bacardio.com

BACARDI SILVER, Premium Malt Beverage - www.bacardisilver.com

BACARDI BREEZER, Less Alcohol Flavored Beverage: www.bacardi-breezer.com

BAILEYS IRISH CREAM - www.baileys.com

BARTENDER FOUNDATION, INC. - www.bartenderfoundation.org - Non-profit organization to raise scholarship money for bartenders and their children. Pledge your support!

BARTENDER MAGAZINE - www.bartender.com

BARTON BRANDS - www.bartonbrands.com

BAR RAGS - www.barrags.com - Your complete line of T-shirts, designed to promote bars, pubs, taverns, saloons and restaurants

BASS ALE - www.bass.com

BECK'S BEER - www.becksbeer.com

BEEFEATER - www.beefeatergin.com

BLAVOD - www.blackvodka.com

BOMBAY SAPPHIRE GIN - www.bombay.com

BORU VODKA - www.greatspirits.com

BUD ICE - www.budice.com

BUDWEISER - www.budweiser.com

BUDWEISER SPECIALTY BREWING GROUP - www.hopnotes.com

BUFFALO TRACE - www.bourbonwhiskey.com

BULLEIT BOURBON - www.bulleit.com

BUMPER TUBE COMPANY - www.bumpertube.com - Manufacturing and selling coin-operated pool tables and shuffleboards, parts and supplies

BUSHMILLS - www.bushmills.com

CABO WABO TEQUILA - www.cabowabo.com

CAMPARI - www.campari.com

CANADIAN CLUB WHISKEY - www.canadianclub-whiskey.com

CANADIAN MIST - www.canadianmist.com

CAPTAIN MORGAN - www.rum.com

CARAVELLA - Authentic Italian Spirits - www.caravellaus.com

CAROLANS IRISH CREAM LIQUEUR - www.carolans.ie

CASA NOBLE TEQUILA - www.casanoble.com

CELTIC CROSSING - www.greatspirits.com

CHAMBORD - www.chambordonline.com

CHARTREUSE LIQUEURS - www.chartreuse.fr

CHIVAS REGAL - www.chivas.com

CICLÓN - www.ciclonrum.com

CIROC - www.ciroc.com

COCO LOPEZ - www.cocolopez.com - "It's more than a drink, it's paradise."

COCKTAILRIGHT - www.cocktailright.com - Have you ever created an ORIGINAL DRINK only to have someone else take credit for it? Well, now you can register your cocktail!

COINTREAU - www.cointreau.com

COORS - www.coors.com

COORS LIGHT - www.coorslight.com

CORONA - MODELO - www.corona.com

COURVOISIER - www.courvoisier.com

CRILLON IMPORTERS LTD. - www.crillonimporters.com

CROWN ROYAL - www.crownroyal.com

CRUZAN RUM - www.cruzanrum.com

CUERVO - www.cuervo.com

CUTTY SARK - www.cutty-sark.com

DEKUYPER - www.dekuyperusa.com

DEWARS - www.dewars.com

DISARONNO AMARETTO - www.disaronno.com

DRAMBUIE - www.drambuie.com

DRI-DEK SHELF LINERS - www.dri-dek.com - Interlocking
tiles that are easy, fast and fun to install!

EARLY TIMES WHISKEY - www.earlytimes.com

FAMOUS GROUSE - www.famousegrouse.com

FERNET BRANCA - www.brancaproducts.com

FINLANDIA VODKA - www.finlandiavodka.com

FOSTER'S LAGER - www.fostersbeer.com

FRANGELICO - www.frangelico.com

FRIS - www.frisvodka.com

GEORGE DICKEL TENNESSEE WHISKEY - www.dickel.com

GLENFIDDICH SINGLE MALT WHISKEY - www.glenfiddich.com

GLENLIVET - www.theglenlivet.com - Glenlivet 18 Year Old and the Glenlivet Cellar Collection.

GLENMORANGIE - www.glenmorangie.com

GOLDSCHLAGER - www.schlager.com

GOSLINGS BLACK SEAL RUM - www.goslingsrum.com

GRAND MARNIER - www.grand-marnier.com

GROLSCH - www.grolsch.com

GUINNESS - www.guinness.com

HEINEKEN - www.heineken.com

HENNESSY - www.hennessy-night.com

HIRAM WALKER - www.pernod-ricard-usa.com

ICEBERG VODKA - www.icebergvodka.net

IRISH MIST - www.irishmist.com

J&B SCOTCH WHISKEY - www.jbscotch.com

JACK DANIEL'S - www.jackdaniels.com

JÄGERMEISTER - www.jagermeister.com

JIM BEAM BRANDS - www.jimbeam.com

JOSE CUERVO - www.cuervo.com

JOHNNIE WALKER & CLASSIC MALT SCOTCH - www.scotch.com

KAHLUA - www.kahlua.com

KENTUCKY BOURBON CIRCLE - www.smallbatch.com

KETEL ONE VODKA - www.ketelone.com

KILLEPITSCH - www.killepitsch.de

KNOB CREEK Kentucky Straight Bourbon Whiskey - www.knobcreek.com

KORBEL - www.korbel.com

LABATT - www.labatt.com

LABATT BLUE - www.labattblue.com

LAPHROAIG - www.laphroaig.com

LAIRD AND COMPANY - www.lairdandcompany.com

LEROY NEIMAN ART - www.bartender.com

LEVEL VODKA - www.levelvodka.com

LICOR 43 - www.licor43.com

MAGELLAN GIN - www.magellangin.com

MAKERS MARK - www.makersmark.com

MALIBU RUM - www.malibu-rum.com

MCCORMICK DISTILLING COMPANY -

www.mccormickdistilling.com

MILLER BREWING COMPANY - www.milleradvantage.com
- Liquor Industry link for bartenders and retailers;
www.millerbeer.com - Consumer link.

MIDORI - www.midori-world.com

MOLSON - www.molson.com

MOUNT GAY RHUM BARBADOS - www.mountgay.com

NATIONAL ALCOHOL BEVERAGE CONTROL ASSOCIA-
TION (NABCA) - www.nabca.org

NATIONAL BEER WHOLESALERS ASSOCIATION, INC.
(NBWA) - www.nbwa.org

NATIONAL RESTAURANT ASSOCIATION -
www.restaurant.org

NICHE - www.ourniche.com - Imported Spirit Specialties.

OLD MILWAUKEE - www.oldmilwaukee.com

OLD PULTENEY SCOTCH - www.oldpulteney.com

ORONOCO RUM - www.thebar.com

PABST BREWING COMPANY - www.pabst.com

PALM BAY IMPORTS - www.palmbayimports.com

PAULANER - www.paulaner.com/bier

PASSOA - www.passoa.com

PATRON TEQUILA - www.patronspirits.com

PERNOD - www.pernod.net; www.pernod-ricard.com

PLAYERS EXTREME - www.playersextreme.com - Flavor Infused Vodkas.

PLYMOUTH GIN - www.plymouthgin.com

PRECISION POURS - www.precisionpours.com

Q GIN - www.qgin.com

QUIK N' CRISPY - www.q-n-c.com

REBEL YELL BOURBON - www.rebelyellbourbon.com

REMY MARTIN - www.remy.com

Design Remy Lounge - www.remylounge.com

RHUM BARBANCOURT - www.crillonimporters.com

ROMANA SAMBUCA - www.thebar.com

SAUZA TEQUILA - www.sauzatequila.com

SAZERAC - www.sazerac.com

SCOTCH WHISKEY GROUP - www.scotchwhiskey.com

SEA WYNDE POT STILL RUM - www.greatspirits.com

SERVESAFE ALCOHOL - www.nraef.org/countingdrinks/bartender

SOUTHERN COMFORT - www.southerncomfort.com

SKYY VODKA - www.skyy.com

SMALL BATCH BOURBONS - www.smallbatch.com

SMIRNOFF VODKA (Heublein)- www.smirnoff.com

SOHO LYCHEE - www.soholychee.com

SOUTHERN COMFORT - www.SouthernComfort.com

STIRRINGS COCKTAILS - www.stirrings.com

STOLICHNAYA RUSSIAN VODKA - www.stoli.com

SVEDKA VODKA - www.svedka.com

SV SUPREME VODKA - www.svvodka.com

TABASCO - www.tabasco.com

TALAPA MEZCAL REPOSADO -
www.crillonimporters.com

TANQUERAY - www.tanqueray.com

TARANTULA AZUL - www.tarantulaazul.com

TETON GLACIER POTATO VODKA -
www.glaciervodka.com

THREE OLIVES - www.threeolives.com

TIA MARIA - www.tiamaria.net

TUACA LIQUORE ITALIANO - www.tuaca.com

TULLAMORE DEW - www.tullamoredew.com

U.S. BARTENDER - www.usbartender.com

VAN GOGH VODKA - www.vangoghvodka.com

VOX VODKA - www.voxvodka.com - Vox Raspberry Vodka
too.

WEBWISER, INC. - www.webwiser.com (ask for Eileen). Web design and information, web graphics, logos and more.

WEDGE - The Ultimate Slicer - www.wedgeonline.com

WHALER'S ORIGINAL RUM - www.whalersrum.com

WHITE ROCK DISTILLERS - www.whiterockdistilleries.com

WILD TURKEY - www.wildturkey.com

WINE AND SPIRITS WHOLESALERS OF AMERICA - www.wswa.com

WORMWOOD-ABSENTE (Herbal Liquid Extract) - www.wormwood-absente.com

99 BRANDS - www.99schnapps.com

Index of Cocktails

T

U

Index of Brand Names

K

L

M

W

About the Author

Ray Foley has been a bartender for more years than he wants to admit. He is the publisher of *Bartender* Magazine and the author of *Bartending for Dummies, How to Run a Bar for Dummies, The Best Irish Drinks, The Ultimate Little Martini Book*, and *The Ultimate Little Shooter Book*. He has appeared on numerous television shows and has had articles published in many national magazines. Ray resides in New Jersey with his wife and partner, Jaclyn, and his son Ryan. He can be contacted on his website, www.bartender.com, or his e-mail, Barmag@aol.com.